D0287704

American Architects from the Civil War to the First World War

ART AND ARCHITECTURE INFORMATION GUIDE SERIES

Series Editor: Sydney Starr Keaveney, Associate Professor, Pratt Institute Library

Also in the Art and Architecture Series:

AMERICAN PAINTING—*Edited by Sydney Starr Keaveney*

COLOR THEORY—*Edited by Mary Buckley and David Baum*

AMERICAN ARCHITECTS FROM THE FIRST WORLD WAR TO THE PRESENT—*Edited by Lawrence Wodehouse**

INDUSTRIAL DESIGN—*Edited by J. Roger Guilfoyle***

ART THERAPY—*Edited by Josef Garai***

ART EDUCATION—*Edited by Clarence Bunch**

PHOTOGRAPHY—*Edited by Diana Edkins***

PRINTS AND PRINTING—*Edited by Jeffrey Wortman***

CERAMICS—*Edited by James E. Campbell***

AMERICAN SCULPTURE—*Edited by Janis Ekdahl**

MODERN EUROPEAN PAINTING—*Edited by Ann-Marie Bergholtz***

BRITISH ARCHITECTS—*Edited by Lawrence Wodehouse***

AMERICAN DRAWING—*Edited by Lamia Doumato***

LATE NINETEENTH—CENTURY EUROPEAN PAINTING AND DESIGN—*Edited by Timothy Daum***

STAINED GLASS—*Edited by Darlene A. Brady and William M. Serban***

*in press
**in preparation

The above series is part of the
GALE INFORMATION GUIDE LIBRARY

The Library consists of a number of separate Series of guides covering major areas in the social sciences, humanities, and current affairs.

General Editor: Paul Wasserman, Professor and former Dean, School of Library and Information Services, University of Maryland

American Architects from the Civil War to the First World War

A GUIDE TO INFORMATION SOURCES

Volume 3 in the Art and Architecture Information Guide Series

Lawrence Wodehouse

Professor of Architectural History
Pratt Institute

Gale Research Company
Book Tower, Detroit, Michigan 48226

Library of Congress
Cataloging in Publication Data

Wodehouse, Lawrence.
American architects from the Civil War to the First World War.

(Art and architecture information guide series; v.3) (Gale information guide library)
1. Architecture--United States--Bibliography. 2. Architecture, Modern--19th century--United States--Bibliography. 3. Architecture, Modern--20th century--United States--Bibliography. 4. Architects--United States--Bibliography. I. Title.
Z5944.U5W63 016.72'092'2 73-17525
ISBN 0-8103-1269-7

VITA

Lawrence Wodehouse is by training an architect, city planner, and architectural historian with degrees from the universities of Durham (England), London, and Cornell respectively. His major field of interest is nineteenth-century American architecture, notably of architects who designed public buildings. He has published more than a score of articles in journals of learned societies including: ANTIQUES, ART JOURNAL, HISTORIC PRESERVATION, JOURNAL OF THE SOCIETY OF ARCHITECTURAL HISTORIANS, and OLD TIME NEW ENGLAND. He has also contributed sixteen entries to the McGRAW HILL DICTIONARY OF WORLD BIOGRAPHY, 1973. His most recent research has centered around the work of Stanford White of the architectural firm of McKim, Mead and White; an introductory paper was given at the annual symposium of the Victorian Society of America in conjunction with Winterthur Museum and the University of Delaware, 1974, to be published as "Stanford White and the Mackays: A Case Study in Architect-Client Relationships," in WINTERTHUR PORTFOLIO 11 (1975). One of the two 1976 issues of OLD TIME NEW ENGLAND will include another article entitled "Ammi Young, Stanford White and the Villard Mansion." At present Lawrence Wodehouse is on a year's leave of absence, lecturing at the Department of Architecture, Jordanstone College, University of Dundee, Scotland.

CONTENTS

INTRODUCTION

In preparing an annotated bibliography of American architecture, several problems immediately become self-evident. One problem is where in history to start, since American settlement patterns began with Spanish, French, Dutch, and English immigrants, to be followed by other nationalities up to the present. This is a broad time span covering 400 years, part of which has already been well covered by Frank J. Roos, Jr. in his WRITINGS ON EARLY AMERICAN ARCHITECTURE, 1943. His revised updated BIBLIOGRAPHY OF EARLY AMERICAN ARCHITECTURE, 1968, contained 4,377 entries, an addition of almost 1,600 entries beyond the 1943 edition of WRITINGS ON EARLY AMERICAN ARCHITECTURE, with next to no annotative data, in 389 pages. Since Roos used the Civil War as his cutoff point, and since he was so thorough, it seemed reasonable not to duplicate his major contribution. More architects have practiced in the United States after 1860 than existed prior to the Civil War and obviously more structures have been constructed. Thus, an annotated bibliography from the period of the Civil War to the First World War would be much more extensive than Roos. Further limitations have of necessity therefore been made, restricting this volume to biographical data on architects. The presentation of architects from the First World War to the present and of building types, stylistic developments, and regional characteristics will be included in a second, and possibly a third volume.

A perusal of Henry F. and Elsie Rathburn Withey's BIOGRAPHICAL DICTIONARY OF AMERICAN ARCHITECTS (DECEASED), will show a presentation of 2000 architects who lived from 1740 to 1952. Frank Lloyd Wright, who died in 1959, was not included, even though his architectural practice dates back to the late 1880's, and notable architects of the Chicago School such as George W. Maher were omitted. THE PRAIRIE SCHOOL REVIEW, which dates back to 1964 under the excellent editorship of W.R. Hasbrouck, has done much to remedy a gap in our knowledge of significant but lesser known names. This Gale Research volume includes an annotation of all relevant articles that the REVIEW has offered over a decade. There will, however, be more omissions in this annotated volume than the 2,000 entries in Withey and Withey because the author has had to be selective, concentrating on the most representative architects of each era and those that historians and critics have thought worthy enough to research and comment upon. The author has attempted to be as objective as possible, including only those architects who have gained sufficient attention to have been included in architectural histories, periodicals, and journals such as the JOURNAL OF THE SOCIETY OF ARCHITECTURAL HISTORIANS. Most publication and periodical entries can be found, but not in annotated form, in the AVERY INDEX TO ARCHITECTURAL PERIODICALS, 1973, or the CATALOG OF THE AVERY ARCHITECTURAL LIBRARY OF COLUMBIA UNIVERSITY, 1968. The Avery Memorial Library is the most outstanding architectural library in the world and has the most complete collection of books, periodicals, pamphlets, and other material on American architecture.

This volume cannot hope to include a listing of all that the Avery Library has to offer or even a minute fragment, but for those who do not have access to that library or its expensive catalog, this volume has attempted to annotate a limited number of books and periodicals on American architects. Other bibliographers have attempted to be definitive, including the late Harrye Black Lyons of the School of Design Library, North Carolina State University at Raleigh, who compiled a bibliography of every mention of Frank Lloyd Wright in books, periodical and newspaper articles up to 1968 and had over 3,000 listings. Bernard Karpel, then Librarian of the New York Museum of Modern Art, produced a bibliography on Wright consisting of 330 listings for the November 1955 issue of HOUSE BEAUTIFUL. Four years later, in October 1959, he added a further 120 items. James R. Muggenburg listed 134 books, catalogues, and general works; 414 periodical articles; and 15 obituaries on Wright from 1959, the year of Wright's death, to 1970, in the ninth issue of THE AMERICAN ASSOCIATION OF ARCHITECTURAL BIBLIOGRAPHERS.

In compiling this Gale Research Information Guide, the author had generally limited listings to articles on architects or evaluations of their works by critics. Magazine coverage of specific buildings, consisting of photographs, plans, annotations, and descriptions have not generally been included, unless the analysis is signed: if a particular architect or building has been the subject of a signed article, it has been listed. This volume could thus be considered to be an interpretation of architects and their works as seen through the eyes of historians and critics--writers who have generally been thorough in their task. Architectural critic Montgomery Schuyler is well known through the two-volume analysis of his writings by William Jordy and Ralph Coe. Likewise, Henry Van Brunt's works have been evaluated by William A. Coles. There are other noteworthy critics but their names have become less well-known due to the passing of time. Herbert Croly was one and the architect Peter Bonnett Wight was another. But others such as Claude Bragdon, who first forewoded and edited the writings of Louis Sullivan; Glenn Brown, historian and one-time secretary of the American Institute of Architects; W. Franklyn Paris, who wrote so many monographs for the AMERICAN SOCIETY OF THE LEGION OF HONOR MAGAZINE and THE HALL OF AMERICAN ARTISTS; Russell Sturgis, one of the seven American pre-Raphaelite brothers and editor of NEW PATH, THE JOURNAL FOR THE ADVANCEMENT OF THE CAUSE OF TRUTH IN ART; and F.S. Swales, A.C.

David, and Henry Desmond are worthy of mention. Of more recent vintage is Ada Louise Huxtable, architectural critic of THE NEW YORK TIMES since May 1963; and Sibyl Moholy-Nagy, who has had a considerable impact upon the professions of architecture and city planning. These then, are a few of the critics, but what about the historians? There are too many to list without fear of omission. However, some early biographers are of undisputed significance such as Mariana Griswold Van Rensselaer, whose 1888 book on H.H. Richardson was the second biography of an American architect, and was followed by Harriet Monroe's biography of John Wellborn Root in 1896. Mrs. Van Rensselaer was also a commentator and critic as her "American Country Dwelling" in the May 1866 issue of THE CENTURY ILLUSTRATED MONTHLY MAGAZINE well illustrates. Again in the realm of modern research, THE PRAIRIE SCHOOL REVIEW has nurtured a whole field of investigation, stimulating historians to wider and more detailed research into the lives of lesser-known designers. Likewise the California School has gained prominence through the writings of Jean Murray Bangs (Mrs. Harwell Hamilton Harris), Esther McCoy, and David Gebhard. The names of Greene and Greene and of Bernard Maybeck are in common usage today and appear in many general histories, while only a quarter of a century ago they were comparatively unknown nationally. The architecture of Newsom and Newsom is little known today, but in the not too distant future exhibitions and catalogues organized and written by Gebhard will stimulate an interest in an exotic Californian architecture slightly earlier than that of the Greene Brothers and Maybeck, and which possibly had an impact upon their works.

The evolutionary aspect of American architecture becomes apparent as one surveys the listings in this volume. For example, Thomas U. Walter employed R. M. Hunt who employed George B. Post and Charles D. Gambrill who practiced together before Gambrill associated with Richardson who employed Charles Follen McKim and Stanford White. The firm McKim, Mead, and White employed Carrere and Hastings and Henry Bacon. William Rutherford Mead of the firm, who was first employed by Russell Sturgis and worked in that office under George Fletcher Babb, later employed Babb who subsequently set up as Babb, Cook and Willard. Frank Furness, from the office of Hunt, employed Louis Sullivan, who also studied under William Ware (from Hunt's office) at the Massachusetts Institute of Technology. Thereafter the links of the chain pass from Wright through to Marion Mahony, Walter Burley Griffin, William Drummond, Arthur Drexler, and numerous other notable designers. When Wright was asked in 1941 whom he considered to be America's best architect, he named Albert Kahn. It is interesting that a romantically-inclined architect could admire another who designed primarily for the automobile industry of Detroit, although it must be allowed that Kahn was a Gothicist at heart, as can be seen in his early sketches in Europe and in his domestic architecture. Kahn's architectural engineering projects are thus very much a part of this bibliography, and so too are the works of Raphael Guastavino, a Spanish architect who settled and practiced in the United States, although he is famed for the development of Catalan vaulting methods. James B. Eads of the St. Louis bridge fame and John A. and Washington Roebling are included as having designed "a tension structure never surpassed and seldom equaled" (James Marston Fitch). James Bogardus--machinist, eccentric mill-maker, and manufacturer of cast-iron structures--also has a place.

Another problem which arises is of the architect who practiced prior to the Civil War but lived on to the third and fourth quarters of the century, without necessarily practicing architecture. In the case of Ammi Burnham Young (1798-1874), for example, all of his projects for the Treasury Department were designed prior to 1860, even though some were not completed until 1865 and after by his successor Isaiah Rogers. Young designed nothing after 1860, thus he has not been included. Some two dozen architects have been listed who began the practice of architecture prior to the First World War, but who continued to practice into the 1920's, 1930's, 1940's and 1950's. All references and articles of their works have been included for convenience of reference. Generally speaking, each architect is provided with a brief biographical sketch, listing selected information where it is actually known--including name, dates of birth and death, education and training, employment, partnerships, writings by the architect if any, deposits of drawings, obituaries, and a notation of any thesis written on the architect. Doctoral dissertations have been annotated separately, but master's theses and unavailable dissertations (such as Francis R. Kowsky's contribution on Frederick C. Withers, which has not yet been released by Johns Hopkins University) have been listed under the biographical entry. Depositories of drawings have been abstracted from George S. Koyl, AMERICAN ARCHITECTURAL DRAWINGS. A CATALOG OF ORIGINAL AND MEASURED DRAWINGS OF BUILDINGS OF THE U.S.A. TO DEC. 31, 1917, and obituaries have generally been located in Adolf K. Placzek, AVERY OBITUARIES INDEX OF ARCHITECTS AND ARTISTS. Reference should be made to Koyl for in-depth descriptions. Both publications are listed in Section I: General Reference Works. Each architect is given a number beginning with 1:1 for Ackerman, Frederick Lee, and each subsequent entry concerning Ackerman is given a follow up number as 1:2, 1:3 and so on. This will make index notations easier to locate, since each reference will be linked not to a page containing approximately five annotations, but to a particular annotation.

Section 1

GENERAL REFERENCE WORKS ON AMERICAN ARCHITECTS AND THEIR ARCHITECTURE

Section 1

GENERAL REFERENCE WORKS ON AMERICAN ARCHITECTS AND THEIR ARCHITECTURE

Andrews, Wayne. ARCHITECTURE, AMBITION AND AMERICANS. New York: Harper and Brothers, 1955. 315 p.

> Although surveying American architecture, this book is really a history of residential architecture by architects overcommitted to the design process for wealthy clients who required an outward expression of their (for the most part) newly-acquired affluence. Quotations are apt and to the point and the illustrations, mostly by the author, enhance the text by the very fact that they were taken with the text in mind. As in Hitchcock's publications, there is an objectivity in judging the Victorian styles.

_____. ARCHITECTURE IN AMERICA, A PHOTOGRAPHIC HISTORY FROM THE COLONIAL PERIOD TO THE PRESENT. New York: Atheneum Publishers, 1960. 182 p.

> Russell Lynes wrote an introduction to this history which has 262 illustrations, many of razed monuments, with reasons given for their demise. It expands upon and complements ARCHITECTURE, AMBITION AND AMERICANS, an earlier work by the same author (see above).

Burchard, John, and Bush-Brown, Albert. THE ARCHITECTURE OF AMERICA, A SOCIAL AND CULTURAL HISTORY. Boston: Little, Brown and Co., 1961. 595 p.

> Part I, consisting of 112 pages, is devoted to American architecture to 1860. Thereafter, the most recent hundred years is carefully portrayed linking architectural, art, social, cultural, and intellectual history. The American-ness of American architecture of the late nineteenth century and the waves of European impact in the twentieth form the major emphasis in the book, which devotes more space to architecture between the two world wars than possibly any other single source. Invaluable for this aspect alone.

Coles, William A., and Reed, Henry Hope, Jr. ARCHITECTURE IN AMERICA:

A BATTLE OF STYLES. New York: Appleton-Century-Crofts, Inc., 1961. 412 p.

An anthology of essays on architecture written by authors ancient and modern, American and non-American. Part one is devoted to the aims of architecture and part two to five controversies of modern American architecture, including classicism, glass boxes, and vertical structures.

Collins, Peter. CHANGING IDEALS IN MODERN ARCHITECTURE 1750 - 1950. Montreal: McGill University Press, 1965. 308p.

This historical survey of 200 years relates the history of ideas to the forms of buildings. It carefully explains all the movements in architecture, American and European, beginning with the Romantic-Classicists and continuing through nineteenth-century movements to "Rationalism." Engineering and the Industrial Revolution is examined in relation to its impact upon architecture. The Society of Architectural Historians considered this book of sufficient excellence for the Alice Davis Hitchcock Award.

Condit, Carl W. AMERICAN BUILDING ART-THE NINETEENTH CENTURY. New York: Oxford University Press, 1960. 371 p.

"A comprehensive history of structural forms and techniques in the United States...as they developed into the structural basis of modern building." Condit explains various structural methods, materials, and systems including those of the skyscraper and wide spans necessary notably in New York City and Chicago in the late nineteenth century.

_____. AMERICAN BUILDING ART-THE TWENTIETH CENTURY, New York: Oxford University Press, 1961. 427 p.

A continuation of the history of civil engineering in relation to architecture in the nineteenth century. This volume carries the skyscraper, railroad terminal, and the bridge into the twentieth century. But the automobile as a twentieth-century phenomena had a different effect upon engineering feats of road and bridge construction. Dams, reclamation projects, and concrete shell constructions are discussed, in addition to the complex engineering innovations demanded by the ingenious architect. All are well illustrated with 134 figures.

_____. AMERICAN BUILDING, MATERIALS AND TECHNIQUES FROM THE BEGINNING OF THE COLONIAL SETTLEMENTS TO THE PRESENT. Chicago: University of Chicago Press, 1968. 329 p. 112 illus.

The third and fourth parts of the book on "The Rise of the Industrial Republic, 1865-1900" and "The Industrial and Urban Expansion in the Twentieth Century" will be of major interest to those concerned with architecture after 1860. Part three is Condit's special period of research although the fourth part represents half of the book. This layman's book is strong on American innovations although Europe forwarded developing traditions of most modern building materials.

_____. THE CHICAGO SCHOOL OF ARCHITECTURE: A HISTORY OF COMMERCIAL AND PUBLIC BUILDINGS IN THE CHICAGO AREA, 1875-1925. Chicago: University of Chicago Press, 1964. 238 p.

"Architecture in the Nineteenth Century" and "Chicago: 1871" are the introductory chapters of a book devoted to the major architects of the late nineteenth and early twentieth centuries within an historical, economic, social, cultural, and business setting. The pioneers of iron, steel, and concrete construction and their respective achievements are considered as a major contribution to American architecture.

_____. THE RISE OF THE SKYSCRAPER, THE GENIUS OF CHICAGO ARCHITECTURE FROM THE GREAT FIRE TO LOUIS SULLIVAN. Chicago: University of Chicago Press, 1952. 255 p.

Although this book emphasizes a building type of a particular regional area, it is included in this list because of the architects and firms involved in the construction of high-rise buildings, mainly in Philadelphia, New York, and Chicago.

Creighton, Thomas H. AMERICAN ARCHITECTURE. The America Today Series. Washington: Robert B. Luce, Inc., 1964. 85 p.

This very brief volume, illustrated by pen and ink drawings, contains not only a survey history of American architecture but also a section on "The Architectural Scene Today," analyzing buildings by type. Creative developments have come into American architecture from other areas of the world due to imagination and transference of ideas. Names of outstanding architects are listed by derivation: Germanic, Scandinavian, Japanese and so on.

Early, James. ROMANTICISM AND AMERICAN ARCHITECTURE. New York: A.S. Barnes, 1965. 171 p.

Developed from a doctoral dissertation at Harvard, the book quotes and discusses romantic philosophical theory without specific links to architectural works. It basically covers only the medieval and Gothic phases of the nineteenth-century revival styles to the exclusion of all others, which in themselves are part of the eclecticisms in the totality of romantic architecture.

Edgell, G.H. THE AMERICAN ARCHITECTURE TODAY. New York: Charles Scribner's Sons, 1928. 401 p.

Written for the layman by an art historian, critic, and observer of beauty, this book discusses monuments as examples of type. Although the works covered are not necessarily the best, those considered bad are totally ignored. When this book was prepared in the 1920's from a series of lectures, the author considered that architecture was on the "threshold of a great Renaissance." The book is divided into four parts, "The Development of American Architecture," "Domestic and Academic," "Ecclesiastic and Monumental," and "Commercial" up to the cathedral-like verticality of skyscrapers of the 1920's.

Fitch, James Marston. AMERICAN BUILDING: THE HISTORICAL FORCES THAT SHAPED IT. Boston: Houghton Mifflin Co., 1948. Reprint. Boston: Houghton Mifflin, 1966. 382 p. Illus.

A chronological history of American architecture discussing each historic period in relation to the environmental, technical, and aesthetic forces that shaped the expression of buildings.

_____. AMERICAN BUILDING 2: THE ENVIRONMENTAL FORCES THAT SHAPED IT. Rev., enl. ed. Boston: Houghton Mifflin Co., 1971. 349 p. 104 illus.

The technologies of environmental controls have had a profound impact upon twentieth-century architecture and much of the outstanding architecture has taken advantage of these forces (heating, air conditioning, lighting, sound insulation).

_____. ARCHITECTURE AND THE AESTHETICS OF PLENTY. New York: Columbia University Press, 1961. 304 p.

A series of published articles brought together under one cover, with subjects ranging over the past 200 years, but with an emphasis on Wright, his early beginnings, his association with the sculptor, Alfonso Iannelli, plus essays on Gropius and Mies.

Gowans, Alan. IMAGES OF AMERICAN LIVING, FOUR CENTURIES OF ARCHITECTURE AND FURNITURE AS CULTURAL EXPRESSION. Philadelphia: J. B. Lippincott, 1964. 498 p.

This outstanding work which won the Alice Davis Hitchcock Award from the Society of Architectural Historians in 1964 combines, as the title suggests, "The Decorative Arts with Architecture." Gowans taught at the University of Delaware, in close vicinity to Winterthur Museum, Wilmington, which created the scene and the stimulus for such a book. But the strength of the publication is not only to be found in the juxtaposition of these two art forms. Client-architect relationships, the role of the builders, social implications, and many cultural attitudes are discussed in assessing 400 years of architectural history.

Greiff, Constance M. LOST AMERICA. Vol. 1. FROM THE ATLANTIC TO THE MISSISSIPPI; vol. 2. FROM THE MISSISSIPPI TO THE PACIFIC. Princeton: The Pyne Press, 1971. Vol. 1, 244 p.; vol. 2, 243 p.

James Biddle, President of the National Trust for Historic Preservation, wrote the introduction to this photographic study which includes captions plus brief statements organized by building type describing structures in America destroyed in the name of progress. These examples "represent only a small sample of the rich and diverse delights that have vanished from the American scene."

Hamlin, Talbot Faulkner. THE AMERICAN SPIRIT IN ARCHITECTURE. The Pageant of America Series, vol. 13. New Haven: Yale University Press, 1926. 353 p.

The span of American architecture from the log cabin to the future of American architecture as envisioned in the mid 1920's is the subject of this volume. It moves from the Victorian era which comprises two thirds of the book, through the "American Renaissance, 1880 to 1900," and thereafter studies buildings by type, with chapter essays and photographs with captions.

Hiller, Carl E. FROM TEPEES TO TOWERS. A PHOTOGRAPHIC HISTORY OF AMERICAN ARCHITECTURE. Boston and Toronto: Little, Brown & Co., 1967. 106 p.

A very selective, brief, pictorial overview of American architecture with just over half of the book devoted to the period after 1860.

Hitchcock, Henry-Russell. AMERICAN ARCHITECTURAL BOOKS. Minneapolis: University of Minneapolis Press, 1962. 130 p.

Updated from the 1946 edition, this publication is subtitled "A List of Books, Portfolios, and Pamphlets on Architecture and Related Subjects Published in America before 1895," beginning with the American Revolution. There are 1461 entries and a good index which list building types and elements in addition to names and places.

______. ARCHITECTURE: NINETEENTH AND TWENTIETH CENTURIES. Baltimore: Penguin Books, 1958. 498 p.

Architecture worldwide is divided into three sections covering the periods 1800 to 1850, 1850 to 1900, and 1900 to 1950, with the second portion being richest in new research. This book thus becomes a fundamental source for all research of the period since, however briefly the material is covered, it does present a basic listing of architects and their major contributions. Individual chapters are devoted to the Second Empire, High Victorian Gothic, and neo-Gothic, in addition to the outstanding architects such as Richardson or McKim, Mead and White.

Joedicke, Jurgen. A HISTORY OF MODERN ARCHITECTURE. New York:

Frederick A. Praeger, 1959. 243 p.

A history of European and American architecture from the "Age of the Pioneers" through to "Masters of Modern Architecture." Frank Lloyd Wright's work up to his Johnson Wax complex, Racine, Wisconsin, is contained in one chapter.

Jordy, William H. AMERICAN BUILDINGS AND THEIR ARCHITECTS: PROGRESSIVE AND ACADEMIC IDEALS AT THE TURN OF THE TWENTIETH CENTURY. American Buildings and Their Architects Series, vol. 3. Garden City, N.Y.: Doubleday and Co., Inc., 1972. 420 p.

This is the third in a four-volume series devoted to "American Buildings and their Architects," although it is the second one off the press. Volume one is by William H. Pierson, Jr., on the colonial and neo-classical styles, and volume two by the same author should span from volumes one to three. Jordy devotes a chapter to topics concerned with Chicago and the commercial style, the works of Sullivan, Wright, Greene and Greene, Irving Gill, Bernard Maybeck, and Charles McKim, but in each case a building type or a single building is meant to represent an architect's work, as McKim's Boston Public Library, for example.

Jordy, William H., and Coe, Ralph. AMERICAN ARCHITECTURE AND OTHER WRITINGS BY MONTGOMERY SCHUYLER. Vol. 1. Cambridge, Mass.: Harvard University Press, 1961. 328 p.

This first of a two-volume series of Schuyler's writings is a reprint of an 1892 edition of his AMERICAN ARCHITECTURE - STUDIES, which, in turn, was a collection of periodical articles. AMERICAN ARCHITECTURE contains essays on "Modern Architecture," the "Heritage of Victorian Gothic," and the "Richardson Interlude." Photographs and line illustrations from the magazine articles are used.

______. AMERICAN ARCHITECTURE AND OTHER WRITINGS BY MONTGOMERY SCHUYLER. Vol. 2. Cambridge, Mass.: Harvard University Press, 1961. Pp. 329-664.

Montgomery Schuyler was the best-known and most outstanding architectural critic from 1880 to his death in 1914. This volume has a thorough and lengthy introduction, numerous illustrations, and a complete bibliography of all of his periodical articles. Chapters are concerned with bridges, skyscrapers, Beaux Arts reaction, and the works of Sullivan and Wright.

Kaufmann, Edgar, Jr. THE RISE OF AN AMERICAN ARCHITECTURE. New York: Metropolitan Museum of Art, 1970. 241 p.

Published to complement an exhibition at the Metropolitan Museum as part of its centennial celebrations, this book consists of an introduction by Kaufmann and four major essays. Hitchcock writes on

"American Influence Abroad," Albert Fein on "The American City," Winston Weisman on "The Skyscraper," and Vincent Scully on "The American House." All four essays attempt to update material in their respective fields, the Fein contribution reflecting a renewed interest in the park and the work of Olmsted and his contemporaries.

Kimball, Fiske. AMERICAN ARCHITECTURE. Indianapolis and New York: The Bobbs-Merrill Co., 1928. 262 p.

About half of this history is pre-Civil War, but, although the historicism of the late nineteenth century and the 1893 Chicago World's Fair is discussed, the second half looks toward the modern movement which is termed "an affirmation of a different principle of style...the supremacy of form, and worked in the classical spirit of unity, uniformity and balance." Pennsylvania Station, New York City, is seen, for example, as constructed of steel which is "a hidden means to achieve a grandiose scenic effect."

Koyle, George S. AMERICAN ARCHITECTURAL DRAWINGS. A CATALOG OF ORIGINAL AND MEASURED DRAWINGS OF BUILDINGS OF THE U S A TO DEC. 31, 1917. 5 vols. Philadelphia: Philadelphia Chapter American Institute of Architects, 1969. Unpaged.

The destruction of buildings designed in Philadelphia by Frank Furness led the Philadelphia Chapter, American Institute of Architects, to compile listings of architectural drawings. Funding came from Kress Foundation and other sources. The catalog lists 6000 buildings, both by geographic area and alphabetically by the architect concerned. The cutoff point is 1917.

Lancaster, Clay. ARCHITECTURAL FOLLIES IN AMERICA. Rutland, Vt.: Charles E. Tuttle Co., 1960. 243 p. 79 pls.

A "folly" is a building either built as a whim or as an extravagant structure of fantasy, as the French word "folie" translates. The book covers early non-American examples followed by a sampling by regional area such as Massachusetts, Pennsylvania, and the South.

Maass, John. THE GINGERBREAD AGE. New York: Bramhall House, 1957. 212 p.

An interesting essay on American architecture after the Civil War, with a few earlier examples of Gothic cottages and Tuscan villas. "The Mansardic Era" is concerned with the General Grant period when the architectural forms were derived from France, but the "Gingerbread" resulted in the vernacular American wood tradition. The book is well illustrated with photographs and woodcuts of the period.

Massey, James C. SOURCES FOR AMERICAN ARCHITECTURAL DRAWINGS IN FOREIGN COLLECTIONS. A PRELIMINARY SURVEY CARRIED OUT UNDER A GRANT FROM THE FORD FOUNDATION. Washington, D.C.: 1969. 140 p.

Only thirty copies were printed (Avery Library, Columbia University, has one). An archive report with bibliography is provided for twelve countries and a drawing list for eight. Most of the listings are of the eighteenth century, but there are some nineteenth-century drawings, and the Royal Institute of British Architects, London, as one example, "is continuing, in a small way, to collect recent U.S. drawings by prominent architects."

Mumford, Lewis. THE BROWN DECADES; A STUDY OF THE ARTS IN AMERCA 1865-1895. New York: Harcourt, Brace and Co., 1931. 266 p.

Based upon the Guernsey Center Moore lectures at Dartmouth College for 1931, Mumford shows an interest in the California School in addition to the names and works of the big guns of the period. It is an attempt to stimulate re-evaluation of the period and not be dominated by negative attitudes. Works of landscape architecture, of structural innovations, and the beginnings of modern architecture of this period were "a fulfillment of the past and a starting point for the future."

_____. ROOTS OF CONTEMPORARY AMERICAN ARCHITECTURE. New York: Grove Press, 1959. 454 p. (There are several editions from the first of 1952).

Mumford's introduction begins with American independence at the Revolution and traces through architectural writings which antedate new building forms. Discussion emphasizes the impact of Emerson, Hawthorne, Thoreau, Whitman, Melville, Downing, Olmsted, Furness, Richardson, Sullivan, and Wright. Then follows a series of essays by designers and theorists on sources of form and roots, the role of the machine, the importance of Chicago through to the future. At the end of the book are twenty-eight biographical sketches of moulders of modern design including one of a guy called Mumford!

_____. STICKS AND STONES; A STUDY OF AMERICAN ARCHITECTURE AND CIVILIZATION. New York: W.W. Norton and Co., 1924. 238 p.

Mumford states in his 1933 edition that "when STICKS AND STONES appeared in 1924, no history of American architecture as a whole was in existence...except for the period before 1840." THE BROWN DECADES takes up where STICKS AND STONES stops. Illustrations have been omitted to encourage readers to investigate the classic and romantic traditions and the pioneer and machine age expressions. The book began as a series of unsuccessful lectures which were ahead of their time.

Noffsinger, James P. THE INFLUENCE OF THE ECOLE DES BEAUX-ARTS ON

THE ARCHITECTS OF THE UNITED STATES. Doctoral dissertation, Catholic University of America, 1955. 123 p.; published in book form, Washington, D.C.: Catholic University of America, 1955. 123 p.

From the period of the Civil War, before which no architecture schools existed in the United States, Americans began to study in Paris at the Ecole des Beaux-Arts, beginning with R.M. Hunt. The school remained a strong force influencing American architecture well into the twentieth century. This thesis lists all American students at the Ecole and is thus a basic research source. It has a bibliography.

Placzek, Adolf K. AVERY OBITUARY INDEX OF ARCHITECTS AND ARTISTS. Boston: G.K. Hall and Co., 1963. 338 p.

Approximately 13,500 entries taken from major American and English journals on architecture from 1865 to 1963, in addition to THE NEW YORK TIMES.

Pevsner, Nikolaus. PIONEERS OF MODERN DESIGN, FROM WILLIAM MORRIS TO WALTER GROPIUS. London: Faber and Faber, 1936 (1st ed.); Baltimore: Penguin Books, 1960. 256 p.

This book is concerned essentially with European movements, but briefly mentions Sullivan and Wright in Chapter 7: "The Modern Movement before 1914." It should be remembered that Wright had a profound influence in Germany and Holland and upon Gropius and the Bauhaus. Pevsner's THE SOURCES OF MODERN ARCHITECTURE AND DESIGN (New York: Praeger, 1968) contains similar material.

Reed, Henry Hope, [Jr.] THE GOLDEN CITY. Garden City, N.Y.: Doubleday & Co., Inc., 1059. 160 p.

In praise of all that is classical, and a damning criticism of most of the modern movement of "Secessionism" or the "rational." This subjective short thesis upholds the theory of a return to classicism, an ideal held by a whole Classical America Society which publishes a journal, CLASSICAL AMERICA, forwarding its ideas. An appendix is entitled "On the Trail of Picturesque Secessionism."

Roos, Frank J., Jr. BIBLIOGRAPHY OF EARLY AMERICAN ARCHITECTURE. Urbana, Ill.: University of Illinois Press, 1968. 389 p. (1st ed., 1943).

Subtitled "Writings on Architecture Constructed before 1860 in Eastern and Central U.S.," this bibliography has 4,377 entries, approximately 1,600 more than the 1943 edition. It is an invaluable source book although the material covered predates the beginning of this Gale Research volume. It is worthy of mention however, since this Gale Information Guide on architecture is intended to be a continuation of source material as begun, in non-annotated form, by Roos.

Scully, Vincent. AMERICAN ARCHITECTURE AND URBANISM. New York: Praeger, 1970. 275 p.

Scully's interests have evolved from the scholarship of his THE SHINGLE STYLE, concerned with residential architecture of the late nineteenth century, to a concern for society and its inherent problems in the urban areas of present day America. Architecture is no longer the concern of a wealthy client or a benevolent committee in relation to the architect, Scully wirtes. Architects of today and tomorrow will become more involved in the social, economic, and political aspects of society, if the urban areas are to improve and if American culture is to survive.

______. THE SHINGLE STYLE: ARCHITECTURAL THEORY AND DESIGN FROM RICHARDSON TO THE ORIGINS OF WRIGHT. New Haven: Yale University Press, 1955. 181 p.

Architectural styles of the 1840's and '50's evolved from the earlier revivals of the nineteenth century into a period of egalitarian architecture for all. Paralleling this was an attempt at space flow within an open plan, especially as seen in the works of Richardson after the Civil War, partially derived from the arts and crafts movement in England. The Queen Anne style gained impetus after 1876, which, translated into wood construction of America, led the way to a personalized colonial revival and the Shingle style. Richardson had his impact upon a style of "rough stone base supports, loose and rambling wood frame, covered with natural shingles." (p. 99). Many notable architects of the period practiced in the style with its numerous variants.

Tallmadge, Thomas E. THE STORY OF ARCHITECTURE IN AMERICA. London: George Allen and Unwin Ltd., n.d. 311 p.

This history spans the period from Colonial America to "Today and Tomorrow," the period of the 1930's; a little over half the book covers the period after 1860. Historical, political, economic, cultural, and social implications in relation to architecture and stylistic trends are divided into chapters on "The Parvenu Period, 1860-80"; "The Romanesque Revival, 1876-93"; "The World's Fair, 1893"; "Louis Sullivan and The Lost Cause"; and "Eclecticism, 1893-1917."

Tunnard, Christopher, and Reed, Henry Hope. AMERICAN SKYLINE. Boston, Houghton Mifflin Co., 1955. 269 p.

Part 4 of this book, "The Age of Steam and Iron," covers the period 1850-80, and thus is relevant for us. The book is concerned with the growth of urban America, the townscape and the resultant effect of industry, highways, parking lots, skyscrapers, hotels, residences. Towns rely upon industry, government, education, and the railroad whether on the prairie, in the mountains, or along the coastline.

Whiffen, Marcus. AMERICAN ARCHITECTURE SINCE 1780: A GUIDE TO THE STYLES. Cambridge, Mass.: The M.I.T. Press, 1969. 313 p.

Only eighty-three pages are devoted to the pre-1860 styles, the remainder to the numerous stylistic changes after the Civil War. The book is invaluable to those who wish for clear-cut definitions and an explanation of the eclecticisms of American architecture. It is well illustrated with good examples, has an extensive bibliography of source material and a glossary.

Withey, Henry F. and Elsie R. BIOGRAPHICAL DICTIONARY OF AMERICAN ARCHITECTS (DECEASED). Los Angeles: New Age Publishing Co., 1956. 678 p. Facsimile edition by Hennessey and Ingalls, Los Angeles, 1970.

The only dictionary of its kind listing 2000 architects from 1740 to 1952. Each architect had to have died prior to 1952 to be included. Thus Frank Lloyd Wright, who died in 1959, is not even mentioned. There are other errors such as the spelling of Stanford White's name. The dictionary is, however, valuable as a basic source of information upon which to build. It has proved extremely useful in the compilation of this annotated biographical bibliography of American architects.

Section 2

SELECTED ANNOTATED BIOGRAPHICAL BIBLIOGRAPHY OF AMERICAN ARCHITECTS FROM THE PERIOD OF THE CIVIL WAR TO THE FIRST WORLD WAR

Section 2

SELECTED ANNOTATED BIOGRAPHICAL BIBLIOGRAPHY OF AMERICAN ARCHITECTS FROM THE PERIOD OF THE CIVIL WAR TO THE FIRST WORLD WAR

1:1 **ACKERMAN, FREDERICK LEE (1878-1950)**

Educated at Cornell and became partner of Alexander S. Trowbridge 1906-20. During the First World War, he was appointed chief of the Department of Housing and Planning of the United States Shipping Board under Robert Kohn.

Publications: THE HOUSING FAMINE, 1920; THE HOUSING PROBLEM IN WAR AND PEACE, 1918; A NOTE ON SITE AND UNIT PLANNING, 1937; GEORGIAN ARCHITECTURE, 1930.

Obituary: AMERICAN INSTITUTE OF ARCHITECTS' JOURNAL 14 (December 1950): 249-54.

1:2 Mumford, Lewis. ROOTS OF CONTEMPORARY AMERICAN ARCHITECTURE. New York: Reinhold Publishing Corp., 1952. P. 420.

> Ackerman "was perhaps, with Grosvenor Atterbury and John Irwin Bright, the first important architect, after Louis Sullivan, to be fully alive to the social responsibilities - and the economic conditioning - of architecture." His work is to be seen at Sunnyside Gardens, New Jersey; Radburn, New Jersey; and also at colonial houses in Manhasset, Long Island.

2:1 **ADLER, DANKMAR (1844-1900)**

Trained in Detroit under John Schaeffer and E. Willard Smith, and in Chicago under Augustus Bauer and O.S. Kinney. Joined Ashley Kinney in partnership, and from 1871 partnered with Edward Burling. By 1878, when Louis Sullivan joined the firm, he was practicing alone. Sullivan became a partner 1881-95.

Obituary: AMERICAN ARCHITECTURE 68 (April 21, 1900): 17.

2:2 Elstein, Rochelle S. "The Architecture of Dankmar Adler." JOURNAL OF THE SOCIETY OF ARCHITECTURAL HISTORIANS 26 (December 1967): 242-49.

Adler and Sullivan were partners from 1881-95. Adler's independent work was for the most part straightforward, functional, honest, and mostly commercial.

2:3 McLean, Robert Craik. "Dankmar Adler." INLAND ARCHITECT AND NEWS RECORD 35 (May 1900): 26-27, 32.

Adler died of apoplexy at noon on April 16, 1900. This obituary is a brief survey of his life and architecture, his family and his profession. In the plates section at the end of this May 1900 issue is a magnificent photographic set of Sullivanesque decorations.

2:4 Mumford, Lewis. ROOTS OF CONTEMPORARY AMERICAN ARCHITECTURE. New York: Reinhold Publishing Corp., 1952. Pp. 420-21.

Adler's "sense of civic responsibility, his immense grasp of practical detail, his theoretic interest in dominant technical problems of his day, all combined to make him an exemplary figure in his profession." Early life, education, and background briefly surveyed.

2:5 Saltzstein, Joan W. "Dankmar Adler: The Man, The Architect, The Author." WISCONSIN ARCHITECT, July-August 1967, pp. 15-19; September 1967, pp. 10-14; November 1967, pp. 16-19.

Mrs. Saltzstein is the grand-daughter of Adler.

3:1 ADLER AND SULLIVAN (Partnership 1881-95)

See also: Dankmar Adler (1844-1900) and Louis Sullivan (1856-1924).

Avery Library, Columbia University, has three sheets of drawings of the Auditorium Building, Chicago.

3:2 Adler and Sullivan. "The Decoration of McVicker's Theatre, Chicago." AMERICAN ARCHITECT AND BUILDING NEWS 23 (February 11, 1888): 70-71.

A letter from the architects clarifying a statement in the January 28th issue of AMERICAN ARCHITECT AND BUILDING NEWS by a Mr. Twyman: "The work was executed under my charge and dictation, and was my own conception without control of architect or owner." The contractors were McGrath and McVicker, and Twyman was only a superintendent.

3:3 ARCHITECTURAL FORUM. "Chicago: Veto Demolition on Esthetic Grounds."

Vol. 113 (October 1960): 9, 11, 14.

Judge McKinlay of the Cook County Superior Court acted to prevent the razing of the Schiller Building, Chicago, containing the Garrick Theater. Judge McKinlay introduced the problem of compensation for the owner; a policy not covered in the ordinances of the city of Chicago. Subsequent history illustrates that the preservationists were not ultimately able to prevent the building being razed.

3:4 _____. "Chicago's Auditorium is Fifty Years Old." Vol. 73 (September 1946 Supplement): 10-12.

This is as much a character study by Frank Lloyd Wright of Dankmar Adler and his handling of building contractors and office architectural assistants as it is an article on the auditorium.

3:5 _____. "Shards: Chicago's Architectural Heritage." Vol. 137 (November 1972): 29-33.

"The decimation of the old Stock Exchange...was fundamentally a cop-out on the economic and potential of a living, working landmark....Sullivan himself might have taken it philosophically. We take it insufferably."

3:6 Garczynski, E.R. . AUDITORIUM. New York: Exhibit Publishing Co., 1890. 59 p.

3:7 Hasbrouck, Wilbert R. "Chicago's Auditorium Theater." THE PRAIRIE SCHOOL REVIEW 4 (Third Quarter, 1967): 7-21.

The auditorium was opened December 9, 1889, but was closed during the Depression, became a USO Club during the Second World War, and Roosevelt University in 1947. The second great opening was on October 31, 1967, for the New York City Ballet, and this was only possible after careful restoration by an army of craftsmen and architects. Plans, sections and numerous photographs of the refurbishing.

3:8 HISTORIC PRESERVATION. "The Auditorium Building." Vol. 10, no. 2 (1958): 61-62.

A history of the building to the period when Roosevelt University acquired it for educational purposes and began restoration.

3:9 Huxtable, Ada Louise. "Acoustical Hall." THE NEW YORK TIMES, June 5, 1960, section 5, p. 18.

The acoustics of Carnegie Hall, New York, are as much due to Adler and Sullivan as to its architect William Burnet Tuthill, claims this letter to the editor.

3:10 ______. "The Chicago Style - on Its Way Out?" THE NEW YORK TIMES, November 29, 1970, section 2, p. 27.

Two buildings in the Loop of Chicago--the Stock Exchange by Adler and Sullivan, and the Carson, Pirie, Scott store by Sullivan after the dissolution of the partnership--are compared in relation to preservation. The Chicago Historical and Architectural Landmarks Commission requested landmark status from the owners who refused. The City Council agrees with the realtors lobby and thus, the Stock Exchange will be lost. The store is in no immediate danger and thus landmark status has been approved.

3:11 ______. "In St. Louis, the News is Better." THE NEW YORK TIMES, Sunday, March 10, 1974, section 2, p. 21.

Adler and Sullivan's Wainwright Building is being preserved as a part of the city center revitalization in St. Louis. Other examples of successful and not so successful preservation in other cities are mentioned.

3:12 Johnson, Richard D. "The Gage Panels: from Contractor's Scrap to Museum Display," THE PRAIRIE SCHOOL REVIEW 1 (Third Quarter, 1964): 15-16.

Discusses the removal and preservation of the cast-iron decorative frieze panels from the Gage Building, Chicago.

3:13 Ritter, Betty J. "Rebirth of Chicago's Auditorium." AMERICAN INSTITUTE OF ARCHITECTS' JOURNAL 47 (June 1967): 65-68.

Restoration began on a "pay-as-you-go basis" with a fund of $1.75 million. The ups and downs of the building and even a latent lack of interest are mentioned.

3:14 Schuyler, Montgomery. "Great American Architects Series." ARCHITECTURAL RECORD (February 1896 Supplement): 2-48.

The article begins with a survey of conditions affecting the work of architects in the Chicago area. Brief biographical sketches of both architects precede a listing and discussion of all of their major works. Some of Sullivan's terra-cotta ornamentations are also illustrated in detail.

3:15 Sprague, Paul E. "Adler and Sullivan's Schiller Building." The Garrick Theater. THE PRAIRIE SCHOOL REVIEW 2 (Second Quarter, 1965): 5-20, 31.

Banister Fletcher is quoted by Sprague ["American Architecture Through English Spectacles." ENGINEERING MAGAZINE 7 (June 1894): 318] as comparing the Schiller Building to the Parthenon, Athens, but "progress" led to its demolition in 1961. Construction and demolition photographs, drawings, plans, sections, details of ornamentation. Lengthy bibliography p. 31.

3:16 Twose, G. "Schiller Building: Steel and Terra-Cotta Buildings in Chicago and Some Deductions." THE BRICKBUILDER 3 (January 1894): 4.

The weak point in the design of the building was apparently "the difficulty of harmonizing the imperatively necessary large openings in the first story with the massiveness of the superstructure." Twose also thought that the building lacked unity.

3:17 Wofford, Theodore J., and Cotton, W. Philip. RECOMMENDATIONS FOR RESTORING AND REJUVENATING THE WAINWRIGHT BUILDING. St. Louis, Mo.: St. Louis Chapter, American Institute of Architects, 1966. 7 p.

Prepared for the Preservation Committee of the St. Louis Chapter, American Institute of Architects, essentially to prevent the building from being demolished. Restoration and rejuvenation must be well coordinated and sympathetic to original design considerations in its approach. Certain minimum recommendations were made, hopefully intended for immediate implementation, with the idea that long term improvements would be undertaken by a competent architect.

4:1 AIKEN, WILLIAM MARTIN (18?-1908)

Educated at the University of the South and Massachusetts Institute of Technology (1879), worked for H.H. Richardson in Boston, and later for James McLaughlin in Cincinnati. Practiced in New York City from 1886 until 1895 when he was appointed Supervising Architect of the Treasury Department by President Grover Cleveland.

National Archives, Washington, has numerous drawings of ten government buildings, mainly post offices, designed when Aiken was Supervising Architect.

Obituary: AMERICAN ARCHITECT AND BUILDING NEWS 94 (1908): 215.

4:2 AMERICAN ARCHITECT AND BUILDING NEWS. "In Memoriam, William Martin Aiken." Vol. 94 (December 23, 1908): 213-14.

A memorial meeting was held in the office of the Supervising Architect of the Treasury Department, a post which Aiken held from 1895-97 "at a time when Federal architecture was the subject of much public criticism and his constant aim while Supervising Architect was to improve conditions as he found them. . . ."

5:1 ALDEN AND HARLOW (n.d.)

Alden, Frank E. (1859-1908), and Harlow, Alfred B. (1857-1927). Also known as Longfellow, Alden and Harlow (see).

Alden's obituary: AMERICAN ARCHITECT AND BUILDING NEWS 94 (October 14, 1908): 16.

5:2 Ferree, Barr. "The Art of High Building." ARCHITECTURAL RECORD 15 (May 1904): 445-66.

> "High building of today - the typical and most noteworthy architectural creation of our time." Alden and Harlow's Farmer's Deposit Bank Building, Pittsburgh, is illustrated.

5:3 Van Trump, James D. "The Triumphant Stone. A Study of the Foyer of the Carnegie Music Hall." CARNEGIE MAGAZINE 31 (May 1957): 167-75.

> "There is no doubt that the Foyer was amply conceived even by the standards of an ample age, and very richly executed, at a time when richness was considered a sine qua non of the architecture of public buildings." Size, style, use, materials, and historic precedents are cited.

6:1 BABB, GEORGE FLETCHER (1843-1916)

Of Babb, Cook and Willard.

Began work with Russell Sturgis where he was mentor of the young William R. Mead (later of McKim, Mead and White). Montgomery Schuyler gives him credit for the design in Sturgis' office of the Mechanics National Bank, Albany, 1876 [ARCHITECTURAL RECORD 25 (1909): 146]. Peter B. Wight also mentions him [ARCHITECTURAL RECORD 26 (August 1909): 123-31]. See also Charles Baldwin, STANFORD WHITE; Charles Moore, THE LIFE AND TIMES OF CHARLES FOLLEN MCKIM; Homer Saint Gaudens, REMINISCENCES OF AUGUSTUS SAINT-GAUDENS; and Louis Hall Tharp, AUGUSTUS SAINT-GAUDENS AND THE GILDED AGE.

6:2 Berg, Louis de Coppet. "Iron Construction in New York City Past and Future." ARCHITECTURAL RECORD 1 (April-June 1892): 448-69.

> Babb, Cook, and Willard's New York Life Insurance Co. building in Minneapolis is illustrated, p. 467.

6:3 Strugis, Russell. "The Carnegie Libraries in New York City." ARCHITECTURAL RECORD 17 (Mary 1905): 237-46.

This is a review of several branch libraries by various architectural firms, and the judgment of Sturgis is that the fronts are "conservative, school-taught, Paris inspired, neo-classic facades of an approved form." The buildings are on narrow frontages because of the expense of land and thus have a highly studied front facade and large functional windows at the rear. The plans for Babb, Cook and Willard's library at 328 East 67th Street are carefully analyzed.

6:4 _____. "A House in Brooklyn." ARCHITECTURAL RECORD 17 (January 1905): 62-63.

Critical analysis of the form and design elements of a house for Mr. E.E. Jackson, 424 Clinton Street. The house has classical elements, but the stepped gable is strongly reminiscent of forms derived from the medieval period.

6:5 _____. "The Warehouse and the Factory in Architecture." ARCHITECTURAL RECORD 15 (January 1904): 1-17.

A warehouse is defined as being "devoted to the rougher kind of business enterprise. . .not primarily where professional men sit quietly. . .but where goods are piled up for loading and unloading." Three warehouses by Babb, Cook and Willard are listed: 175 Duane Street, 1877; Hanan Building at White and Center Streets; and the DeVinne Press Building, Lafayette Place, 1885. Sturgis praises them for functional brick massing, unbroken vertical lines, and for being "greatly more architectural in character."

7:1 BACON, HENRY (1866-1924)

Educated University of Illinois, 1884, and worked for McKim, Mead and White, ?-1891. Associated with James Brite (see) 1897-1902; thereafter both worked alone.

Avery Library, Columbia University, has eight sketches, three elevations, and perspective views of the Massachusetts Monument, St. Mihiel, France. The American Institute of Architects, Washington, has drawing of three monuments and one house, and the National Archives has 155 sheets of the Lincoln Memorial.

Obituaries: ARCHITECTURAL RECORD 55 (March 1924): 274-76; AMERICAN ARCHITECTURE 125 (January-March 1924): 196; AMERICAN INSTITUTE OF ARCHITECTS' JOURNAL 12 (1924): 151, 276, 401; NEW INTERNATIONAL YEARBOOK 924: 508.

7:2 AMERICAN ARCHITECTURE. "Henry Bacon, 1866-1924." Vol. 125 (1924): 195-96.

Background, education, training, and professional and other awards are enumerated in this tribute obituary.

7:3 Brown, Glenn. "The Lincoln Memorial in Washington, D.C." AMERICAN ARCHITECTURE 118 (October 20, 1920): 489-99, 503-6; 118 (October 27, 1920): 523-33, 537-39.

Situated on an extension of the mall in an area of what had been 700 acres of marshland, the Lincoln Memorial terminates the long axis of the United States Capitol. This was not the first site discussed in relation to the memorial but became the final selection when the architect was appointed. Another site, on the axis of North Capitol Street, was suggested with a design prepared by John Russell Pope. Congressional opinion, costs, and technical data are all included in this well-illustrated article.

7:4 Concklin, Edward F. THE LINCOLN MEMORIAL, WASHINGTON. Washington: United States Government Printing Office, 1927. 94 p.

An historical illustrated description of President Lincoln precedes the reports of the Lincoln Memorial Commission and a description of the architecture, sculpture, reliefs, landscaping, and construction. Settlement in the foundations and cracking of concrete beams necessitated additional underpinning. Progress photographs span from the untouched site, a marshy area along the Potomac, to the dedication.

7:5 Cram, Ralph Adams. "The Lincoln Memorial, Washington, D.C." ARCHITECTURAL RECORD 53 (June 1923): 478-508.

Cram praises the classicism of the Lincoln Memorial stating that the age of Lincoln was "without a vestige even of architectural decency." The article is thoroughly illustrated but literary and poetic in its presentation.

7:6 Embury, Aymar. "Henry Bacon, 1866-1924." ARCHITECTURAL RECORD 55 (March 1924): 274-76.

An assessment of his qualities: "He hated meanness, hypocrisy, self-seeking and bigotry with a fiery contempt."

7:7 Swales, F.S. "Henry Bacon as a Draftsman." PENCIL POINTS 5 (May 1924): 42-62.

"Henry Bacon had only reached his zenith as a draftsman as well as architect at the time of his death." His early drawings in this country were "dry but never hard in technique"; they developed in Europe and in the offices where he worked. His influence in those offices was considerable. His association with painters and sculptors added to his development. Career, partnerships, office work, and eulogistic tributes are quoted from other sources. Representative examples of his free hand and architectural draftsmanship and watercolor work are illustrated.

8:1 BARNETT, GEORGE INGHAM (1815-98)

Studied architecture in England under Sir Thomas Hine. Settled in St. Louis, where he worked for M. Lewis Clark, thereafter setting up practice independently.

8:2 Burnett, Tom P. "George I. Barnett, Pioneer Architect of the West." WESTERN ARCHITECT 18 (1912): 13-25.

A biographical and pictorial essay of Barnett's work in St. Louis, in a variety of flavors of the Gothic and classic idioms.

8:3 Van Ravensway, Charles. "Antiques in Domestic Setting." ANTIQUES 43 (February 1943): 70-71.

"In the year 1854, Colonel Ferdinand Kennett commissioned the English-trained St. Louis architect, George I. Barnett, to build a great sprawling mansion for him on the...Mississippi." The mansion, which cost $125,000, is well illustrated inside and out in this article.

9:1 BEMAN, SOLON SPENCER (1853-1914)

Trained in office of Richard Upjohn but began practicing independently in Chicago, 1879.

Obituary: AMERICAN INSTITUTE OF ARCHITECTS' JOURNAL 2 (1914): 348.

9:2 Jenkins, Charles E. "A Review of the Works of S.S. Beman." ARCHITECTURAL REVIEWER 1 (March 31, 1897): 47-101.

This was a short-lived publication devoted to "leading architects of the West, and, as far as possible gives an illustrated review of what they have done." Beman was born in Brooklyn but was selected at the age of twenty-six by George M. Pullman to design buildings at the company town in Illinois. He built most of the public buildings there in a mixture of styles before settling in Chicago with a practice in commercial and residential architecture, but not exclusively so. He designed the Pullman car for the 1893 Columbian Exposition.

10:1 BENARD, HENRI JEAN EMILE (1844- ?)

10:2 Daniels, Mark. "University of California Administration Building, Berkeley. Arthur Brown, Jr., Architect." ARCHITECT AND ENGINEER 151 (November 1942): 12-18.

Originally won in competition by Henri Jean Emile Benard, the plan for the University of California has changed over the years by a succession of well-known local California architects including Arthur Brown who designed the administration building, which is simple, dignified, individualistic, and classical.

11:1 BERRY, PARKER NOBLE (1888-1918)

One of Sullivan's last assistants. Worked for his father, a building contractor, until 1907, when he enrolled at the University of Illinois which he left dissatisfied in 1909.

11:2 Hoffmann, Donald L. "The Brief Career of a Sullivan Apprentice: Parker N. Berry." THE PRAIRIE SCHOOL REVIEW 4 (First Quarter, 1967): 7-15.

Berry was hired as a draftsman by Sullivan in 1909, just prior to Elmslie's departure, and remained until 1917. He practiced in Princeton, Illinois, building there the Adeline Prouty Old Ladies Home, as well as the Henry C. Adams Building in Algona, the First State Bank of Manlius, and the Interstate Bank of Hegewish, all Sullivanesque. Berry died at the age of thirty in 1918, thus his career was brief and his buildings few, but of significant interest.

12:1 BOGARDUS, JAMES (1800-74)

Manufacturer of cast-iron structures.

Published: CAST IRON BUILDINGS: THEIR CONSTRUCTION AND ADVANTAGES, New York, 1856.

12:2 Bannister, Turpin C. "Bogardus Revisited." JOURNAL OF THE SOCIETY

OF ARCHITECTURAL HISTORIANS 15 (December 1956): 12-22; 16 (March 1957): 11-18.

Divided into two parts, these articles are subtitled "The Iron Fronts" and "The Iron Towers." On either side of Center Street several iron-works manufactories were situated, including that of Bogardus who began iron construction in a modest way and in 1848 changed his City Directory listing from machinist to eccentric mill-maker. He built his factory in 1849, and thereafter constructed several noteworthy New York landmarks, few of which remain. His towers included those for making cannon balls, a lighthouse, and a fire alarm bell tower. The footnotes of these articles are extensive and contain a wealth of information for anyone researching the field.

12:3 Higgins, Daniel Paul. "Centenary of a Structural Revolution." EMPIRE STATE ARCHITECT 8 (March-April 1948): 11-22.

The Centenary celebrated the erection of the first cast-iron building in New York City at 63 Center Street, between Pearl and Worth. The article also discusses the introduction and development of cement in England.

12:4 Huxtable, Ada Louise. "Harper and Brothers Building. 1854, New York" PROGRESSIVE ARCHITECTURE 38 (February 1957): 153-54.

After the publisher's earlier building burned, this new structure of 1854 incorporated fire prevention devices not only in the structural detailing but also in the planning and separation of the building's functions. I-section beams made by Peter Cooper's Works at Trenton were used here, the year before Cooper Union in 1855.

12:5 O'Gorman, James F. "A Bogardus Original." ARCHITECTURAL REVIEW 5 (February 1970): 155-56.

The Laing Store at Washington and Murray Streets, New York City, 1849, was scheduled for demolition and re-erection elsewhere. It was designed "being cast and fitted so that each piece may be put up as fast as it is brought on the ground...taken down, removed and put up again in short time."

12:6 Sturges, Walter Knight. "Cast-iron in New York." ARCHITECTURAL REVIEW 114 (October 1953): 232-37.

"The surviving pocket of iron facades in central New York, where James Bogardus did pioneer work..." is illustrated with photographs of his buildings, extant and now razed and drawings of his patent of "certain new and useful improvements in the method of constructing Iron Houses."

13:1 **BRAGDON, CLAUDE FAYETTE (1866-1946)**

Trained under Bruce Price. Established his own office in Rochester, 1901.

Publications: THE ARCHITECTURAL LECTURES, 1942; ARCHITECTURE AND DEMOCRACY, 1918; THE BEAUTIFUL NECESSITY, 1910; DETAILS FROM ITALIAN PALACES, 1897; FOUR DIMENSIONAL VISTAS, 1916; THE FROZEN FOUNTAIN, 1932; MINOR ITALIAN PALACES, 1896; MORE LIVES THAN ONE, 1938; A PRIMER OF HIGHER SPACE, 1913; PROJECTIVE ORNAMENT, 1915.

Gave some of the Scammon Lectures at the Chicago Art Institute, SIX LECTURES ON ARCHITECTURE, 1915 (published in 1917); prefaced Carl F. Schmidt's COBBLESTONE ARCHITECTURE, 1944; wrote foreword to Louis Sullivan's THE AUTOBIOGRAPHY OF AN IDEA, 1926; and edited Louis Sullivan's KINDERGARTEN CHATS ON ARCHITECTURE, EDUCATION AND DEMOCRACY, 1934.

Avery Library, Columbia University, has one sheet of "The Application of Musical Ratios and of Regulating Lines to Architecture," two plates of "New York Central Station at Rochester, 1913," and one sheet of the entablature around "Waiting Room of Rochester Station."

Obituaries: ARCHITECTURAL FORUM 105 (November 1946): 140. MICHIGAN SOCIETY OF ARCHITECTS WEEKLY BULLETIN 20 (December 10, 1946): 2.

13:2 Bragdon, Claude, "Salvaged from Time; Extracts from the Autobiography of Claude Bragdon." AMERICAN ARCHITECTURE 149 (November 1936): 79-82; 149 (December 1936): 81-84; 150 (January 1937): 79-82; 150 (February 1937): 81-84; 150 (March 1937): 85-88.

Bragdon worked for Harvey Ellis and Bruce Price prior to various partnerships and travel in Europe. In 1909, he was given the $2 million commission for the New York Central Railroad Station at Rochester where he attempted to link musical ratios to architectural design. This led to the publication of ART AND GEOMETRY by William Ivins. He collaborated with an engineer on bridge design and became interested in Sullivan and his Prudential Building, Buffalo.

13:3 Erville, Costa. "Claude F. Bragdon, Architect, Stage Designer and Mystic." ROCHESTER HISTORY, October 1967, pp. 1-20.

13:4 Mumford, Lewis. ROOTS OF CONTEMPORARY AMERICAN ARCHITECTURE. New York: Reinhold Publishing Corp., 1952. Pp. 422-23.

One of the few easterners of the 1890-1930 period to be inspired by the Chicago School. He designed the

New York Central Railroad Station, Rochester, while practicing there. His philosophy paralleled Sullivan's but was muddled with Theosophy.

13:5 Smith, M.B. "Master Draftsmen XX; Claude Bragdon." PENCIL POINTS 8 (1927): 201-16.

Bragdon's drawings vary from competition entries, caricatures, cartoons, book illustrations, stage sets, scenery, costumes, and book plates in a wide variety of media.

14:1 BRIGHAM, GEORGE (1869- ?)

Educated Massachusetts Institute of Technology, 1910-13, where he later taught, prior to moving to California in 1920. He worked there for various firms including Ernest Kump.

14:2 Eaton, Leonard K. "George Brigham, A Quiet Force in Domestic Architecture," PROGRESSIVE ARCHITECTURE (April 1969): 142-45.

His domestic work began in 1926 in California, with later work in Michigan. He experimented in prefabricated construction.

15:1 BRITE, JAMES (d. 1942)

Trained in the office of McKim, Mead and White. Associated with Henry Bacon, 1897-1902, and thereafter practiced alone.

15:2 McCabe, L.R. "Darlington, a Jacobean Manor in New Jersey." ARCHITECTURAL RECORD 32 (October 1912): 496-509.

"The literal or quasi-grafting of Old World historic homes on to American soil, is one of the most significant phases in the development of modern domestic architecture." Brite was a pupil of McKim, Mead and White. Darlington was one of his most ambitious buildings in private practice. The source of the building and qualities of each area of the building are enumerated.

16:1 BRUNNER, ARNOLD W. (1857-1926)

Educated at Massachusetts Institute of Technology and worked for George B. Post. Entered into partnership with Thomas Tryon in 1896 and at times collaborated with William M. Aiken (see).

Publications: A CITY PLAN FOR ROCHESTER, 1911; COLLAGES;

OR HINTS ON ECONOMICAL BUILDINGS, 1884; INTERIOR DECORATION, 1891; PRELIMINARY REPORT FOR A CITY PLAN FOR GRAND RAPIDS, 1909; PROPOSED CHANGE OF MAP FOR RIVERSIDE DRIVE EXTENSION, 1913; STUDIES FOR ALBANY, 1914.

16:2 AMERICAN ARCHITECTURE. "Arnold W. Brunner, FAIA, 1857-1925." Vol. 127 (1925): 167.

An obituary providing details of early life and education, architectural output, service to the profession, and work on various committees and commissions.

16:3 Croly, Herbert. "The United States Post-Office, Custom House and Court House, Cleveland, O." ARCHITECTURAL RECORD 29 (March 1911): 193-213.

A building such as this can only be built by the skill of the architect, willingness of the federal government and the determination of Cleveland's concerned citizens. These public-spirited men of Cleveland used the Chamber of Commerce in creating a core of civic structures based upon recommendations of D.H. Burnham. Models, full scale mock-ups, interiors and sculpture groups are illustrated to complement a discussion of post office needs and the manner in which the architect has expedited his commission.

16:4 Haddon, Rawson W. "City Planning Studies for Albany." ARCHITECTURAL RECORD 36 (August 1914): 170-74.

A combined project with landscape architect, Charles Downing Lay, Brunner wanted to create a monumental city entrance bridge, a plaza with terminal points but within a picturesque treatment for an organic city.

16:5 Price, Charles Matlack. "Denison University, Granville, Ohio." ARCHITECTURAL RECORD 54 (October 1923): 298-320.

This picturesque site chosen by Baptists for a college in 1831 was being considerably enlarged by Brunner, with Olmsted as landscape architect in the mid-1920's. The Georgian colonial style was utilized throughout with residential precedents of the Atlantic seaboard for dormitories, a University of Virginia library based upon the Pantheon, and a Wrenian chapel. The article is well illustrated with excellent sketches (of aerial views, perspectives, and details), plans, sections, elevations, and a model of the chapel.

16:6 Sturgis, Russell. "Pavilions in the New York Parks." ARCHITECTURAL RECORD 17 (March 1905): 248-54.

Two pavilions are by Brunner and the one illustrated in Seward Park is derived from the Florentine Renaissance.

16:7 Tozier, Josephine. "An Ideal Hospital." ARCHITECTURAL RECORD 18 (November 1905): 377-83.

Brunner's Mt. Sinai Hospital, New York City, was designed for "convenience and the promptness in caring for the sick" compared to earlier hospitals which tended to do more harm than good. The elevations are severe, but Tozier is more concerned with the arrangement and planning of the building with relation to noise, ventilation, and facilitating the movement of sick patients.

17:1 BRYANT, GRIDLEY JAMES FOX (1816-99)

Trained under Alexander Parris in Boston where he began practice in 1837.

Avery Library, Columbia University, has thirty-two sheets of drawings (preliminaries, sketches, and working drawings) of the B. Stark house in New London, Connecticut, 1866. The Society for the Preservation of New England Antiquities has drawings of Mt. Auburn Cemetery Chapel and dwelling for James H. Beal, Boston. The National Archives has ten sheets on the Custom House, San Francisco.

Obituary: AMERICAN ARCHITECT AND BUILDING NEWS 64 (1899): 97.

17:2 ARCHITECTURAL FORUM. "Old City Hall." Vol. 137 (September 1972): 26-29.

Down-to-earth economics, relating preservation and assets, have been the attitudes adopted towards landmark buildings in Boston and notably the City Hall. This approach is described and the building illustrated with before and after floor plans.

17:3 Bailey, Henry Turner. "An Architect of the Old School." NEW ENGLAND MAGAZINE 25 (November 1901): 326-49.

Bailey was a neighbor of Bryant. He considered that Bryant played a significant role in the design of the Mechanics Bank, South Boston, while in the office of Parris.

17:4 Boston. Committee on Public Buildings. THE CITY HALL, BOSTON. Boston: The City Council, 1866. 130 p.

Published after the dedication, Monday, September 17, 1865. The cornerstone ceremony was on Monday, December 22, 1862. Bryant was associated with Arthur Gilman in this design "described as the Italian Renaissance, modified and elaborated by the taste of the French architects of the last thirty years" (p.v.) A history of the need for a new City Hall is given in addition to a list of accommodations needed. Costs are provided in addition to detailed plans, sections, and elevations.

17:5 Huxtable, Ada Louise. "Commercial Buildings - c. 1850-1870. Boston, Mass. Gridley James Fox Bryant, Architect." PROGRESSIVE ARCHITECTURE 39 (August 1958): 105-6.

The fire of 1872 destroyed 152 Bryant-designed structures and thereafter he was commissioned to rebuild 111 of them. This short article contains interesting details of Bryant's life and the city in which he lived and worked.

17:6 _____. "A Funny Roll of the Dice." THE NEW YORK TIMES, Sunday, December 27, 1970, section 2, p. 27.

The Boston City Hall was being saved from destruction by being converted into commercial use which would produce revenue for its upkeep. Huxtable praises this approach as opposed to that of the General Services Administration of the federal government which prohibits commercial uses for buildings no longer in use by the federal government. The article discusses other preservation projects.

17:7 _____. "Granite Wharf, Warehouse, Office Buildings. c. 1823-1872." Boston, Mass. PROGRESSIVE ARCHITECTURE 39 (June 1958): 117-18.

Huxtable provides street addresses of early buildings and mentions Bryant's edifices of the 1850's and 1860's. Large monolythic slabs rather than individually cut stones were the order of the day in early construction, although Bryant is known for ashlar construction.

17:8 _____. "Old City Hall in Boston Gets a New Life." THE NEW YORK TIMES, Saturday, October 21, 1972, p. 39.

The Boston City Hall, 1862-65, had been refurbished into modern offices with a French restaurant in the basement (on foundations of an earlier building by Bulfinch), instead of being demolished. The article is a detailed account of the steps in preserving the building. "Those who said it couldn't be done are enjoying tournedos and a good little burgundy at Maison Robert," the basement restaurant.

17:9 Wrenn, George L. III "The Boston City Hall." JOURNAL OF THE SOCIETY OF ARCHITECTURAL HISTORIANS 21 (December 1962): 188-92.

Bryant won a limited competition in 1860 for a City Hall to be built on the same site as an earlier one by Bulfinch. Its cost, estimated at $160,000, was $100,000 under the final sum.

18:1 BUFFINGTON, LEROY SUNDERLAND (1847-1931)

Trained in offices of Anderson and Hannaford of Cincinnati.

Obituaries: THE WESTERN ARCHITECT (March 1931): 9, 22; ARCHITECTURAL FORUM 54 (March 1931): 23; AMERICAN ARCHITECT 139 (April 1931): 106.

18:2 AMERICAN ARCHITECT AND BUILDING NEWS. "Claim for Infrigement of Patent Covering Principle of Steel Frame Construction." Vol. 38 (December 10, 1892): 157-58.

> Buffington began civil suits against those "who unmindful or ignorant of his monopoly, have erected such buildings" in steel. He wanted 5 percent on the cost of all buildings erected under his patent. In Chicago alone, this would amount to $4.5 million!

18:3 Upjohn, Everard Miller. "Buffington and the Skyscraper." ART BULLETIN 17 (March 1935): 48-70.

> Upjohn attempts to sift through arguments and claims concerning the first skyscraper, 1882, supporting Buffington's conception which predated Jenny's Home Insurance Building, Chicago, 1883-85. Drawings are illustrated to forward this viewpoint, and are supplemented by quotations from Buffington's MEMORIES. Jenny can be credited with the first skyscraper but Buffington had an earlier concept of skeletal high-rise construction in his twenty-eight-story design.

19:1 BURNHAM, DANIEL HUDSON (1846-1912)

Apprenticed to William Le Baron Jenney, 1868, and worked for several firms including Carter, Drake and Wight where he met John Wellborn Root (see) his partner 1873-91. After Root's death the firm was known as D.H. Burnham, 1891-96...and Co. 1896-1912.

Publications: REPORT ON A PLAN FOR SAN FRANCISCO, 1905; REPORT ON IMPROVEMENTS FOR MANILA, 1905; REPORT ON THE PROPOSED PLAN OF THE CITY OF BAGUIO, 1905; WHITE CITY AND CAPITAL CITY, 1902; THE GROUP PLAN OF THE PUBLIC BUILDINGS OF THE CITY OF CLEVELAND, 1903; PLAN OF CHICAGO, 1909.

Burnham Library has 59 sheets of drawings of the Ashland Block, Chicago; Simmons Library has 4 sheets of Simmons Memorial Library, Kenosha, Wisconsin (D.H. Burnham and Co.); and Pennsylvania Railroad Co., Philadelphia, 532 sheets of Union Station, Washington.

Obituaries: AMERICAN ARCHITECT AND BUILDING NEWS 101 (June 1912): 5; ARCHITECTURAL RECORD 31 (1912): 175-85, 192; 33 (1913): 36; ROYAL INSTITUTE OF BRITISH ARCHITECTS JOURNAL 19 (1911-12): 576; NEW INTERNATIONAL YEARBOOK, 1912, p. 113; WESTERN ARCHITECT 18 (July 1912): 74.

19:2 AMERICAN INSTITUTE OF ARCHITECTS' JOURNAL. "The Little-Known Plan That Burnham Proposed." Vol. 59 (May 1973): 48-51.

Burnham prepared a comprehensive plan for San Francisco, which incorporated more than 200 pages of suggestions. It was submitted just prior to the April 1906 earthquake and fire. Recommendations included the setting up of an art commission, the adornment of streets, tree planting, settings for public and religious buildings, cornice heights, pavements, cutting into hills, restricting heavy traffic, and water supply. What a plan in such a situation! But it was almost completely ignored.

19:3 David, A.C. "The Building of the First National Bank of Chicago." ARCHITECTURAL RECORD 19 (January 1906): 48-58.

In praise of constructing skyscrapers above banking accommodations for leasing to other businesses, rather than merely building a two-story structure exclusively for bank use. As such, the First National Bank of Chicago is "business-like and sensible," and the architecture utilitarian and not a pastiche of a renaissance church, or over-decorated as earlier skyscrapers.

19:4 Desmond, Harry W. "Rationalizing the Skyscraper." ARCHITECTURAL RECORD 17 (May 1905): 422-25.

Quoting Russell Sturgis as saying that we need "a period of fasting in architecture," meaning a less florid style of building, Desmond praises the idea of "a meagre diet" as seen in Burnham's Railway Exchange Building, Chicago. Desmond believes that Burnham will be condemned for his design, but that the attitude will ultimately prevail, as it has!

19:5 Gilbert, Cass, et al. "Daniel Hudson Burnham: An Appreciation." ARCHITECTURAL RECORD 32 (1912): 175-86.

Burnham is described as an experimenter in an ecclectic age by Gilbert. Other appreciations by his contemporaries are included, notably one by Frank Lloyd Wright who claimed, "He was not a creative architect but he was a great man."

19:6 Hill, George S. "A Plea for the Burnham Plan." ARCHITECT AND ENGINEER 161 (June 1945): 23-25.

Burnham prepared his plan for San Francisco prior to the

great earthquake disaster of 1906. After the conflagration, City Hall, which was the focal point of the Burnham plan, was moved and thus the plan changed. Hill advocated certain changes in respect to vehicular traffic and objected to the great cost of certain parts of the project.

19:7 Huxtable, Ada Louise. "Lessons in the Death of Style." THE NEW YORK TIMES, December 21, 1969, section 2, p. 36.

"The railroad age is over," and thus, not only is the Pennsylvania Station, New York City, of 1903-7 gone, but others are threatened and are not being replaced with anything resembling excellence. Burnham's Pittsburgh Station, 1898-1902, has lost its railroad sheds, and the new projected development may not even include the station's famed rotunda.

19:8 Karlowicz, Titus M. "D.H. Burnham's Role in the Selection of Architects for the World's Columbian Exposition." JOURNAL OF THE SOCIETY OF ARCHITECTURAL HISTORIANS 29 (October 1970): 247-54.

The National Commission for the Exposition, charged with the selection of a site and planning the buildings, wanted architects experienced and able to design specific types of exhibition architecture. Burnham and Root were appointed consultant architects, but Richard Morris Hunt of New York was also considered for this position. Choosing non-Chicagoan architects was thus not a "sell-out" by Burnham as is usually reported. After agreeing on "direct selection" of architects, it is not surprising that four New York firms, one Boston, one Kansas City, plus Chicago firms of note, were chosen.

19:9 Kennedy, Roger G. "Daniel Burnham: Tycoon of Western Architecture." THE AMERICAN WEST, September 1968, pp. 4-15.

19:10 Moore, Charles. DANIEL H. BURNHAM, ARCHITECT, PLANNER OF CITIES. Boston and New York: Houghton Mifflin Co., 1921. 238 p. Reprint. New York: Da Capo Press, 1968. 238 p.

Chapter three covers the period of 1875-91 when Burnham associated with the great innovator, John Wellborn Root, but the emphasis of the book concerns Burnham after Root's death when the former organized the 1893 World's Columbia Exposition and became as famous in the midwest as McKim, Mead and White on the East Coast. Burnham was a great city planner as well as architect and his City Beautiful schemes for Washington, Cleveland, Chicago, San Francisco, and Manila are all covered in great detail.

19:11 Paris, W. Francklyn. "Daniel Hudson Burnham." AMERICAN SOCIETY

OF LEGION OF HONOR MAGAZINE 24 (Summer 1953): 125-48.

"A Success Story. . .a story completely in the American vein because its subject was completely in the American Tradition." He succeeded because he did not recognize failure. He was a tycoon of the profession, a great organizer encouraging his fellow architects to produce schemes of bold magnificence. He collected people, organized them, and produced outstanding results.

19:12 ______. "Daniel Hudson Burnham." THE HALL OF AMERICAN ARTISTS. New York: New York University Press, 1953. Pp. 35-58.

The growth of Chicago after the 1871 fire mirrored the success of the career of Burnham, who was a good businessman, and a colleague and trainer of young architects. The 1893 Columbian Exposition brought him into greater prominence after the death of his partner, John W. Root. The fair began a new era of classicism in America notably by eastern architects, although encouraged by Burnham. Toward the end of his career he forwarded the City Beautiful movement and contributed to those ideals in significant city planning schemes.

19:13 Parsons, William E. "Burnham as a Pioneer in City Planning." ARCHITECTURAL RECORD 38 (1915): 13-32.

Factors of comprehensive redevelopment encompassing open space, relocating railroads, and suburbs in relation to urban areas must be considered in city planning and Burnham is a master of this approach. City planning in Washington, Chicago, and other cities is Burnham's legacy to the future.

19:14 Pond, Irving K. "Daniel H. Burnham, Planner of Cities." AMERICAN ARCHITECTURE 120 (December 7, 1921): 417-20.

This is a review of Charles Moore's biography of Burnham. His work and his partnerships are discussed as are his professional associates in architecture, sculpture, and landscape. Burnham was the last major figure of his generation.

19:15 Rebori, A.N. "The Work of Burnham and Root." ARCHITECTURAL RECORD 38 (1915): 32-168.

"It would take volumes of closely printed matter to properly review the life and deeds of the late Daniel Hudson Burnham, and as this article is to be concerned principally with the buildings executed by him and his associates. . . the appreciation must be brief. The article is mainly concerned with the skyscraper, a field in which Burnham was an innovator and master in all aspects of its development throughout the country.

19:16 Saylor, Henry H. "Make No Little Plans. Daniel Burnham Thought It but Did He Say It?" AMERICAN INSTITUTE OF ARCHITECTS' JOURNAL 28 (March 1957): 95-99.

Burnham forwarded the idea but did not actually say what Moore quoted in his biography of Burnham. The idea came from the London City Planning Conference of 1910 and the quotation was used by Willis Polk, an employee of Burnham, on a Christmas card of 1912 after Burnham's death on June 1, 1912. Moore took the quotation from Polk as being a verbally accurate quotation.

19:17 Schuyler, Montgomery. "Daniel Hudson Burnham." Great American Architects Series. ARCHITECTURAL RECORD (February 1896 Supplement): 49-71.

A brief biographical sketch of Burnham and his significance leads into a discussion of the works of Burnham and Root prior to Root's death in 1891. "The commercial buildings of Burnham and Root were in the main... Romanesque in origin and suggestion," with the possible exception of Root's Monadnock Building, Chicago, which impressed Schuyler.

19:18 Starrett, Theodore. "Daniel Hudson Burnham." ARCHITECTS' AND BUILDERS' MAGAZINE 13 (1912): 281-83.

Personal reminiscences by Starrett as a young office boy meeting Burnham for the first time and later being hired by the firm Burnham and Root. "Root was an artist draftsman, Burnham just a plain businessman." Their partnership, the death of Root, and the World's Fair of 1893 are touched upon.

19:19 _____. "The Washington Terminal." ARCHITECTURAL RECORD 18 (December 1905): 434-46.

Burnham's building complements and extends the classical ideas for Washington as envisaged by L'Enfant. It is also one of many railroad stations of notable design built throughout the country at this period. Statistics, cost, materials, and dimensions of railroad and passenger accommodations are given. Its scale is monumental as well as grandiose: it is longer than the United States Capitol.

19:20 Sturgis, Russell. "The New Thomas Music Hall." ARCHITECTURAL RECORD 16 (August 1904): 161-64.

Essentially an analysis and appreciation of the thoroughly-studied facade treatment of this Boston building. Style, function, materials, and the down-to-earth practical attitudes of Burnham's atelier complement the discussion.

19:21 Wight, Peter Bonnett. "David Hudson Burnham and His Associate." ARCHITECTURAL RECORD 38 (July 1915): 1-12.

An excellent insight into the workings of the Burnham office from the time of the partnership with Root in 1873 through a whole succession of able partners in the years after 1891. Many works of the firm are listed.

19:22 Wilson, F.L. "Some Features of the Ellicott Square, Buffalo." AMERICAN ARCHITECT AND BUILDING NEWS 6 (January 6, 1900): 3-5.

The Ellicott Square Company Building was large and innovative for its period and deserved the detailed study which it received. Structure, fireproofing, decoration, interiors, elevators, and mechanical equipment are subjects covered in this study. Only one small illustration is provided, and it is that of the cornice.

19:23 Wrigley, Robert W., Jr. "Daniel H. Burnham, Architect and City Planner." AMERICAN INSTITUTE OF ARCHITECTS' JOURNAL 35 (March 1961): 68-73.

Burnham's City Beautiful philosophy is expounded in a series of quotation. "Make no little plans," (see 19:16) nor "limit suggestions to present available means." Highlights of Burnham's career include the experience gained at the World's Fair, Chicago, 1893; the Senate Park Commission; and the plans for Chicago and other cities.

20:1 BURNHAM AND ROOT (Partnership 1873-91)

See Daniel Hudson Burnham (1846-1912), and John Wellborn Root (1850-91).

Burnham Library, Chicago, has drawings of the following Chicago buildings: Rookery, Phoenix, First Regiment Armory, Armour Memorial Hall, Masonic Temple, and Monadnock-Kearsarge.

20:2 Hoffman, Donald. "Root's Board of Trade Building, A Doomed Landmark of the Chicago School." ARCHITECTURAL FORUM 5 (December 1967): 54-59.

Occupied by the Board of Trade from its inception in 1888 to 1925, this bold structure, praised by many architects and historians, is likely to be demolished. It is carefully described in relation to the firm's work, and well illustrated.

20:3 Jenkins, Charles E. "A White Enameled Building?" ARCHITECTURAL

RECORD 4 (January-March 1895): 299-306.

John Root designed the sixteen-story Reliance Building, Chicago, in 1890, but after his death, Charles Atwood, a partner of Burnham, decided upon the use of white terra-cotta as an external material for fireproofing and thus had a major part in the design of the building. Detailed considerations of the iron construction are described.

21:1 BYRNE, BARRY (1833- ?)

Of Barry Byrne, Ryan and Co. and Willatzen and Byrne.

Avery Library, Columbia University, has nine miscellaneous drawings.

21:2 Chappell, Sally Anderson. "Barry Byrne, Architect: His Formative Years." THE PRAIRIE SCHOOL REVIEW 3 (Fourth Quarter, 1966): 5-23.

Byrne worked for Wright and in 1913 substituted for Walter Burley Griffin when he left his practice to go to Australia. In Europe he became acquainted with Mies, Mendelsohn, Loos, and Poelzig, and one can detect the impact of Irving Gill in his work. Most of his work was residential but he designed churches, schools, and college buildings. The article has good photographic coverage and some plans.

21:3 _____. BARRY BYRNE, ARCHITECTURE AND WRITINGS. Doctoral dissertation, Northwestern University, 1968. 346 p.

The second generation of the Chicago School spawned the Prairie School, which also was dominated by Wright. Byrne directed the principle of Wright's organic architecture to religious structures for the Catholic Church, pulling together nave and chancel and thus linking laity and priesthood in the act of worship. The New Liturgy of the 1960's was needed to break down conservative attitudes toward this type of design for the religious building. Chapter 3 discusses his publications and Chapter 4 his nonreligious architecture.

21:4 Lavanoux, Maurice. "More Western Observations." LITURGICAL ARTS 8 (January 1940): 27-34.

The article is primarily concerned with the arrangement of the various functions in a Catholic Church. It illustrates, among others, the Church of Christ, Tulsa, Oklahoma, 1927, a building which was a "refreshing departure from the stereotyped structure," solving the architectural problems and fitting well into the landscape.

21:5 Ryan, John F. "Modernism goes to Church." AMERICAN ARCHITECT 138 (November 1930): 50-53, 86.

Four church designs by Byrne battering "on the doors of convention" to produce lines, angles, pilasters "which are very much like nothing that ever happened before in the way of churches." Changing Roman Catholic liturgy, functionalism, and geometry are discussed. Included in the discussion, with illustrations and plans, are churches in Tulsa, Oklahoma; Racine, Wisconsin; and Cork, Ireland.

21:6 THE WESTERN ARCHITECT. "The Evolution of a Personal Style as Shown in the Work of Barry Byrne and Ryan Company." Vol. 33 (March 1924): 30-31, 35.

A philosophical essay on Byrne as a creative, as opposed to an imitative, architect. The sixteen plates and commentary support the contention that Barry Byrne and Ryan Co., architects, were creative (in the Wrightian sense, that is).

22:1 CADY, JOSIAH CLEVELAND (1837-1919)

Educated Trinity College, 1860, and worked for Town and Davis; in the 1880's joined in partnership with William S. Gregory and Milton See.

Cady's library and records of commissions are in the Trinity College Library, Hartford, Connecticut.

Obituaries: AMERICAN ARCHITECTURE 115 (1919): 583; AMERICAN INSTITUTE OF ARCHITECTS' JOURNAL 7 (1919): 226.

22:2 Schuyler, Montgomery. "The Work of Cady, Berg and See." ARCHITECTURAL RECORD 6 (April-June 1897): 517-53.

This is one of those valuable and useful articles by Schuyler on which the architectural historian must rely at the beginning of any research project on a particular architect or architectural firm. Schuyler lists and illustrates residential and public buildings, including libraries, and religious and commercial structures. The firm specialized in school and college buildings--notably at Yale, Williams and Wesleyan--but is famous for the Museum of Natural History and the Metropolitan Opera of New York City.

22:3 Van Rensselaer, Mariana Griswold. "The Metropolitan Opera House, New

York." AMERICAN ARCHITECT AND BUILDING 15 (February 16, 1884): 76-77; 15 (February 23, 1884): 86-89.

Cady's Metropolitan was inspired, well planned and detailed, with a "dignity of quiet size and the force of good structural designing." European methods of opera house design are mentioned, Mr. Cady having been forced to accept the Italian vogue of keeping the auditorium free from obstructions. Planning, arrangement, layout, ornamentation, and acoustics are discussed.

23:1 CARRERE, JOHN MERVEN (1858-1911)

Born in Brazil and educated in Switzerland and the Ecole des Beaux Arts, Paris. Worked for McKim, Mead and White, 1882-84, and there met Thomas Hastings (see) his partner.

Publications: PRELIMINARY REPORT FOR A CITY PLAN FOR GRAND RAPIDS, 1909, (with Arnold W. Brunner); two articles in THE ART COMMISSION OF THE CITY OF NEW YORK, 1908.

Obituaries: AMERICAN ARCHITECT AND BUILDING NEWS 99 (1911): 131-32; ROYAL INSTITUTE OF BRITISH ARCHITECTS' JOURNAL 18 (1910-11): 352.

23:2 Paris, W. Franklyn. "John M. Carrere." NEW YORK UNIVERSITY HALL OF AMERICAN ARTISTS 10 (1955): 63-77.

Carrere was an artist, gentleman, and man of affairs with solid qualifications who became a partner of Hastings (another graduate of the Ecole des Beaux Arts, Paris) from the mid-1880's until his death in 1911. "Their methods were those of the French Ecole and their style was that of the French Eighteenth Century." Their major project, the Ponce de Leon Hotel, St. Augustine, Florida, which they designed for Henry M. Flagler, is one of many notable works of the firm discussed.

23:3 Swales, F.S. "John Merven Carrere, 1858-1911. An Appreciation." ARCHITECTURAL REVIEW 29 (1911): 283-93.

An appreciation of "the most alive, most ambitious, the most strenuous artist among the architects. . . ." The article is as much an appreciation of the office or atelier of McKim, Mead and White where Carrere and many other notable architects gained their professional experience. Several structures by Carrere are illustrated and mentioned, but the article is equally concerned with Carrere's attitudes and associations.

24:1 **CARRERE AND HASTINGS (Partnership 1884-1911)**

See also John Merven Carrere (1858-1911), and Thomas Hastings (1860-1929).

Avery Library, Columbia University, has sketch of A.I. Dupont Chapel, Wilmington, Delaware, 1928; A.I. Dupont Fountain, Wilmington, Delaware, 1926; forty-six drawings of A.I. Dupont residence, Roslyn, Long Island, 1916-17; sixty-five sheets of Central Presbyterian Church, Montclair, New Jersey, 1921-22; seven sheets on proposed changes for Senate Chamber of United States Capitol, 1928-29; fifteen drawings Durand-Ruel Building, New York City, 1912; thirty-eight sheets estate and boat house for C. Ledyard Blair, Harrington Sound, Smith's Parish, Bermuda, 1928-29; three sheets Henry Hudson Memorial Bridge; forty-four drawings house for E.H. Harriman, New York, 1915-16; thirty-six drawings house for David A. Reed, Washington, D.C. 1930; twenty-five drawings house for William R. Castle, Jr., Washington, D.C., 1930; forty-four drawings house for W. Deering Howe, Jericho, Long Island, New York, 1926; seven sheets of miscellaneous details of Carnegie libraries; thirty-seven drawings passenger station for Union Pacific Railroad, Boise, Idaho, 1924; proposed fountain, Central Park; plan for New York Public Library; sketch Triborough Bridge, New York; two sheets Lafayette College, Easton, Pennsylvania; ninety-five sketches residence Mrs. Allan McLane, Jr., Locust Valley, Long Island, 1924-29; eight drawings residence of Julian A. White, Mill Neck, Long Island; sketch for an eagle, Senate Chamber, United States Capitol; twenty-one sheets stable for Mrs. F.E. Guest, Roslyn, Long Island, 1928; seven layouts Sutton Place and yacht basin, New York; twenty-two sheets tennis courts for Mrs. Bradley-Martin, Old Westbury, Long Island, 1921-22. Other library holdings of drawings: Firestone Library, Princeton.

Publications: A PLAN FOR THE CITY OF HARTFORD, 1912; FLORIDA, THE AMERICAN RIVIERA, 1887; THE NEW THEATRE, 1887.

24:2 Condit, Carl W. "The Pioneer Concrete Buildings of St. Augustine." PROGRESSIVE ARCHITECTURE, September 1971, pp. 128-33.

The Ponce de Leon Hotel, 1885-87, was to be one of a chain in the Florida hotel boom. The Moorish influence it displays was due as much to Bernard Maybeck, an assistant in the office of Carrere and Hastings, as to the architects themselves. The structural principles of the building were based upon Spanish precedents, closely allied to concrete. Aggregate replaced coquina and hydraulic cement substituted for oyster lime. The Alcazar Hotel followed in the same vein as well as several churches in the area. These "Carrere and Hastings designs must be regarded as important pioneer works. . .[in an] endlessly useful material."

24:3 Cottrell, Charles H. "The Architecture of a Christian Science Church."

ARCHITECTURAL RECORD 15 (February 1904): 158-71.

What is to be the architectural expression of a Christian Science Church? "The Protestant Congregational meeting house is, of course, the obvious answer." Cottrell sees this New York City church as of the highest import! A background history is provided as well as costs, architectural criticism, and a discussion, with illustrations, of internal spaces.

24:4 David, A.C. "The New York Public Library." ARCHITECTURAL RECORD 28 (September 1910): 145-72.

"The most important building erected since the American architectural revival began," partially because it fits into the American dream of education. Churches and city government buildings are apparently by their association no longer representative of the American ideal. Its aspirations, site, planning, and dignity but nonmonumentality are topics touched upon in this critical essay. Well illustrated, with plans, details, and numerous interior shots, especially of elaborate screen, door, and ceiling treatments.

24:5 Desmond, H.W. "A Beaux-Arts Skyscraper: The Blair Building, New York City." ARCHITECTURAL RECORD 14 (December 1903): 436-43.

"The architects have avoided, if not disregarded, the fundamental problem. Such design as the building exhibits is an architectural expression at the surface only." Although not rationalist, the building is expressive of structural steel construction. Choice of materials and the judgment used in their placement are highly praised.

24:6 Hastings, Thomas. "John Merven Carrere." THE NEW YORK ARCHITECTURE 5 (May 1911): 65-72.

Personal reminiscences by one partner of another, in a partnership which had a profound effect upon the profession. Early student associations, early collaboration, and finally partnership from 1885 and their early commissions are discussed.

24:7 ______. "A Letter from Thomas Hastings, Reminiscent of the Early Works of Messrs. Carrere and Hastings, Architects." AMERICAN ARCHITECT AND BUILDING NEWS 96 (July 7, 1909): 3-4.

Both worked for McKim, Mead and White, where Hastings met: "Mr. Carrere who superintended an important house in Baltimore, while I was working on the plans of the same house." Henry M. Flagler commissioned from them a hotel for St. Augustine, Florida, which led to other commissions including a church and residence for Flagler.

24:8 Morris, Harrison S. "America at Home." ART AND PROGRESS 2 (October 1911): 362-69.

Carrere and Hastings designed the Pavilion at Rome for the art exhibition there in 1910. Brief description and one photograph.

24:9 Paris, W. Francklyn. "John M. Carrere." AMERICAN SOCIETY LEGION OF HONOR MAGAZINE, Spring 1946, pp. 313-28.

Qualities of an architect are epitomized in the life and work of Carrere and his partner. His training and later contribution to American architecture is eulogized as seen in his hotels, libraries, and theaters--a few of the building types on which he was engaged.

24:10 Price, C. Matlack. "A Renaissance in Commercial Architecture, Some Recent Buildings in Uptown New York." ARCHITECTURAL RECORD 31 (May 1912): 449-69.

Exclusive shopping establishments along Fifth Avenue and Forty-second Street began replacing the earlier standardized commercial structures after the turn of the century. They vary in style, but this is a quality that the reviewer admires. Carrere and Hastings' building at 556-58 Fifth Avenue, is illustrated.

24:11 Pryor, Roy Thomas. "Lattice: Its Use and Adaptation." AMERICAN ARCHITECTURE 106 (December 30, 1914): 397-404, 407-9.

Lattice and trellis work, a necessary adjunct to the garden, have been given considerable attention in the work of Carrere and Hastings. Usually of carved wood, but marble and other materials are occasionally used.

24:12 Schuyler, Montgomery. "Recent Church Building in New York." ARCHITECTURAL RECORD 13 (June 1903): 508-34.

"What is the right architectural expression of Christian Science we do not pretend to know," reports Schuyler in discussing the First Church of Christian Science at Central Park West and Ninety-sixth Street.

24:13 Stuart, Percy C. "Recent Domestic Architecture in Washington, D.C." ARCHITECTURAL RECORD 10 (April 1901): 425-37.

Domestic architecture for entertainment and as a backdrop for social gatherings and politics. Luxurious interiors suggest seventeenth-century France rather than the late nineteenth-century republic of America.

25:1 CLINTON AND RUSSELL (Partnership 1873-91)

Charles W. Clinton (1838-1910), and William Hamilton Russell (1854-1907).

Clinton worked for Richard Upjohn and Edward T. Potter. Russell began in 1878 with his great-uncle, James Renwick, becoming a member of Aspinwall, Renwick and Russell until 1894 when he joined Clinton.

Obituary of Clinton: AMERICAN ARCHITECT AND BUILDING NEWS 98 (December 7, 1910): 3.

Obituaries of Russell: AMERICAN ARCHITECT AND BUILDING NEWS 92 (1907): 33-34; ARCHITECTURAL RECORD 7 (1879-78): 533; ARCHITECTS' AND BUILDERS' MAGAZINE 8 (1906-7): 614.

25:2 AMERICAN ARCHITECT. "Architecture and Decoration in the Modern Office." Vol. 128 (July 1, 1925): 15-20.

"The necessity for congenial environment in the office as we have in the home." Carrere and Hastings were the architects of the building and Clinton and Russell the interior designers, using variations of medieval and Jacobean styles with antlers and andirons.

25:3 ARCHITECTURAL RECORD. "Over the Drafting Board. Opinions Official and Unofficial." Vol. 11 (October 1901): 705-16.

A diatribe on the nineteenth-century styles as used by Clinton and Russell, even to the extent of terming the Gothic Revival "a vain thing." Sullivan's dictum of "total abstinence from indulgence in ornament is repeated, but the writer(s) do not want stereotyped architecture. Rather, quality, as in some model tenements by Ernest Flagg and Howells and Stokes. They quote Professor Pite, an architect who forwards the idea of "beauty of economy of material."

25:4 Hutchins, William. "New York Hotels." ARCHITECTURAL RECORD 12 (October 1902): 459-71; 12 (November 1902): 621-35.

The first article is devoted to an historical consideration of hotel design in New York City and the second includes the design of the Astor on Long Acre Square, New York City, by Clinton and Russell. One of many huge hotels by several notable architects at the beginning of the century, the Astor, a modern renaissance structure, had high mansard roofs (p. 627), and functional services and arrangement of rooms.

25:5 Schuyler, Montgomery. "Two New Armories." ARCHITECTURAL RECORD 19 (April 1906): 259-64.

The Armory by Clinton and Russell was at 34th Street and Park Avenue (demolished 1973). The article is concerned with the design of armories generally, forwarding the idea that architects excel in armory design even though they may fail in all else.

25:6 Sturgis, Russell. "The Reverse of the Broad Exchange Building." ARCHITECTURAL RECORD 17 (February 1905): 142-46.

Sturgis prefers the rear of the building, "a really delightful bit of picturesque effect with interesting shadows and shaded sides illuminated by reflected light."

25:7 _____. "A Review of the Works of Clinton and Russell, Architects." ARCHITECTURAL RECORD 7 (October-December 1897): 1-61.

The work of the firm was almost wholly involved in high-rise commercial buildings for New York City, with an occasional religious structure, or country or town residence. Sullivan's ideal of base, shaft, and cap as the three stages of a skyscraper was clearly expressed by Clinton and Russell, invariably terminating the lines of the shaft by rows of arches. Most structures were utilitarian but decoration was used where possible even to the extent of sculptures by J. Massey Rhind.

25:8 _____. "The Warehouse and the Factory in Architecture." ARCHITECTURAL RECORD 15 (January 1904): 1-17; 15 (February 1904): 122-33.

Achievements of simple, commercial warehouse design are emphasized and a factory by Clinton and Russell at 16th Street and Seventh Avenue, New York City, is illustrated. It has "a gravity of design not to be surpassed by anything that we have consulted in this study," except for two shop windows at the ground level.

26:1 COBB, HENRY IVES (1859-1931)

Educated at Massachusetts Institute of Technology and Harvard University. Worked for Peabody and Stearns. Partnership with Charles S. Frost in Chicago.

26:2 Jenkins, Charles E. "The University of Chicago." ARCHITECTURAL RECORD 4 (October-December 1894): 229-46.

Founded by John D. Rockefeller and with donations from local citizens, President Harper and the board chose Cobb as its architect in 1891. An aerial view of the four block scheme and the individual buildings in a functional collegiate Gothic style are illustrated. Internally there is a mixture of medieval craftsmanship and exposed cast and wrought iron.

26:3 Schuyler, Montgomery. "Great American Architects Series." ARCHITECTURAL RECORD, February 1896 Supplement, pp. 72-110.

"Mr. Cobb's work is the most conspicuous exception to the rule of the practice of architecture in Chicago, that it consists of designing dwellings and tall commercial buildings," the former tending toward the early French Renaissance in style and the latter of an arts and crafts flavor. (The fifteen-story Owings Building has the top five floors within a gable.) The Fisheries Building was in a delicate Romanesque, although the Chicago Historical Society was thoroughly Richardsonian.

27:1 CODMAN, OGDEN (1863-1951)

27:2 Codman, Florence. THE CLEVER YOUNG BOSTON ARCHITECT. Augusta, Me.: Florence Codman, 1970. 43 p.

Architect of Edith Wharton's "Lands End" at Newport, Rhode Island, and a collaborator with her on THE DECORATION OF HOUSES. His architecture was of the Colonial Revival and Beaux Arts styles.

28:1 COPE, WALTER (1860-1902)

Education at Friends School in Germantown and trained under T.P. Chandler. In the late 1880's, he formed a partnership with John and Emlyn Stewardson (see). See also Cope and Stewardson.

Obituaries: AMERICAN ARCHITECTURE 78 (November 8, 1912): 41; INLAND ARCHITECT 40 (November 1902): 35; AMERICAN ARCHITECT AND BUILDING NEWS 78 (1902): 41; AMERICAN INSTITUTE OF ARCHITECTS' JOURNAL 3 (Quarterly Bulletin, January 1903): 184; INLAND ARCHITECT AND NEWS RECORD 41 (February 1903).

28:2 Seeler, Edgar V. "Walter Cope, Architect." ARCHITECTURAL REVIEW (Boston) 9 (1902): 289-300.

A memoir on Cope's background, association with Emlyn Stewardson, and his intense interest in education and travel. Cope and Stewardson are perhaps best remembered for their medieval vernacularisms at Bryn Mawr, Pennsylvania, and Washington University, St. Louis, but other structures tended toward classicism, the Mannerist period of the sixteenth century, and Spanish and French Provincial.

29:1 COPE AND STEWARDSON (Partnership 1884-1902)

Walter Cope (1860-1902); John Stewardson (1859-96) (see). Partnership from 1884. Emlyn Lamar Stewardson (1863-1936) joined in 1886 and the firm remained Cope and Stewardson until Cope's death in 1902. E.L. Stewardson associated with George Bispham Page (1870-1948) from 1927-36.

Princeton University, Department of Grounds, has seventeen drawings of Blair Hall. Pennsylvania University, Department of Grounds, has sixteen sets of numerous sheets of buildings at Pennsylvania (one by Cope, Stewardson and McIlvaine).

29:2 Cram, Ralph Adams. "The Work of Messrs. Cope and Stewardson." ARCHITECTURAL RECORD 16 (October 1904): 407-38.

> Cope and Stewardson are justifiably famous for their English medieval and renaissance styled university halls at Bryn Mawr, Pennsylvania; Princeton; and Washington University, St. Louis. "Personally, we must grieve forever over the loss of two altogether lovable men; professionally we can say, and without irreverence 'Lord, now lettest Thou Thy servants depart in peace, according to Thy Word; for our eyes have seen Thy salvation.'" Other structures are also illustrated including an institution for the blind in a pseudo-Byzantine style.

29:3 Fisher, C.P. "The New Building for the College of Physicians of Philadelphia." AMERICAN ARCHITECT AND BUILDING NEWS 94 (December 9, 1908): 185-86.

> "The style of architecture is English, of about the end of the seventeenth century." After a brief history of the college, the structure, accommodations, and materials are listed.

29:4 Nolan, Thomas. "Recent Suburban Architecture in Philadelphia and Vicinity." ARCHITECTURE RECORD 19 (March 1906): 167-93.

> "The suburbs of Philadelphia. . .have been often compared. . .to the English counties in the Southwest especially Devonshire and parts of Somerset." These qualities are to be found in a wide range of Philadelphia suburban architecture by many firms of architects but notably Cope and Stewardson.

29:5 Study, Guy. "Washington University, St. Louis, Mo." ARCHITECTURAL RECORD 37 (January 1915): 64-75.

> A brief background history of this educational institution is provided up to 1900 when a competition was held. The English Tudor style won out and eight buildings were immediately commenced on the 3000-acre site.

Historic precedents and stylistic trends are described in addition to the plan arrangement and location of the various departments within the scheme.

30:1 CRAM, RALPH ADAMS (1863-1942)

In 1887 formed partnership with Charles Wentworth (1861-97); in 1891 Bertram G. Goodhue joined Cram and Wentworth. At Wentworth's death, Frank W. Ferguson joined; Goodhue withdrew in 1910. (See Goodhue, Bertram Grosvenor). After 1910, the firm was known as Cram and Ferguson (see).

Has published on religious architecture, American and foreign, in his time and in the historic past; on the Gothic period; Japanese architecture; Christian art; farm houses; and proposals for Boston.

Avery Library, Columbia University, has two sheets of drawings of a proposed Boston Civic Center and three preliminary sketches for an island in the Charles River.

Obituaries: MICHIGAN SOCIETY OF ARCHITECTS WEEKLY BULLETIN 16 (September 29, 1942): 3; ARCHITECTURAL FORUM 77 (October 1942): 104; ROYAL INSTITUTE OF BRITISH ARCHITECTS' JOURNAL 49 (October 1942): 226; THE OCTAGON 15 (February 1943): 13-15.

Anne M. Daniel is working on a doctoral dissertation at the University of North Carolina on Cram's churches and early writings.

30:2 Allen, George N. "Cram, The Yankee Medievalist." ARCHITECTURAL FORUM 55 (July 1931): 79-80.

Described as an architect, artist, author, lecturer, romanticist, academician, and idealist, Cram was educated at Exeter, Williams, and Notre Dame and received a Doctor of Letters degree from Princeton and Doctor of Laws degree from Yale. His inspiration came from Richardson, Japan, England, France, and Spain. His partner, Goodhue, considered him a "well-fed genius," rather than one who starved in a garret.

30:3 Bryant, H. Stafford. "Classic Ensemble." ARTS IN VIRGINIA, Winter 1971, pp. 18-25.

An essay on Cram's design for Sweet Briar College, Virginia.

30:4 Cram, Ralph Adams. MY LIFE IN ARCHITECTURE. Boston: Little, Brown and Co., 1936. 325 p.

An autobiography covering his own training and development in relation to the profession in America at the period. However, Cram's major training ground was Europe, where he spent considerable time in study. His partnerships, competitions, and practice are discussed, as is his philosophy of design. In his chapter on tradition plus modernism, he forwards the idea of certain styles for particular building types. He thought it "absurd and perfectly pointless and ungrammatical to couch a school of liberal arts, a library or college chapel in terms of a garage." He had some respect for the modern movement.

30:5 North, Arthur Tappan. CONTEMPORARY AMERICAN ARCHITECTS: RALPH ADAMS CRAM (CRAM AND FERGUSON). New York: McGraw-Hill Book Co. Inc., 1931. 115 p.

In praise of Cram's approach to Gothic architecture for religious buildings and away from the Romanesque trend. Cram's Gothic is not an archaeological reproduction but has the religious, aesthetic, and structural principles of the medieval period. Modern architecture was rejected as an unhistoric arbitrary style from France and Germany!

31:1 CRAM AND FERGUSON (Partnership 1910- ?)

See also Cram, Ralph Adams (1863-1942).

Also associated with Goodhue (1897-1910), and Wentworth, 1887-97, and Frank W. Ferguson (1861-1926).

Avery Library, Columbia University, has drawings of All Saints' Church, Peterborough, New Hampshire, 1913; Church of the Holy Rosary, Pittsburgh, Pennsylvania; picture gallery for William E. Atwood, East Gloucester, Massachusetts; Rollins College Chapel, Winter Park, Florida, 1931; St. Mary's Church, Redford, Michigan, 1925-29.

31:2 Allen, Harris C. "A Western Parthenon by the Pacific, Grace Cathedral in San Francisco." CALIFORNIA ARTS AND ARCHITECTURE 35 (May 1929): 21-23.

A brief history of the church precedes the ideas and philosophies of Cram presented in a series of lengthy quotations. Sketches, plan, and a photo montage.

31:3 Cram, R.A. "House of Paul Watkins, Winona, Minn." AMERICAN ARCHITECTURE 134 (August 20, 1928): 223-35.

The house was designed for the owner's collection of arts and crafts of Europe: paintings, furniture, tapestries, rugs, metal, and glassware. The residence was thus designed in the Tudorbethan style with a huge, open, timber-roofed great hall separated from the other rooms of the house as in the case of an English Manor hall with later additions, thus making it a residence as well as a museum.

31:4 Eberlein, Harold Donaldson. "All Saints Church, Peterborough, New Hampshire." ARCHITECTURAL RECORD 58 (September 1925): 278-88.

"A modern example of the transitional phase from Norman style to the Early English ecclesiastical manner." It is described as honest, direct, and appropriate to needs. Classical versus romantic discussion is entered into, with a strong bias toward this particular flavor of the Gothic. It is well illustrated with plans and sections.

31:5 Frohman, Philip Hubert." The Cathedral of St. Peter and St. Paul, Washington, D.C." AMERICAN ARCHITECTURE 127 (April 22, 1925): 355-68.

Henry Vaughan was the architect until 1917, Frohman Robb and Little since 1919, with Cram and Ferguson, consultants. (See same article under Vaughan.)

31:6 Loring, Charles G. "The Boston Federal Building." AMERICAN ARCHITECTURE 143 (November 1933): 15-19.

"It was designed by Cram and Ferguson, but does not conform to Mr. Cram's philosophy of Architecture.... A New England Colonial was out of the question on an office building 338 feet high, so Mr. Cram selected what he terms 'Modern'."

32:1 CRAM, GOODHUE AND FERGUSON (Partnership 1897-1910)

Frank W. Ferguson (1861-1926). See also Cram, Ralph Adams and Goodhue, Bertram Grosvenor.

Avery Library, Columbia University, has drawings of Grammar Schoolhouse, Mather District, Meetinghouse Hill, Boston, Massachusetts, July 1903; Richmond College, Richmond, Virginia, mens' dormitory, library, and academic group; and an unidentified country church. Additionally, Williams College, Williamstown, Massachusetts, has thirty drawings of Grace Hall; Princeton University buildings and grounds, Campbell Hall and Graduate College buildings; American Institute of Architects, Washington; one sheet of St. Stephen's Church, Cohasset, Massachusetts.

32:2 Bottomley, H.L. "The Story of St. Thomas' Church." ARCHITECTURAL RECORD 35 (February 1914): 100-31.

After the destruction by fire of old St. Thomas at Fifth

Avenue and 53rd Street, New York City, a limited competition was held for a Gothic structure. Cram, Goodhue and Ferguson were given freedom to develop the Gothic for a church, the size of which would have been unheard of in the thirteenth century. Trials and tribulations in the rebuilding are described, as are the planning of certain areas and the details in stone, wood, and wrought iron.

32:3 Byre, A.G. "The First Baptist Church, Pittsburgh, Pennsylvania." ARCHITECTURAL RECORD 32 (September 1912): 193-208.

Modern Gothic was, according to the author, synonymous with the work of this firm, who have adapted the French Gothic in a nonliteral, nonarchaeological mode, with a Romanesque plan. All aspects and details are carefully analyzed. The undercroft, or basement, is used as an assembly room and has an extremely low tile cross vault.

32:4 Pawtucket, R.I., Deborah Cook Sayles Public Library. THE DEBORAH COOK SAYLES PUBLIC LIBRARY, PAWTUCKET, R.I. Providence, R.I.: Standard Printing Co., 1903. 102 p.

The cornerstone was laid in 1899, and the library which houses up to 75,000 volumes was opened in 1902. It was innovative in introducing the idea of open shelves. Addresses, orations, and benedictions at the various ceremonies are reproduced in full. The building is well illustrated inside and out and floor plans provided for this Greek Revival structure.

32:5 Pittsburgh, First Baptist Church. THE FIRST BAPTIST CHURCH OF PITTSBURGH. Pittsburgh: William Ensign Lincoln, 1925. 91 p.

Described from its foundation in 1812, its growth with the community and city of Pittsburgh, the building and rebuilding of school and meeting rooms through to "Contemporary Descriptions." Architectural criticism, symbolic detailing, and numerous plans and photographs of all details of architecture, sculpture, glass, reliefs, furnishings, and even the kitchens are explained.

32:6 Price, C.M. "The Chapel of the Intercession, New York City." ARCHITECTURAL RECORD 35 (1914): 527-43.

The creative genius of this firm expresses itself in the Gothic, described as being "...virile and massive without being heavy, and delicate without being trivial and essentially scholarly without being archaeological." The existing graveyard provides an authentic setting for this modern Gothic structure, which is illustrated in detail.

32:7 ______. "Panama-California Exposition, San Diego, California." AR-

CHITECTURAL RECORD 37 (March 1915): 229-51.

A general article discussing the role of exhibition architecture: festive, colorful, expressing local or national traditions. San Diego was meant to "express and typify the history, resources, prosperity, industries and products as well as the golden lined future promise of the Southwest. It is an attempt to embody the romance of old Spanish civilization..." austere, primitive, complex, rich. Goodhue had visited Mexico, illustrated a book on its architecture in 1901 and created a city based upon colonial Spanish precedents.

32:8 Schuyler, Montgomery. "The Architecture of West Point." ARCHITECTURAL RECORD 14 (December 1903): 463-92.

The firm won the competition for West Point against outstanding architects of the period including McKim, Mead and White, and C.C. Haight. Competition drawings are illustrated to complement a lengthy discussion especially of Memorial Hall, the earlier classical design by McKim, Mead and White.

32:9 _____. "The Works of Cram, Goodhue and Ferguson...1892-1910." ARCHITECTURAL RECORD 29 (January 1911): 1-112.

A well-illustrated survey of the firm's work, beginning with a discussion of the partnership in which Ferguson acted as a foil to the two major designers. The second part of the article relates the whole nineteenth-century movement of the Gothic Revival to their secular and miscellaneous buildings, with a third section on ecclesiastical works. The last section is devoted wholly to their work at the United States Military Academy, West Point, won in competition in 1903, again in the Gothic style evoking the desires of that period for educational structures in that style.

32:10 Spelman, Roger. "Chancels, Their Arrangement and Furniture, with Illustration from the New York Offices of Cram, Goodhue and Ferguson." AMERICAN ARCHITECTURE 105 (February 18, 1914): 65-74; 105 (April 15, 1914): 165-72, 175-76; 106 (July 1, 1914): 1-7; 106 (September 2, 1914): 129-36, 139-41; 106 (October 7, 1914): 209-16, 219-20; 106 (November 11, 1914): 285-92.

Laity and clergy have jointly demanded care and attention to detail in religious art and architecture. Cram, Goodhue and Ferguson have provided generous spacial arrangements for religious ritual. Plans, sections, and plates illustrate the different varieties of Gothic expression.

33:1 CRAM AND WENTWORTH (Partnership 1887-91)

Charles F. Wentworth (1861-97). See also Cram, Ralph Adams.

Avery Library, Columbia University, has drawings of projected house, Boston; Rockingham County Courthouse, New Hampshire; Fellner House, Chestnut Hill, Massachusetts; Methodist Church, Newton Corner, Massachusetts. (Cram, Wentworth and Goodhue).

34:1 CRET, PAUL PHILLIPPE (1876-1945)

Born in France, where he studied at the Ecole des Beaux Arts. Taught at the University of Pennsylvania until 1907, when he began a practice with Albert Kelsey, and associated with Zantzinger, Borie and Medary. Avery Library, Columbia University, has drawings of Perry Memorial at Put-in-Bay, Lake Erie, Ohio, 1913; Federal Reserve Board Building and Folger Shakespeare Library, Washington, D.C.; Hartford County Building, Hartford, Connecticut; and miscellaneous designs and studies.

Obituary: AMERICAN INSTITUTE OF ARCHITECTS' JOURNAL 4 (December 1945): 281-88.

34:2 Adams, Payne. "Paul Phillippe Cret." ARCHITECTURE 63 (May 1931): 263-68.

Italian Gothic and the reading of Viollet-le-Duc's DICTIONARY preceded Cret's acceptance of classical architecture. The article includes sketches and drawings by Cret and his draftsmen.

34:3 Allen, George H. "The Little Master of the Arts, Paul Phillippe Cret of Philadelphia, of Pennsylvania and of the World at Large." ARCHITECTURAL FORUM 54 (April 1931): 483-84.

Unassuming, diminutive, academic, an epigrammist and teacher--these are all descriptions assigned to Cret. Lyons born, Paris Beaux Arts trained, and American by adoption, "he abhors cheese and hand rolls his cigarettes." George Allen's articles are generally inane, as he tries to give architects the charisma of movie stars.

34:4 ARCHITECTURE. "The Buildings of the Barnes Foundation at Merion, Pennsylvania." Vol. 53 (January 1926): 1-6.

"The Barnes Foundation is an educational institution in which is conducted research in art, more particularly modern art and its derivation from earlier art." The museum inspired by the Italian Renaissance is limited in scale fitting the size of the collection. Spaces are provided for sculpture, but roof lighting has been avoided to attain lighting values similar to the conditions under which the paintings were executed.

34:5 Chase, C.E. "The Delaware River Bridge." AMERICAN ARCHITECTURE 131 (March 5, 1927): 329-35.

Stretching 1750 feet over the harbor at Philadelphia at a cost of $36 million, this is an example of collaboration between architect Cret and Ralph Modjeski, engineer.

34:6 Delaware River Bridge Joint Commission of Pennsylvania and New Jersey. REPORT...1923. Burlington, N.J., 1923. Folded plates, tables and diagrams.

Contains sketches and photographs mainly of construction and machinery, but also contracts for piers, anchorages, towers, cables, investigations, and tests.

34:7 THE FOLGER SHAKESPEARE LIBRARY, WASHINGTON. Washington: Trustees of Amherst College, 1933. 2 p. 36 pl.

A description with plates of the building, including plans, sections, internal and external photographs, details, sculptures, and finishes; it is preceded by an essay on Folger and the establishment of the library.

34:8 Harbeson, John. "Paul Cret and Architectural Competitions." JOURNAL OF THE SOCIETY OF ARCHITECTURAL HISTORIANS 25 (December 1966): 305-6.

Harbeson was taught by Cret at the University of Pennsylvania and practiced with him. Cret's student awards are enumerated and his position as juror of and entrant in competitions is assessed. After 1913 Cret associated with Zantzinger, Borie and Medary.

34:9 Price, C. Matlack. "The Pan American Union and its Annex, Washington, D.C." ARCHITECTURAL RECORD 34 (November 1913): 385-457.

Cret associated with Albert Kelsey in the design of a building for twenty-one American republics to foster understanding, friendship, and economic development. All details were adapted from historic American sources and the whole building, basically classical in feeling, is illustrated in detail. Initial sketches, plans, sections and elevations, working drawings and photographs of the completed structure, descriptions and criticism provide an in-depth study of a special type of building.

34:10 Reid, Kenneth. "Paul Phillippe Cret, Master of Design." PENCIL POINTS 19 (October 1938): 608-38.

Cret's French training which emphasized the historic past provided the foundation for his architectural work. He also visualized his designs in section and prepared numerous full-size details. "He still believes there is a deal of beauty to be discovered within the realms of symmetry," as numerous photographs of his work attest. Most of his work was educational or for the federal government, but he also desined bridges, memorials, and the interiors of railroad cars.

34:11 Swales, F.S. "Draftsmanship and Architecture as Exemplified by the Work of Paul Phillippe Cret." PENCIL POINTS 9 (November 1928): 688-704.

His Paris training grounded him well for a teaching and practicing career in Philadelphia. He was placed in several competitions, and some of these are illustrated. His achievements are listed and many examples of his draftsmanship, in a variety of media, are illustrated.

34:12 Zantzinger, C.C. "In Memory of Paul Phillippe Cret." AMERICAN INSTITUTE OF ARCHITECTS' JOURNAL 10 (September 1948): 109-11.

A memoir on Cret the educator, and his service to the profession, the cities of Philadelphia and Washington, and to America, his chosen country.

35:1 DANA, RICHARD HENRY (1879-1933)

Educated at Harvard, Columbia, and the Ecole des Beaux Arts, he worked from 1906 to 1908 for Delano and Aldrich before setting up in practice with H.K. Murphy from 1908 to 1920, and thereafter worked alone.

35:2 Dana, Richard H., Jr. RICHARD HENRY DANA, (1879-1933) ARCHITECT. New York: Richard H. Dana, Jr., 1965. Unpaged.

"That he worked within Colonial, Georgian and Federal traditions seems less important now than how he used these vocabularies. The variety of his solutions provided comfortable and commodious country houses..." writes Harmon H. Goldstone in his introduction. Seventy-four plates serve to illustrate his work, a complete list of which is provided at the end of the book.

36:1 DAY, FRANK MILES (1861-1918)

Educated University of Pennsylvania, and the Royal Academy School of Architecture, London, and began practice in Philadelphia, 1887. From 1892-1912 he practiced with his brother, H. Kent Day, and after 1912 with Charles Z. Klander. Wrote AMERICAN COUNTRY HOUSES OF TODAY, 1911; also on city planning and improvements for Detroit and the outer park system of American cities. Pennsylvania University, Department of Buildings and Grounds, has six sheets of Gymnasium, and forty-eight sheets, Houston Hall, Pennsylvania University. Fine Arts Library has fifty sheets of Offices for the American Baptist Publication Society.

Obituaries: ROYAL INSTITUTE OF BRITISH ARCHITECTS' JOURNAL 25 (1917-18): 206; AMERICAN INSTITUTE OF ARCHITECTS' JOURNAL 6 (1918): 311, 383-94; NEW INTERNATIONAL YEARBOOK, 1918, p. 167.

36:2 Cram, Ralph Adams. "The Work of Messrs. Frank Miles Day, and Brother." ARCHITECTURAL RECORD 15 (May 1904): 397-421.

> "Purest in blood of all the greater American cities," Philadelphia ultimately sired "men who produced work of infinite refinement, who had the faculty of instilling their own high principles into their followers." The work of the Day Brothers is highly praised as work fitting into this category. Domestic architecture by the firm is praised at the expense of late eighteenth and early nineteenth-century houses which are subjectively classified as clumsy. Examples of their public and private works are illustrated and discussed, notably the Archaeological Museum of Philadelphia in association with Wilson Eyre and Cope and Stewardson.

36:3 West, Andrew F. "Frank Miles Day, A Remembrance." AMERICAN INSTITUTE OF ARCHITECTS' JOURNAL 6 (1918): 383-94.

> A poetic memorial on Day with illustrations of his house near Philadelphia and a good sampling of drawings from his student sketch books.

37:1 DESPRADELLE, CONSTANT DESIRE (1862-1912)

Born in France and educated at the Ecole des Beaux Arts (diploma 1886), he taught at Massachusetts Institute of Technology and formed a partnership with Stephen Codman.

Obituaries: AMERICAN ARCHITECT AND BUILDING NEWS 102 (September 11, 1912): 5; NEW INTERNATIONAL YEARBOOK, 1912, p. 185; WESTERN ARCHITECT 18 (October 1912): 103.

37:2 Bourne, F.A. "On the Work of the Late Desire Despradelle." ARCHITECTURAL RECORD 34 (1913): 185-89.

> Many notable American architects eulogized Despradelle at this retrospective exhibition of the architect's achievements. They spoke of his "sympathy and enthusiasm and notably of the power, so rare in a teacher, of being able

to develop the student's own abilities." Some of his works are discussed and his "Beacon of Progress," which won the 1900 First Gold Medal in Paris at the Luxembourg Gallery, is illustrated.

37:3 Swales, F.S. "Master Draftsman, XI, Desire Despradelle." PENCIL POINTS 6 (May 1925): 58-70.

Born in France, Despradelle taught at Massachusetts Institute of Technology, was on various commissions and designed several buildings. Details of his education and submissions for various prizes are listed and illustrated. Most of them are of a gigantic grandeur.

37:4 TECHNOLOGY ARCHITECTURAL RECORD. "The 'Beacon of Progress,' a Monument to Glorify the American Nation. . . ." Vol. 6 (1912): 3-5.

This tribute describes and illustrates the Beacon of Progress and publishes letters received by Despradelle after his award of first medal in the Paris Salon of 1900 for his drawings of the project.

38:1 DRUMMOND, WILLIAM (1876-1948)

Trained in engineering at the University of Illinois, Drummond began as an architectural assistant to Wright, 1899-1909, although during 1901 and 1903-4 he worked for Richard E. Schmidt and D.H. Burnham, respectively. Associated with Guenzel, 1910-15, and thereafter practiced alone intermittently until 1945.

38:2 Ganschinietz, Suzanne. "William Drummond I, Talent and Sensitivity." THE PRAIRIE SCHOOL REVIEW 6 (First Quarter, 1969): 5-19.

Drummond worked on and off for Wright from 1899-1909. The article lists projects by Wright upon which Drummond worked and others in which he contributed to the design (all based upon the authority of Drummond's son, Dr. Alan Drummond). In practice, Drummond's reliance upon Wright's idiomatic style is evident, as seen in perspectives, plans, photographs, and drawings which accompany the article.

38:3 _____. "William Drummond II. Partnership and Obscurity." THE PRAIRIE SCHOOL REVIEW 6 (Second Quarter, 1969): 5-19.

After Wright closed his practice in 1910, Drummond aided Von Holst, but soon established his own practice and joined Guenzel in 1910. Guenzel was the businessman and Drummond the designer who continued in the Wrightian idiom even after the dissolution of the partnership. Illustrations include Drummond's Chicago Tribune

Building competition entry. He was still working in 1945.

39:1 EADS, JAMES BUCHANAN (1820-87)

Obituary: BUILDING 6 (March 19, 1887): 112.

39:2 Huxtable, Ada Louise. "Eads Bridge, 1868-1874, St. Louis Missouri." PROGRESSIVE ARCHITECTURE 38 (April 1957): 139-42.

This bridge, built from 1869 to 1871, was the first to be constructed of steel. It was also the site of the first use of pneumatic-caissons sunk ninety-five feet to bedrock. Numerous problems involved in the construction are described.

40:1 EIDLITZ, CYRUS L.W. (1853-1921)

Trained in father's office (Leopold Eidlitz) and in Switzerland and Germany.

40:2 Schuyler, Montgomery. "The Evolution of a Skyscraper." ARCHITECTURAL RECORD 14 (November 1903): 329-43.

Pros and cons of skyscraper construction are forwarded leading to an analysis of the New York Times building by Eidlitz, "an unmistakable skyscraper," with a fifty-five-foot deep basement for subways and the mechanical equipment involved in newspaper publishing. Problems of building on a trapezoid-shaped site at Broadway and 42nd Street are described and several sketches serve as illustrations in the evolution of the design.

40:3 ______. "The Works of Cyrus L.W. Eidlitz." ARCHITECTURAL RECORD 5 (April-June 1896): 411-35.

Some of the residential architecture and railroad stations of Cyrus Eidlitz reflect his German background and European education, although he was born in New York City, the son of architect Leopold Eidlitz. His high-rise and commercial structures are eclectic, as was typical of the period, with stylistic trends from numerous sources but with interestingly detailed textures and decorative effects.

41:1 EIDLITZ, LEOPOLD (1823-1906)

Born in Prague and trained in the United States under Richard Upjohn. Practiced with Blesch prior to independent practice.

Avery Library, Columbia University, has drawings of Broadway Tabernacle, New York City, 1859; Christ Church, St. Louis, Missouri, 1859; Clergy House, St. George's Church, New York City, 1887; competition design for the New York Crystal Palace, 1852; assembly corridor of New York State Capital, Albany, 1878; and a photographic portfolio of nineteenth-century architecture. He wrote THE NATURE AND FUNCTION OF ARCHITECTURE, 1881.

Obituaries: AMERICAN ARCHITECT AND BUILDING NEWS 93 (April 1, 1908): 17; ROYAL INSTITUTE OF BRITISH ARCHITECTS' JOURNAL 15 (1907-8): 653.

Walter E. Langsman is working on a doctoral dissertation at Yale on the New York State Capitol, Albany. H. Allen Brooks wrote a master's thesis in 1955 on Eidlitz, Yale University.

41:2 Roseberry, Cecil. CAPITOL STORY. Albany, N.Y.: State of New York, 1964. 128 p.

The contribution of Eidlitz is described and illustrated in great detail, in addition to the work of those who began the building, contemporaries of Eidlitz, and his successors.

41:3 Schuyler, Montgomery. "A Great American Architect." ARCHITECTURAL RECORD 24 (September 1908): 164-79; 24 (October 1908): 277-92; 24 (November 1908): 365-78.

St. George's, Stuyvesant Square, New York City, was the first structure by Blesch and Eidlitz, a Bavarian and a Bohemian, who designed the exterior and interior respectively. This article by Schuyler illustrates examples of the work of Eidlitz in the "stick" style in wood, stone, and brick construction through to the High Victorian Gothic of Holy Trinity, Madison Avenue and 42nd Street. The second article discusses the commercial and public buildings mainly of the Italianate style; and the third article is devoted wholly to the Capitol at Albany, a Romanesquoid structure, designed in collaboration with Richardson.

42:1 **EISENMANN, JOHN (1851-1924)**

Of Eisenman and Smith (George H.)

Educated University of Michigan, 1871, in engineering and later at the Polytechnics at Munich and Stuttgart before returning to Cleveland to teach at the Case School of Applied Science.

42:2 Huxtable, Ada Louise. "The Cleveland Arcade, 1888-90, Cleveland, Ohio." PROGRESSIVE ARCHITECTURE 37 (September 1956): 139-40.

"Industry and transportation created the nineteenth century American city; commerce and technology built its monuments." The Cleveland Arcade exemplified both commercial architecture and metal construction. The editorial of this issue (p. 138) announces this article to be the first of a series, "documenting the significant contributions made to the development of architectural form and meaning in the United States over the past 300 years."

42:3 Schofield, Mary-Peale. "The Cleveland Arcade." ARCHITECTURAL FORUM, September 1967, pp. 60-65.

The arcade consists of two towers, nine stories high, linked by a five-story arcade in the "Romano-Byzantine" style. The roof trusses were partially innovative and are illustrated with a section and a plan of the whole building. Construction and other aspects of the building are described.

42:4 _____. "The Cleveland Arcade." JOURNAL OF THE SOCIETY OF ARCHITECTURAL HISTORIANS 25 (December 1966): 281-91.

A surprisingly elegant iron arcade linking Eneid and Superior Avenues, Cleveland, but with monumental Sullivanesque commercial style red sandstone facades. The article has numerous construction drawings, plans and photographs, and, at footnote no. 17, biographical data on Eisenmann.

43:1 ELLIS, HARVEY (1852-1904)

Worked for Eckel and Mann, St. Louis, and L.S. Buffington, Minneapolis.

Eileen Michels wrote a master's thesis at the University of Minnesota in 1953 entitled "The Architectural Designs of Harvey Ellis."

Obituaries: WESTERN ARCHITECT 3 (February 1904): 15. AMERICAN ARCHITECT AND BUILDING NEWS 85 (1904): 25-26.

43:2 Bragdon, Claude. "Harvey Ellis: A Portrait Sketch." ARCHITECTURAL REVIEW (Boston) 15 (December 1908). Rpt. THE PRAIRIE SCHOOL REVIEW 5 (First-Second Quarter, 1968): 19-35.

A superb watercolorist, Ellis was a Gothicist who evolved into Richardsonian Romanesque and was definitely not a classicist. The article is poetic but does have good coverage of drawings, plans, elevations and perspectives, watercolors, and photographs.

43:3 Garden, Hugh M.G. "Harvey Ellis, Designer and Draughtsman." ARCHITECTURAL REVIEW (Boston) 15 (December 1908). Reprint. THE PRAIRIE SCHOOL REVIEW 5 (First-Second Quarter, 1968): 36-39.

"A glutton for work when it had to be done, he was nevertheless incredibly lazy....His architectural designs are generally reminiscent. He generally picked up some suggestion, generally medieval...and twisted it to suit his own purpose." His fame as a draughtsman is emphasized and several watercolors and unfinished perspectives are utilized to illustrate his capabilities.

43:4 Kennedy, Roger. "Long Dark Corridors: Harvey Ellis." THE PRAIRIE SCHOOL REVIEW 5 (First-Second Quarter, 1968): 5-18.

Ellis is described as spanning the years from Richardson to the Prairie School and of having produced the jewel box and skyscraper aesthetic attributed to Sullivan before Sullivan! Photographs and sketches are reproduced to prove the point. His structures are to be found throughout Minnesota and in St. Louis.

43:5 Purcell, William Gray. "Forgotten Builders - The Nation's Voice." NORTHWEST ARCHITECT. Vol. 8, no. 6-7 (1944): 6-7, 13-14.

A confused article by an old architect who has rather little to say about Harvey Ellis, but much concerning his own ideas. The introduction states that Ellis had a "structural and technological sense and it is from that point on that his genius as a practitioner in the true Fine Art of building begins to sing."

43:6 Rochester, University of. A REDISCOVERY - HARVEY ELLIS: ARTIST ARCHITECT. Rochester, N.Y.: University of Rochester Memorial Art Gallery, 1972 (?).

A catalogue of an exhibition held at the Memorial Art Gallery.

43:7 Swales, F.S. "Master Draftsmen." PENCIL POINTS 5 (July 1924): 49-55, 79.

Praised for his pen and ink, charcoal, and watercolor sketches; his intellect; learning; overall designer, individual and original talent as an architect; Ellis' career, interests, and work methods are commented upon. Selections of sketches and finished drawings are illustrated.

44:1 ELMSLIE, GEORGE GRANT (1871-1952)

See also Purcell and Elmslie.

Obituaries: ARCHITECTURAL RECORD 111 (July 1952): 28; INTERIORS 111 (May 1952): 138; JOURNAL OF THE SOCIETY OF ARCHITECTURAL HISTORIANS 11 (May 1952): 25.

44:2 Gebhard, David. DRAWINGS FOR ARCHITECTURAL ORNAMENT BY GEORGE GRANT ELMSLIE, 1902-1936. Santa Barbara, Calif.: University of Southern California, Santa Barbara Art Gallery.

The notes by Gebhard complement twelve plates of Elmslie's drawings in this edition limited to 250 copies.

44:3 _____. "Louis Sullivan and George Grant Elmslie." JOURNAL OF THE SOCIETY OF ARCHITECTURAL HISTORIANS 19 (May 1960): 62-68.

See Sullivan.

44:4 Hamlin, Talbot Faulkner. "George Grant Elmslie and The Chicago Scene." PENCIL POINTS 22 (September 1941): 575-86.

Hamlin lists the creative architects of Chicago, 1900-30, including Purcell and Elmslie and those of the arts and crafts attitude toward design. Elmslie was Scottish by birth, came to the United States in the 1880's, was employed by Adler and Sullivan, and later partnered with Purcell, a Cornell graduate.

44:5 Hoffman, Donald L. "Elmslie's Topeka Legacy." THE PRAIRIE SCHOOL REVIEW 1 (Fourth Quarter, 1964): 22-23.

Photographs, description, and discussion of Elmslie's Capitol Building and Loan Association, Topeka, Kansas, 1922-24.

44:6 Vaughn, Edward J. "Sullivan and Elmslie at Michigan." THE PRAIRIE SCHOOL REVIEW 6 (Second Quarter, 1969): 20-23.

See Sullivan.

45:1 EMERSON, WILLIAM RALPH (1833-1917)

Publication: THE ARCHITECTURE AND FURNITURE OF THE SPANISH COLONIES, 1901.

Obituary: AMERICAN INSTITUTE OF ARCHITECTS' JOURNAL 6 (1918): 89.

45:2 Emerson, William. "As He is Known, Being Brief Sketches of Contemporary Members of the Architectural Profession." THE BRICKBUILDER 24 (1915): 234.

Education and training are discussed and architectural abilities praised; notably, his use of brick and the improvement of general housing conditions in our cities.

45:3 Zaitzevsky, Cynthia. THE ARCHITECTURE OF WILLIAM RALPH EMERSON. 1833-1917. Cambridge, Mass.: Fogg Art Museum, Harvard University, 1969. 100 p.

Although practicing in the field of mainly residential architecture in the Boston area from 1857 to 1909, this exhibition catalog covers the years 1870-90, since nothing is known of Emerson's work prior to 1870. The exhibition consisted of drawings of fourteen projects, many of which are illustrated with plans and discussion in the catalog. There is also a checklist of buildings and drawings, a bibliographical note, and a genealogy.

46:1 **EYRE, WILSON (1858-1944)**

Educated Massachusetts Institute of Technology, 1876, and worked in Philadelphia for James P. Sims until 1881. Joined J. Gilbert McIlvaine during 1912.

Avery Library, Columbia University, has 10 scrapbooks, 24 folders of correspondence, and architectural drawings of 11 projects. Pennsylvania University Fine Arts Library has sheets of 131 projects; Detroit Fine Arts Library, 13 projects; Free Library of Philadelphia, 5 projects; Historical Society of Pennsylvania, 1 project; and Princeton University Firestone Library, 2 projects.

Obituaries: MICHIGAN SOCIETY OF ARCHITECTS (Weekly Bulletin) 18 (November 7, 1944): 4.

46:2 Harbeson, John F. "Wilson Eyre, 1858-1944." AMERICAN INSTITUTE OF ARCHITECTS' JOURNAL 5 (March 1946): 129-33.

"In 1883, in the midst of a great deal of mediocre building, Wilson Eyre set up practice in Philadelphia." Eyre was part of the new Philadelphia, of fireproof technology in buildings, but he also had a love for the rustic handmade object, most notably seen in his domestic architecture.

46:3 Millard, Julian. "Work of Wilson Eyre." ARCHITECTURAL RECORD 14 (1903): 279-320.

Wilson Eyre spent his first eleven years in Florence prior to education in the United States from 1869 to 1877. The article is well illustrated by his architecture in which "will be found that in every case an exterior is the direct outgrowth of its plan." Structures designed prior to 1889 are discussed as being different in feeling to Eyre's later works, notably his domestic work. Skill, art of composition, use of materials, and the handling of a wide variety of details from different stylistic periods provides, in his work, a sense of originality comparable to that of Frank Furness.

46:4 Swales, Francis S. "Master Draftsmen, 13." PENCIL POINTS 6 (July 1925): 43-54.

Born in Florence, Italy, he returned to Quaker Philadelphia where he practiced. Several of his bold drawings are illustrated.

46:5 Wallick, Frederick. "Fairacres and Some Other Recent Country Houses by Wilson Eyre." INTERNATIONAL STUDIO 40 (1910): 29-36.

Eyre reproduced Pennsylvania colonial or English manor house styles at Fairacres, Jenkinstown, Pennsylvania. "Yet the similarity is only passing. No detail of comfort or convenience has been sacrificed to a strict conformity to style." At Fairacres the major rooms are at the rear of the house with the service rooms at the point of access as in English medieval residential architecture.

47:1 FLAGG, ERNEST (1857-1947)

Educated at the Ecole des Beaux Arts, and practiced in New York City, 1891-1940.

Has written on building regulations, Greek architecture (MS in Avery Library, Columbia University). Small houses and standard details. Cooper Union, New York City, has one sheet of United States Naval Academy Chapel, Annapolis, Maryland.

47:2 Burnham, Alan. "Forgotten Pioneering." ARCHITECTURAL FORUM 106 (April 1957): 116-21.

The Singer Building, New York, 1907, is well illustrated and described, and so too is the earlier 1904 Singer Building by the same architect, which gains higher praise for its functional qualities. The 1907 structure was the world's tallest building for eighteen months.

47:3 Desmond, H.W. "Illustrations and Descriptions of the Chief Works of Ernest Flagg." ARCHITECTURAL RECORD 11 (1901-2): 1-104.

"The first building that brought Mr. Flagg into prominence was the new St. Luke's Hospital on Morningside Heights." During a period of Romanesquoid structures, Mr. Flagg preferred the French style. This article is essentially a photographic essay with a detailed consideration of the Naval Academy on pp. 82-83.

47:4 Dillon, Arthur J. "The Proposed Tilden Trust Library for New York City." ARCHITECTURAL REVIEW (Boston) 1 (September 12, 1892): 67-72.

Tilden's will bequeathed money for a library and Flagg proceeded with a design on the site of the southwest corner of Fifth Avenue and 42nd Street. The scheme is illustrated with plan, sections, elevations, and perspectives.

47:5 Semsch, Otto Francis. A HISTORY OF THE SINGER BUILDING CONSTRUCTION, ITS PROGRESS FROM FOUNDATION TO FLAG POLE. New York: The Trow Press, 1908. 117 p.

"The Tower idea is an entirely new type of office building construction...it is doubtful if an equally magnificent tower will ever be built unless it is a literal copy of the Singer Building." It was forty-seven floors high and a total of 670 feet. Every aspect of the building is covered in minute detail, from the pneumatic caisson foundation, including all mechanical equipment, to the flag on the pole!

47:6 Sturgis, Russell. "Some Recent Warehouses." ARCHITECTURAL RECORD 23 (May 1908): 375-86.

Scribner's Publishing House, New York City, is illustrated at figs. 3 and 4, and discussed on pp. 381-82. Sturgis likes the simple expression of minimal brick structure and open loft windows, an approach to design which he had proposed at a New York American Institute of Architects' Journal meeting in 1865-66.

48:1 FORSTER, FRANK JOSEPH (1866-1948)

Wrote PROVINCIAL ARCHITECTURE OF NORTHERN FRANCE, 1931.

48:2 Forster, Frank J. COUNTRY HOUSES: THE WORK OF FRANK JOSEPH FORSTER. New York: W. Helburn, 1931. 183 p.

Forster condemns the nineteenth-century styles, and praises Bertram Goodhue and his advice on reading Lethaby (the English architect, and then only the last chapter of his ARCHITECTURE). Goodhue states: "In general my work follows the French tradition, and is known by a number of names, Norman Farmhouse, French Provincial, Domestic Gothic, and others, vague or descriptive." Numerous photographs, plans, and woodcuts illustrate a rather fine selection of vernacular designs with an arts and crafts flavoring.

49:1 FROST, CHARLES SUMNER (1856-1931)

Educated Massachusetts Institute of Technology, 1876, and worked for Peabody and Stearns until 1881, when he moved to Chicago and worked with Henry Ives Cobb. Burnham Library, Chicago, has drawings of McKinlock Building and Calumet Club, Chicago.

49:2 Jenkins, Charles E. "A Review of the Works of Charles S. Frost." ARCHITECTURAL REVIEWER 1 (September 30, 1897): 19-47.

ARCHITECTURAL REVIEWER was a short-lived publication devoted to "leading architects of the West, and, as far as possible, gives an illustrated review of what they have best done." After training in Boston, Frost settled in Milwaukee and built numerous small railroad stations in the area, in addition to churches, residences, and commercial and public buildings in a wide variety of styles.

50:1 FULLER, THOMAS W. (1822-98)

Born and trained in England until 1876, when he came to the United States and worked with Augustus Laver. Became Architect to the Dominion of Canada, 1881.

Avery Library, Columbia University, has a photographic portfolio of nineteenth-century architecture including the New York State Capitol.

Obituary: AMERICAN ARCHITECT AND BUILDING NEWS 62 (1898): 37.

50:2 Roseberry, Cecil R. CAPITOL STORY. Albany, N.Y.: State of New York, 1964. 128 p.

All aspects of the New York State Capitol are discussed and illustrated, including the competition-winning designs of Fuller and Laver and Fuller's contribution to the building up to the time of his dismissal.

51:1 FURNESS, FRANK (1838-1912)

Trained in the office of R.M. Hunt and organized a partnership with John Fraser, 1867-71, George W. Hewitt, 1871-75, and Allan Evans, in 1876.

Library Co. of Philadelphia has one sheet of its building; Pennsylvania Historical Society has drawings of six projects; Maryland

Historical Society, one project; University of Pennsylvania, Department of Buildings and Grounds, one project; Van Pelt Library, University of Pennsylvania, one project; and Pennsylvania Hospital, one project. Pennsylvania Academy of Fine Arts has twenty-one sheets of its building by Furness and Hewitt. Charles Savage wrote a master's thesis on Furness at Yale.

51:2 Campbell, William. "Frank Furness, an American Pioneer." ARCHITECTURAL REVIEW 110 (November 1951): 311-15.

The claim that all know of Wright, few of Sullivan, and none of Furness is the basis of this first article of recent vintage on Furness. Furness was an early employer of Sullivan, and Sullivan an early employer of Wright. Several commissions of Furness in Philadelphia are discussed and illustrated with references to the influence from France of Viollet-le-Duc.

51:3 Massey, James C. "Frank Furness in the 1870's: Some Lesser Known Buildings." CHARETTE 43 (January 1963): 13-16.

Massey considers the Provident Life and Trust Co. Bank, Philadelphia, 1879, the most important of a series of major designs by Furness in attempting to achieve an "American Style." The functional tradition and the acclaim by critics are topics discussed in this brief survey article.

51:4 _____. "The Provident Trust Buildings, 1879-1897." JOURNAL OF THE SOCIETY OF ARCHITECTURAL HISTORIANS 19 (May 1960): 79-81.

Written in the year of its demolition, this article by Massey on Provident Trust provides a few scanty facts and a lengthy criticism from PUNCH, previously quoted at length in the Campbell article (above). Massey declares the building to be ugly in that all decorative details were enlarged to twice the size that would normally seem reasonable.

51:5 O'Gorman, James F. THE ARCHITECTURE OF FRANK FURNESS. Philadelphia: Museum of Art, 1973. 212 p.

This catalog to an exhibition held from April 5, to May 27, 1973, has almost 300 illustrations including ten in color, plans, sections, elevations, sketches, photographs, details, and portraits. A list of 375 buildings as a checklist of documented works, attributed and incorrectly attributed works, was prepared by George E. Thomas and Hyman Myers but the introductory essay is by O'Gorman. It attempts a re-evaluation of Furness, a man who died June 27, 1912, "long past his prime, and his passing went almost unnoticed in the architectural press."

52:1 **GARDEN, HUGH MACKIE GORDON (1873-1961)**

Of Schmidt, Garden and Martin.

Obituary: ARCHITECTURAL FORUM 115 (November 1961): 16.

52:2 Garden, Hugh M.G. "The Chicago School." THE PRAIRIE SCHOOL REVIEW 3 (First Quarter, 1966): 19-23.

Reprint of an article published by the Illinois Society of Architects MONTHLY BULLETIN, 1939, pp. 6-7. Written at a time when the significance of the Chicago School was almost forgotten and ignored and prior to post-World War II interest, publications, and THE PRAIRIE SCHOOL REVIEW.

52:3 Greengard, Bernard C. "Hugh M.G. Garden." THE PRAIRIE SCHOOL REVIEW 111 (First Quarter, 1966): 5-18.

A brief survey of Garden's output from the Chicago days of Sullivan and Wright, through the commercial styles to the twentieth-century functionalism of the Montgomery Ward warehouses, Chicago, 1908. Photographs, drawings, sketches, plans, elevations, and details.

52:4 Shank, Wesley I. "Hugh Garden in Town." THE PRAIRIE SCHOOL REVIEW 5 (Third Quarter, 1968): 43-47.

Documentation of a work by Garden, little known until recently: The First Church of Christ, Scientist, in Marshalltown, Iowa, 1902-3. It has a simple Greek-cross plan, and internally has dark stained wood in the Stick style. Externally the steeply pitched gable roofs give the appearance of Wright's Tudorbethan houses.

53:1 **GILBERT, CASS (1859-1934)**

Educated Massachusetts Institute of Technology and worked for McKim, Mead and White after travel in Europe. From 1882 practiced with James Knox Taylor in St. Paul and New York City.

New York Historical Society had drawings of twenty-three projects.

Obituaries: AMERICAN ARCHITECT AND BUILDING NEWS 100 (September 20, 1934): 3; AMERICAN ARCHITECTURE 144 (July 1934): 140-43; ANNUAL REGISTER, 1934, p. 120; ARCHITECTURAL FORUM 60 (June 1934): 6; NEW INTERNATIONAL YEARBOOK, 1934, p. 276.

53:2 Cochran, Edwin A. THE CATHEDRAL OF COMMERCE, THE HIGHEST BUILDING IN THE WORLD. Baltimore: Thomsen-Ellis, 1918. 30 p.

The candlepower of the exterior illuminations is emphasized as much as the architecture for the Woolworth Building, New York, this "Cathedral of commerce." Photographs and color sketches illustrate the building in relation to its immediate and overall surroundings. Internal photographs illustrate the building from boiler rooms to the lavish and luxurious suite for the client, Mr. Woolworth.

53:3 Cortissoz, Royal. "Cass Gilbert: 1859-1934, An Appreciation." ARCHITECTURE NEW YORK 70 (July 1934): 34.

An obituary praising the qualities and listing the awards of an architect who was essentially a classicist but also designed the Woolworth Building, one of his major works, in the Gothic.

53:4 Gauthier, Julia Celina. THE MINNESOTA CAPITOL; OFFICIAL GUIDE AND HISTORY. St. Paul, Minn.: Pioneer Press Manufacture Departments, 1908. 71 p.

Detailed description with plans and photographs of the building, architectural details, sculptures, paintings, private and public apartments, and inscriptions.

53:5 Gilbert, Julia Finch. CASS GILBERT, REMINISCENCES AND ADDRESSES. New York: Privately printed by The Scribner Press, 1935. 118 p.

The book is exactly as the title describes it, with the reminiscences written by Julia Finch Gilbert, Cass' wife. Few illustrations are provided.

53:6 Huxtable, Ada Louise. "New Custom House: Modern, Functional, No Match for the Old." THE NEW YORK TIMES, Thursday, October 4, 1973, pp. 47, 90.

The new Custom House, as part of the World Trade Center, is standard, efficient, mechanical, and bland. Huxtable realizes that this is a sign of the times, but laments the grandeur of the historic, elaborately classical building with its numerous sculptures, paintings, and rich array of finishes and materials of 1907.

53:7 Moore, Charles. "Cass Gilbert, Architect. 1859-1934." AMERICAN ARCHITECT 144 (July 1934): 20.

An obituary of Gilbert who "died on the eve of giving to a waiting public two structures of the highest rank - the United States Supreme Court Building, Washington, and the building for the Federal Courts in New York City."

53:8 Paris, William Francklyn. THE HOUSE THAT LOVE BUILT, AN ITALIAN RENAISSANCE TEMPLE TO ARTS AND LETTERS. New York: The Haddon Press, 1925. 91 p.

A well-illustrated essay on the Detroit Public Library, a renaissance revival building, adorned with sculpture, reliefs, stained glass, mosaics, wrought iron, and a total idea of architectural-artistic collaboration comparable to sixteenth-century Italy. All is described in great detail.

53:9 _____. "Italian Renaissance in Detroit." AMERICAN ARCHITECT 123 (January 3, 1923): 15-19, 21.

In praise of the golden cornice on the exterior and gorgeous colored internal ceilings of the Detroit Public Library. All the mythological and historic symbolism of each ceiling plus the decorative motifs are described in great detail: "The Golden Staircase...is like a rainbow imprisoned in gossamer goldsmith and filigree work."

53:10 _____. "The Mosaics in the Frontal Colonnade of the Detroit Public Library." ARCHITECTURAL RECORD 49 (April 1921): 301-9.

After a survey of the use of mosaic work from the period of the Renaissance, Gilbert's library is highly praised as a unified design both from the general massing and also for the details, most notably in the mosaic apse with a theme based upon Shakespeare's Seven Ages. More historic background is given in praise of the scheme of this art form.

53:11 Schuyler, Montgomery. "The New Custom House at New York." ARCHITECTURAL RECORD 20 (July 1906): 1-14.

A general discussion of the aesthetics of utilizing the classical styles of architecture in government buildings. Isaiah Rogers' Merchants Exchange, later used as a Custom House on Wall Street, and Ammi Young's Boston Custom House are referred to in comparison to Cass Gilbert's new Custom House at Bowling Green. Schuyler justifies architectural expression above the utilitarian functions but is critical of the main north front of Gilbert's building. Sculptures on the building are illustrated.

53:12 _____. THE WOOLWORTH BUILDING. New York: Privately printed, 1913. 25 p.

Several engravings illustrate this essay by Schuyler, dedicated to Cass Gilbert. Schuyler is at his most poetic level.

53:13 Swales, F.S. "Master Draftsmen Cass Gilbert." PENCIL POINTS 7 (1926): 39, 583-98, 613-14.

Education, training, and projects upon which he worked in the firm of McKim, Mead and White are listed prior to Gilbert's successful design for the Minnesota State Capitol in 1896, and other prestigious buildings. His water color sketches, pen and ink drawings, and competition entry drawings are illustrated.

53:14 _____. "The Work of Cass Gilbert." ARCHITECTURAL REVIEW 31 (1912): 3-16.

Written at the time of the construction of the Woolworth Building, Broadway, New York City. Gilbert's most famous structures are listed as designed with "no pronounced predilection for any historical style. His attitude is like Stanford White's before him...."

53:15 Weber, P.J. "A Review of the Works of Cass Gilbert." ARCHITECTURAL REVIEWER 1 (June 30, 1897): 42-65.

This was a short-lived publication devoted to "leading architects of the West, and, as far as possible, gives an illustrated review of what they have done." Cass Gilbert is perhaps best known for his New York commissions, although he had a major practice in Minnesota before returning to New York after his initial training. He used a variant of the Shingle, Gothic, and Romanesque styles for religious and residential buildings, whereas his State Capitol at St. Paul was thoroughly classical.

53:16 Woolworth, Frank Winfield. DINNER GIVEN TO CASS GILBERT, ARCHITECT, BY FRANK W. WOOLWORTH...APRIL 24, 1913. Baltimore: Munder-Thomsen Press, 1913. 140 p.

Contains plates, portraits and an appreciation.

54:1 GILL, IRVING JOHN (1870-1936)

Trained under Louis Sullivan until 1893, when he moved to California for health reasons. Practiced in San Diego from 1895.

Obituary: ARCHITECT AND ENGINEER 127 (1936): 65. Helene Barbara Kallman wrote a master's thesis at Columbia University in 1964 on "Irving Gill, His Past, His Time, the Future He Helped to Shape."

54:2 Huxtable, Ada Louise. "Blue Monday in Los Angeles." THE NEW YORK TIMES, Sunday, March 8, 1970, section 2, p. 23.

After stating that Irving Gill's Dodge House, Los Angeles, 1916, is "one of the 15 most significant houses in the history of American domestic architecture," Mrs. Huxtable relates the tragedy of its demolition. It was compulsorily purchased by the Los Angeles Board of Education so that it could be razed and the site used for a school, which never materialized.

54:3 McCoy, Esther. FIVE CALIFORNIA ARCHITECTS. New York: Reinhold Publishing Corp., 1960. Pp. 59-102.

"Sullivan turned the faces of the young men away from Europe and bade them look to Africa, a land of serene wall, of earth form, of decorative details." Gill was an employee of Adler and Sullivan and equipped with Sullivan's philosophy, became interested in low cost migrant workers housing ("a dangerous kind of work," according to Elmer Gray of San Diego) and tile slab construction of hollow tile and reinforced concrete. His most famed house, simple in form and in all details, including the interior fittings, was the Walter L. Dodge House, Los Angeles, 1916.

54:4 _____. IRVING GILL, 1870-1936. Los Angeles: Los Angeles County Museum, 1958. 59 p.

The son of a Syracuse, New York, building contractor, Gill sought his professional development in the office of Adler and Sullivan. Gill then followed the railroad to San Diego, and it was on the West Coast that he practiced from the time of his first commission in 1895 until his death in 1936. The catalog is well illustrated and provides a chronological list of his known buildings.

54:5 _____. "Roots of California Contemporary Architecture." ARTS AND ARCHITECTURE 73 (October 1956): 14-17, 36-39.

The Los Angeles City Art Department arranged an exhibit of seven California architects and their work, 1900-35, including Gill, who is briefly mentioned. He built more than one hundred houses and fifty large buildings in San Diego.

54:6 Roorbach, E.M. "The Garden Apartments of California." ARCHITECTURAL RECORD 34 (December 1913): 520-30.

"It has taken California to produce a man with imagination brilliant enough to build a home in an apartment house," and that is best seen in the work of Gill. The unity of the scheme, originality of the plan, and an architecture based upon first principles is seen at Bella Vista, Sierra Madre, constructed of hollow tile, reinforced concrete, and an asbestos surfacing. Planting and integration with the landscape is notably emphasized.

55:1 GILMAN, ARTHUR DELEVAN (1821-82)

See G.J.F. Bryant with whom Gilman collaborated, notably on

the Boston City Hall. Partner with Edward H. Kendal in New York from 1868, in association with George B. Post on the Equitable Life Assurance Building.

55:2 Bunting, Bainbridge. "The Plan of the Back Bay Area of Boston." JOURNAL OF THE SOCIETY OF ARCHITECTURAL HISTORIANS 13 (May 1954): 19-24.

The plan approved in 1856 was the work of Gilman. It consisted of a rigid grid but was general enough to allow for gradual change. Back Bay became axial with "wide impressive street corridors and its strong sense of unity" comparable to the work of Haussmann in Paris.

55:3 Stone, Alfred. "The Boston Public Garden." AMERICAN ARCHITECT AND BUILDING NEWS 80 (June 20, 1903): 94-95.

A letter to the editors from Stone, who worked under Gilman when he was proposing improvements to the Boston Commission on the Back Bay area. A letter from Gilman about Commonwealth Avenue and allied areas is quoted from at length.

55:4 Wrenn, George L. "A Return to Solid and Classical Principles." JOURNAL OF THE SOCIETY OF ARCHITECTURAL HISTORIANS 20 (December 1961): 191-93.

Arthur Gilman designed the Arlington Street Church, 1859-61, in the Boston Back Bay area at a cost of over $116,000 as described in an article of December 6, 1861, in the BOSTON EVENING TRANSCRIPT quoted here in full.

56:1 GOODHUE, BERTRAM GROSVENOR (1869-1924)

Trained under James Renwick and became a partner of Cram, Goodhue and Ferguson (see), prior to independent practice in New York City.

Wrote AMERICAN CHURCHES, 1915, on the design, services, and planning as best practiced in the United States. Drawings from the office of James Renwick, Jr., for St. Patrick's Cathedral, New York City, in the Avery Library, Columbia University, are signed by Goodhue. Avery also has two sheets of the San Diego, Panama-California Exposition, of which Goodhue was consulting architect. He helped illustrate Sylvester Baxter's SPANISH COLONIAL ARCHITECTURE IN MEXICO, 1901.

Obituaries: AMERICAN ARCHITECTURE 125 (April-June 1924): 477-78. AMERICAN INSTITUTE OF ARCHITECTS' JOURNAL 12 (1924): 242, 276, 401; NEW INTERNATIONAL YEARBOOK, 1924,

p. 511.

Eric S. McCready is working on a doctoral dissertation on the Nebraska State Capitol, at the University of Delaware.

56:2 Abbott, Lawrence F. "Bertram Goodhue." AMERICAN ARCHITECTURE 125 (May 21, 1924): 478.

A quarter-page obituary on "Bertram Goodhue [who] made an important and notable contribution to this unfailing test of American culture."

56:3 Barber, Donn. "Bertram Grosvenor Goodhue, FAIA, An Appreciation." AMERICAN ARCHITECTURE 125 (May 21, 1924): 477-78.

An obituary of Goodhue who died at the height of his career when major ecclesiastical and university buildings were being contemplated. His Nebraska State Capitol "departed from accepted standards" and was under construction in 1924. Only one week after his death his National Academy of Sciences in Washington was dedicated.

56:4 Colton, Arthur W. "Bertram Grosvenor Goodhue. Architect and Master of Many Arts." ARCHITECTURAL RECORD 59 (January 1926): 95-98.

"Mr. Goodhue's career is an argument for the guild and apprenticeship system of technical education against the school." His greatness is defined and stated in relation to his career, partnerships, and major works.

56:5 Davies, Florence. "Christ Church, Cranbrook; A Work of Art in Which Artists, Craftsmen and Artisans Collaborated." AMERICAN MAGAZINE OF ART 20 (1929): 311-25.

This Bloomfield Hills, Michigan, Gothic church was begun by Goodhue but continued after his death by associates. The church is described and well illustrated with all the art works: stained glass, mosaics, wood carving, sculpture, frescoes, all in the medieval tradition of craftsmen and artists complementing each other's work.

56:6 Goodhue, Bertram Grosvenor. A BOOK OF ARCHITECTURAL AND DECORATIVE DRAWINGS BY BERTRAM GROSVENOR GOODHUE. New York: The Architectural Book Publishing Company, 1914. 104 p.

E. Donald Robb writes an introductory explanation of the purpose of the book: to give the public the enjoyment of seeing Goodhue's sketches and drawings, which his assistants admired to such a great extent in working with the designer on a day-to-day basis. Frank Chouteau Brown wrote the section on "An Architect's Renderings of some of his Works."

56:7 Howland, Eugene B. "The New Virginia Military Institute." ARCHITECTURAL RECORD 36 (September 1914): 231-40.

Two miles out of Lexington, Virginia, stood the first gleaming new buildings, dominated by a four-story barracks in 1914. A history of the Institute is given including the destruction of the Institute by bombardment at the end of the Civil War. A plan provided showing the arrangement of buildings according to topography.

56:8 Imlay, Robert. "The Proposed Nebraska State Capitol." ARCHITECTURAL RECORD 48 (July 1920): 75-78.

This competition-winning design was considered unusual, novel, bold, and original among ten limited submissions. Although only a preliminary design, it is praised as not being based upon St. Peter's, Rome. Three illustrations complement the brief description. It is interesting to note the names of the three jurors--W.B. Wood, James Gamble Rogers, and Willis Polk!

56:9 Kimball, Fiske. "Goodhue's Architecture: A Critical Estimate." ARCHITECTURAL RECORD 62 (December 1927): 537-39.

Goodhue died three years prior to the memorial volume: ARCHITECT AND MASTER OF MANY ARTS, which is here being reviewed. "His early romantic worship of logic and function," was superseded by an attitude of utilizing modern materials such as structural steel and reinforced concrete, with stone and oak of the medieval tradition. His latest structures exhibited a logic of modern function, which provides a niche for him in the realm of modern architecture.

56:10 Mumford, Lewis. "American Architecture Today." ARCHITECTURE 58 (October 1928): 189-204.

This is the third part in a series by Mumford that was devoted to monumental architecture. Goodhue's Los Angeles Public Library is a specific example. This is a critical article of architecture and interior design.

56:11 R., E.D. "Bertram Grosvenor Goodhue." THE BRICKBUILDER 24 (April 1915): 102.

A pen and ink artist, Goodhue utilized picturesque qualities of the sketch to create his major structures. Education and training are listed.

56:12 Swales, Francis S. "Bertram Grosvenor Goodhue, Architect, Designer and Draftsman, 1869-1924." PENCIL POINTS 5 (June 1924): 42-56.

Influenced by English Pre-Raphaelite artists, Goodhue's partnership came into being with the winning of the West Point Competition in 1903. He always gave credit to his assistants and four of those upon whom he relied, when away from the office, are listed, and their work discussed. Pencil drawings, pen and ink sketches, and watercolors are illustrated.

56:13 Updike, Daniel Berkeley. A DESCRIPTION OF THE PASTORAL STAFF GIVEN TO THE DIOCESE OF ALBANY, N.Y. Boston: Merrymount Press, 1900. 6 pl.

The design for this staff was by Bertram Grosvenor Goodhue and was based upon "examples of ecclesiastical art in the South Kensington Museum," London.

56:14 Whitaker, Charles Harris. "Bertram Grosvenor Goodhue." AMERICAN INSTITUTE OF ARCHITECTS' JOURNAL 13 (May 1925): 155.

Goodhue died at a time when he was producing some of his most significant work. A watercolor sketch of "A Persian Reminescence" is used as illustration.

56:15 Whitaker, Charles Harris, and Alexander, H.B. THE ARCHITECTURAL SCULPTURE OF THE STATE CAPITOL AT LINCOLN, NEBRASKA. New York: Press of the American Institute of Architects' Journal, 1926. 16 p. 45 pl.

Essays, plans, and photographs of the architecture and the incorporated sculpture and incised texts, all having a touch of Art Deco.

56:16 Whitaker, Charles Harris, ed., et al. BERTRAM GROSVENOR GOODHUE - ARCHITECT AND MASTER OF MANY ARTS. New York: Press of the American Institute of Architects' Journal, 1925. 50 p. 273 pls.

Biographical essay, the partnerships of Goodhue, his association with sculptors, his designs for the Nebraska State Capitol and the National Academy of Sciences precede the 273 plates. The plates are of Goodhue's designs even though they were the product of firms in which he was a partner: Cram, Wentworth and Goodhue, or Cram, Goodhue and Ferguson. All projects after 1914 were supervised from Goodhue's own office.

56:17 Winslow, Carleton Monroe. THE ARCHITECTURE AND THE GARDENS OF THE SAN DIEGO EXPOSITION...San Francisco: P. Elder Co., 1916. 154 p.

57:1 GREENE AND GREENE (Partnership 1893- ?)

Charles Sumner Greene (1868-1957) and Henry Mather Greene (1870-1954).

Both educated at the Manual Training High School of Washington

University, St. Louis, and at Massachusetts Institute of Technology, 1888. Thereafter Henry worked for Shepley, Rutan and Coolidge before setting up practice in Pasadena, California, 1893.

Obituaries of Charles: ARCHITECTURAL RECORD 122 (August 1957): 24; HOUSE AND HOME 12 (July 1957): 85.

Avery Library, Columbia University, has approximately 500 drawings of about 100 projects which are being carefully catalogued.

57:2 Bangs, Jean Murray. "Greene and Greene, The American House Owes Simplicity and Clarity to Two Almost-Forgotten Brothers Who Showed Us How to Build with Wood." ARCHITECTURAL FORUM 89 (October 1948): 80-89.

The renaissance of these two architects began with such enthusiasts as Miss Bangs and led the California Chapter of the American Institute of Architects to give them an award of merit. Their work in California is a part of the American drama of architecture, as the Chicago School in the Midwest. Their major material was wood, assembled and detailed in the arts and crafts tradition with a touch of the Japanese in the internal spaces and the way in which the bungalows fit into the landscape.

57:3 _____. "Prophet without Honor." AMERICAN INSTITUTE OF ARCHITECTS' JOURNAL 18 (July 1952): 11-16.

The American indigenous house together with its furniture, fabrics, and art pottery was due, according to Jean Murray Bangs, to the brothers, Greene and Greene. Glass walls, patios and the extension of the interior of the house into the landscape, adaptation to climatic conditions, careful orientation of rooms, all leading toward new social thinking, are credited to the brothers. They are even credited with "democratic elements" of design as opposed to European domination!

57:4 Croly, Herbert D. "The Country House in California." ARCHITECTURAL RECORD 34 (December 1913): 483-519.

Croly feels that California does not have a stylistic direction since the Spanish Mission style is ecclesiastical and the building boom in California is in the field of residential architecture. Some old ranch buildings have been converted into houses rather well. Added to this are the facts that the climate is moderate and wood plentiful. The work of Greene and Greene (and the architecture of a few other firms) is illustrated to complement the thesis of the article. The photographs illustrate how well their houses integrate with the landscape and environment.

57:5 David, Arthur C. "An Architect of Bungalows in California." ARCHITECTURAL RECORD 20 (October 1906): 307-15.

The origin of the "bungalow" was India, where Englishmen wanted comfortable temporary accommodations when travelling. California has, however, adopted characteristics of Japanese models, and it is seen "most completely and happily fulfilled in the houses of Messrs. Greene and Greene," where the house complements the landscape. Heavy masonry and wide wood overhangs provide a rural quality which is practical as well as economic.

57:6 Lancaster, Clay. "Some Sources of Greene and Greene." AMERICAN INSTITUTE OF ARCHITECTS' JOURNAL 34 (August 1960): 39-46.

Several of their 540 residences are described and analyzed with sources from Japan, and also from the American vernacular. Chimneys, for example, are not from Japan but from pioneer structures, and from published examples of work by contemporary architects, both in relation to plan and siting and also in some of the detailing.

57:7 McCoy, Esther. FIVE CALIFORNIA ARCHITECTS. New York: Reinhold Publishing Corp., 1960. Pp. 103-48.

Graduating from Massachusetts Institute of Technology, they became eclectic designers in the Queen Anne style, setting up practice where their parents lived, in Pasadena, 1893. Japanese influence is seen in the J.A. Culbertson House, 1902; Irwin, Gamble and Blacker houses, but additionally with Tiffany glass; adobe qualities in the Bandini's bungalow, 1904. With the emergence of the classical styles in California, the golden era of Pasadena and its resultant shingle style began to wane.

57:8 Makinson, Randell L. "Greene and Greene: The Gamble House." THE PRAIRIE SCHOOL REVIEW 5 (Fourth Quarter, 1968): 5-23.

D.B. Gamble of Proctor and Gamble fame, retired with his wife to Pasadena, California, bought a lot, and commissioned Greene and Greene to build a house which cost $50,000. The Gambles went to Japan for the year during which time the house was built, giving the architects carte blanche. The architects designed the house in the spirit of Japanese architecture, plus the furnishings, rugs, light fixtures, and even the decorative glazing which was made by Tiffany Studios, New York.

57:9 _____. "Notes on Greene and Greene." ARTS AND ARCHITECTURE 70 (July 1953): 27, 38.

"Revived interest in craftsmanship leads students back to the great Greene and Greene, who lavished as much care on a trellis as an interior detail. Order and naturalness mark their work, a sincere use of wood and sensitivity to brick and stone." The James A. Culbertson house, 1897, one of three on the Arroyo Seco, is illustrated.

57:10 _____. "Roots of California Contemporary Architecture." ARTS AND ARCHITECTURE 73 (October 1956): 14-17, 36-39.

The Los Angeles City Art Department arranged an exhibit of seven California architects and their work, 1900 to 1935, including the Greene brothers who are briefly mentioned. They developed a "unique design vocabulary. It grew in time into a rich language, which they were to use with great fluency."

57:11 Taylor, Walter A. "Charles Sumner Greene." AMERICAN INSTITUTE OF ARCHITECTS' JOURNAL 28 (November 1957): 402.

Records the award of the Certificate of Merit to Greene and Greene by the Southern California Chapter of the American Institute of Architects.

57:12 Yost, L. Morgan. "Greene and Greene of Pasadena." JOURNAL OF THE SOCIETY OF ARCHITECTURAL HISTORIANS 9 (March and May 1950): 11-19; AMERICAN INSTITUTE OF ARCHITECTS' JOURNAL 14 (September 1950): 115-25.

Greene and Greene were still alive when this article was written, and Yost located them through a daughter of Charles Sumner Greene. The article provides background, the beginnings of their career in architecture, inspiration from Japan, commitment to detail, and comments on some of their designs.

58:1 GRIFFIN, MARION LUCY MAHONY (1871-1962)

Architect and architectural draftsman of distinction and high quality. Worked for Frank Lloyd Wright and executed many of the drawings of projects published by Wright over an eleven-year period. Married Walter Burley Griffin.

Educated Massachusetts Institute of Technology. Published ONE HUNDRED BUNGALOWS, 1912. Burnham Library, Chicago, has one sheet of the Mueller family summer home, Decatur, Illinois, and one sheet of the World Fellowship Center, New Hampshire.

58:2 Griffin, Marion Mahony. "The Magic in America." Unpublished manuscript, New York Historical Society, and Burnham Library, Chicago Art

Institute, 1949.

Frank Lloyd Wright accused Walter Burley Griffin of "highway robbery" and of "sucking his eggs," to which Marion rebutted, claiming that Wright's work was "wholly" hers and that of her husband.

58:3 Van Zanten, David T. "The Early Work of Marion Mahony Griffin." THE PRAIRIE SCHOOL REVIEW 3 (Second Quarter, 1966): 5-23.

Discusses Marion's work as an illustrator but also her independent architectural designs, including All Souls Unitarian Church at Evanston, Illinois, 1903, designed in the Chicago School idiom but later Gothicized at the request of the church (demolished 1960). Other projects were of a residential nature, including the country house for Henry Ford at Dearborn, begun, but not completed.

59:1 GRIFFIN, WALTER BURLEY (1876-1937)

A Prairie School architect who, with his wife, Marion Mahony, worked for Frank Lloyd Wright. He is most famous for his competition-winning design of the Capital of Australia at Canberra.

Both books, by Birrell and Peisch, should be consulted since they complement each other with slightly different material covered in each.

Drawings by Griffin for the landscaping of Wright's house for Adolph Mueller at Decatur, Illinois, plus thirty-seven of Griffin's projects are owned by the Burnham Library, Chicago Art Institute. The Burnham Library also has one residence by Griffin and Byrne and four projects of Griffin and A.A. Fritsch. Avery Library, Columbia University, has miscellaneous drawings and a pamphlet on Griffin's termination as Director of Design and Construction by the government of Australia.

59:2 Birrell, James. WALTER BURLEY GRIFFIN. Brisbane, Australia: University of Queensland Press, 1964. 203 p. Illus.

Well illustrated portfolio of the work of Griffin from his earliest residential architecture (such as the Melson house, Mason City, Iowa, 1912) through his neighborhood planning and landscape designs, to his later domestic and collegiate work in Australia after winning the Canberra Competition.

59:3 Johnson, Donald Leslie. "The Griffin Reico Incinerators." ARCHITECTURAL ASSOCIATION QUARTERLY, Autumn 1971, pp. 46-55.

Concerned with the incinerator buildings at Canberra,

Australia, for the Reverboratory Incinerator and Engineering Company, Griffin replaced "industrial eyesores with public amenities." Most are geometric in design and some appear to have been influenced by Mayan architecture. Most are now dormant (due to high costs) or demolished. At least sixteen were built, many illustrated.

59:4 O'Connor, Peggy. "A Pair of Early Griffin Houses." THE PRAIRIE SCHOOL REVIEW 7 (First Quarter, 1970): 5-13.

The houses in question (now owned by Edward Lechinger and Joseph B. Kovalchik on Magnolia Street, Edgewater, Illinois, on Lake Michigan) are Wrightian in style, cubic, and finished in stucco. Both were built for William F. Temple as speculative houses and are among Griffin's earliest designs. This is a student paper from Professor Paul E. Sprague's class; the class measured the buildings and produced plans, here illustrated.

59:5 Peisch, Mark L. "The Chicago School and Walter Burley Griffin, 1893-1914. Growth and Dissemination of an Architectural Movement and a Representative Figure." Doctoral dissertation, Columbia University, 1969. 279 p.

Griffin is chosen as a lesser representative of the Chicago School, a school which included Sullivan and Wright, because he was an early assistant of Wright and achieved a certain amount of fame in his own right. Maher, Purcell, and Elmslie are considered together with Griffin, who began practice in 1906 with an intense interest in the Garden City Movement, leading to the Canberra Competition of 1911.

59:6 _____. THE CHICAGO SCHOOL OF ARCHITECTURE. New York: Random House, 1965. 177 p.

Sub-titled "Early Followers of Sullivan and Wright," this mistitled book is really about Walter Burley Griffin, who was the subject of Peisch's doctoral dissertation (see), but other minor figures are mentioned. Griffin's links to Ebenezer Howard's Garden City Movement and the American (Burnham) City Beautiful ideals are examined.

59:7 Purcell, William Gray. "Walter Burley Griffin. Progressive." WESTERN ARCHITECT 18 (September 1912): 93-95.

A brief essay on Griffin's work at the University of California. Won in competition.

59:8 Sprague, Paul E. "Griffin Rediscovered in Beverly." THE PRAIRIE SCHOOL REVIEW 10 (First Quarter, 1973): 6-23, with a catalog by

Sprague, pp. 24-32.

A little intuition and research has produced a list of fifteen additional residences by Griffin, almost totally forgotten from the period of their construction. All are illustrated, some with plans, details of chronology and descriptions, and compared with works by Wright.

59:9 Van Zanten, David T. WALTER BURLEY GRIFFIN: SELECTED DESIGNS. Palos Park: Prairie School Press, 1970. 113 p. 54 pls.

An attempt to illustrate Griffin's work mainly through the superb draftsmanship of his wife, Marion Mahony (who also assisted and made numerous drawings for Wright), and to present Griffin's lectures and articles. Drawings by Griffin himself and assistants, Roy Lippincott, George Elge, and others, are also used.

60:1 GUASTAVINO, RAPHAEL (1842-1908)

Wrote: COHESIVE CONSTRUCTION, ITS PAST, ITS PRESENT, ITS FUTURE? Chicago, 1893. 16 p. and ESSAY ON THE THEORY AND HISTORY OF COHESIVE CONSTRUCTION APPLIED ESPECIALLY TO THE TIMBREL VAULT, Boston, 1893. 140 p.

Obituary: AMERICAN ARCHITECT AND BUILDING NEWS 93 (February 12, 1908): 15.

60:2 Collins, George R. "The Transfer of Thin Masonry Vaulting from Spain to America." JOURNAL OF THE SOCIETY OF ARCHITECTURAL HISTORIANS 27, no. 3 (October 1968): 176-201.

A well-illustrated, informative article on thin vault construction using warped tiles, a construction technique utilized in the United States from 1880 to 1940 by most notable architects. Raphael Guastavino introducted the system from Spain, where it was used by Antonio Gaudi in Barcelona, to the northeast area of the United States. Heins and La Farge used it at St. John the Divine, New York, and McKim, Mead and White on their Pantheon inspired dome. Appendix I is a list of publications on Spanish tile vault construction and Appendix II, publications by Guastavino.

60:3 Wight, Peter Bonnett. "The Life and Works of Raphael Guastavino." THE BRICKBUILDER 10 (April, May, September, October, 1901): 79-81, 100-2, 184-88, 211-14.

Part I: born in Valencia, Spain, in 1842, he became an architect winning his first competition in 1866. His interest in structural techniques led him into the field of building. He won competitions and designed and constructed several structures in Barcelona, Spain. Part

II. his interest and expertise was in cohesive construction when forces in structure react with one another rather than countering the forces of gravity. He came to the United States in 1881, after winning a medal for his Spanish architecture at the Philadelphia Exposition, 1876. Parts III and IV are devoted to examples of the practice of architecture and cohesive construction in America.

61:1 GUENZEL AND DRUMMOND (n.d.)

Louis Guenzel (1860-1956), and William E. Drummond (1876-1946) (see), Prairie School architects.

61:2 Hasbrouck, Wilbert R. "The Architectural Firm of Guenzel and Drummond." THE PRAIRIE SCHOOL REVIEW I (Second Quarter, 1964): 5-7, 16-21.

Portraits, photographs, sketches of a firm which was nurtured in the Chicago School, since Guenzel worked for Sullivan, and Drummond discovered Wright's work in Oak Park, Illinois, while he was taking a nightly ramble. After working for R.E. Schmidt, D.H. Burnham, and Wright, Drummond joined Guenzel in practice during 1910.

62:1 HAIGHT, CHARLES COOLIDGE (1841-1917)

Trained in law at Columbia, and after the Civil War, entered the office of Emlyn T. Littel, thereafter opening his own office. Associated at the turn of the century with Alfred M. Githens.

Avery Library, Columbia University, has drawings of eighteen projects and Yale University has four sheets of one project by Haight and Githens.

Obituaries: AMERICAN ARCHITECT AND BUILDING NEWS 111 (1917): 151; ARCHITECTURAL RECORD 41 (1917): 367.

62:2 Githens, Alfred Morton. "Charles Coolidge Haight." ARCHITECTURAL RECORD 41 (April 1917): 367-69.

Trained in law and later a volunteer in the Civil War, Haight practiced in the English Gothic tradition of architecture during a period of "low ebb" in design. His position in the profession is evaluated and a list of his major achievements provided.

62:3 Schuyler, Montgomery. "Great American Architects Series." ARCHITEC-

TURAL RECORD, Supplement to the July 1899 issue, p. 1.

Schuyler remembers Haight as far back as 1870, when a competition was held by A.B. Mullett for the New York post office. Haight's entry was Ruskinian, although by 1874, when he designed his first buildings for Columbia College, he was practicing in the "Victorian Gothic." This style was suitable for "church colleges" as Hobart, Geneva, New York; St. Stephens, Annandale-on-Hudson, New York; and University of the South, Sewanee, Tennessee; as well as Yale and the General Theological Seminary, New York. Other building types in other styles are discussed including competition entries for the New York Public Library and City College of New York.

62:4 _____. "The Architecture of West Point." ARCHITECTURAL RECORD 14 (December 1903): 463-92.

This general article illustrates Haight's unsuccessful competition entry for the extension of West Point. Discussion centers around the earlier classical design of Memorial Hall by Stanford White and the award-winning Gothic scheme by Cram, Goodhue and Ferguson.

63:1 HARDENBURG, HENRY JANEWAY (1847-1918)

Worked for Detlef Lienau, 1865-70, when he set up practice for himself.

Obituaries: AMERICAN ARCHITECTURE 115 (1918): 387; NEW INTERNATIONAL YEARBOOK, 1918, p. 291.

63:2 Bach, Richard F. "Henry Janeway Hardenburg." ARCHITECTURAL RECORD 44 (July 1918): 91-95.

Hardenburg's career spans "the full period from Greek Revival style of the ugly forties, through the still uglier fifties and the gradual improving succeeding decades to the time of the most up to the minute skyscraper innovation." He began in the office of Detlef Lienau. The 1884 Dakota Apartment Building, New York, seems to have been designed when the architect "found" himself after phases of less "remarkable character."

63:3 Frohne, H.W. "Designing a Metropolitan Hotel, The Plaza." ARCHITECTURAL RECORD 22 (September 1907): 349-64.

Accommodations public and private of a transitory or permanent nature are discussed in relation to costs, upkeep, and initial expenses of a hotel. The architects' problems of height, building codes and regulations, space relationships, lighting, and ventilating are all touched upon. The lavish interiors of this New York hotel are illustrated and plans provided.

63:4 Hartmann, Sadekichi. "A Conversation with Henry Janeway Hardenburg." ARCHITECTURAL RECORD 19 (May 1906): 376-80.

Entering Detlef Lienau's office in 1863, Hardenburg was educated in architecture through publications rather than foreign travel. By 1906 there were, however, many publications upon which the younger members of the profession relied too heavily. Strong opinions were held by Hardenburg on style, the dominance of Europe over America, and New York over the rest of the country, the level of the profession, and more specifically his hotel designs.

63:5 Horseley, Carter B. "The Dakota Finds Repairs to a Landmark are Costly." THE NEW YORK TIMES, Sunday, February 17, 1974, section 8, pp. 1, 6.

This fine early apartment building on Central Park West, New York, and now a cooperative, is finding repairs and refurbishing exorbitantly expensive. The whole problem of preserving old structures is discussed and the usual brief history of the building given.

63:6 Schuyler, Montgomery. "Henry Janeway Hardenburg." ARCHITECTURAL RECORD 6 (January-March 1897): 335-75.

Hardenburg's early training under Detlef Lienau and one of his early "interesting and respectable commercial buildings," preface a laudatory essay on some of his more famed buildings including the Dakota Apartments and the several huge New York hotels, which are "of special significance." Numerous lesser-known structures, many of which have long been demolished, are described and illustrated.

63:7 Sturgis, Russell. "The Whitehall." ARCHITECTURAL RECORD 14 (July 1903): 70-73.

Utilitarian in design and without decoration, this New York hotel was designed for a real estate speculator and achieved simplicity through client demands.

64:1 HARTWELL AND RICHARDSON AND DRIVER (Partnership from 1881)

Henry W. Hartwell (1833-1919) practiced in Boston from 1856 and with William C. Richardson (1854-1935) from 1881. James Driver (1859-1923) became a partner in 1895.

64:2 Vogel, Susan Maycock. "Hartwell and Richardson: An Introduction to their Work." JOURNAL OF THE SOCIETY OF ARCHITECTURAL HISTORIANS 32 (May 1973): 132-46.

Their "buildings were neither forward in style nor innovative in interior planning. . . but competently designed, excellently constructed and comfortably up to date in the accepted styles of the day." Early partnerships of Hartwell are mentioned and many of the domestic structures which he designed are described and illustrated, most, in some variety of Richardsonian shingle. Interiors were carefully detailed and some exteriors are quite magnificent, notably the Memorial Library at Acton.

65:1 **HASTINGS, THOMAS (1860-1929)**

Educated Columbia and Ecole des Beaux Arts, and worked for Mc Kim, Mead and White until forming a partnership with John M. Carrere. Carrere died in 1911, but Hastings continued to practice under the joint name. Wrote two of the SIX LECTURES ON ARCHITECTURE for the Scammon Lectures of 1915, with Ralph Cram and Claude Bragdon, and contributed an essay on Beaux Arts influence in America in the ARCHITECTURAL RECORD, January 1901.

Avery Library, Columbia University, has drawings of the A.I. Dupont Chapel, Wilmington, Delaware.

Obituaries: ARCHITECTURAL RECORD 66 (December 1929): 596. AMERICAN ARCHITECTURE 136 (July-December, 1929): 55; ROYAL INSTITUTE OF BRITISH ARCHITECTS' JOURNAL 37 (1929-30): 24-25; ARCHITECTURAL FORUM 51 (December 1929): 35.

65:2 Clute, Eugene. "Master Draftsman." PENCIL POINTS 6 (December 1925): 49-60, 88.

Hastings insisted upon drawing with T-square and triangle and not with thin paper and soft pencil. His work is well illustrated and his career, partnership, and commissions discussed. Listed are his work on comissions, committees, and contributions to the profession and architectural education.

65:3 Gray, David. THOMAS HASTINGS, ARCHITECT: COLLECTED WRITINGS. Boston: Houghton Mifflin Co., 1933.

Twenty-two essays by Hastings, each identified in relation to its source cover various aspects of design, but the first seventy-nine pages are devoted to a memoir providing an appreciation of the work of Hastings, his life history, education, partnership, teaching, philosophy of architectural design, and major achievements.

65:4 Hastings, Thomas. "On the Evolution of Style." AMERICAN ARCHITECT AND BUILDING NEWS 97 (February 9, 1910) 71.

A short quotation justifying the classical approach, taken from the February 1910 issue of THE NORTH AMERICAN REVIEW.

65:5 Waterhouse, Paul. "The Royal Gold Medal... Presented to Mr. Thomas Hastings, Honorary Corresponding Member Royal Institute of British Architects at the General Meeting, June 26, 1922." ROYAL INSTITUTE OF BRITISH ARCHITECTS' JOURNAL 29 (1921-22): 513-22.

Hastings was awarded the gold medal of the Royal Institute of British Architects in 1922, and Waterhouse, as president of that august institute, gave the address on that occasion. Hastings by that time had designed fifty structures of "really cardinal importance." High praise was heaped upon Hastings whose reply was also published. He spoke of ideals in the profession. A biographical sketch and list of his principal works are appended.

66:1 **HATHERTON, EDWARD A. (n.d.)**

Practiced in San Francisco.

66:2 Johnson, Bruce. "How to Treat a Beat City Hall." AMERICAN INSTITUTE OF ARCHITECTS' JOURNAL 47 (March 1967): 71-72.

An attempt to save this Italian Renaissance revival City Hall at Tacoma, California, built in 1894, at a cost of approximately $1 to $1.5 million.

67:1 **HILL, HENRY W. (1852-1924)**

Educated Polytechnic Institute of Hamburg. Practiced in Chicago with James G. Egan and later with Augustus Bauer until 1894; thereafter with Arthur Woltersdorf.

Obituary: AMERICAN INSTITUTE OF ARCHITECTS' JOURNAL 12 (1924): 206.

67:2 Sturgis, Russell. "Factories and Warehouses." ARCHITECTURAL RECORD 19 (May 1906): 369-75.

The Eastman Kodak Company Building, Chicago, has functional and nonfunctional entrances, the latter being an architectural-decorative cover-up of structural steel elements.

67.3 ______. "Some Recent Warehouses." ARCHITECTURAL RECORD 23 (May 1908): 375-86.

Sturgis doesn't seem to like the Parke, Davis and Co. warehouse, Chicago, a building of massive piers throughout six stories with windows at the top as wide as those at the bottom even though not as necessary. Discussion pp. 375-77, illustrated p. 374, 385.

68:1 HOFFMAN, F. BURRALL, JR. (n.d.)

68:2 Klaber, John J. "Planning the Moving Picture Theater." ARCHITECTURAL RECORD 38 (November 1915): 540-54.

General considerations of sight lines, picture screen, and the need for fireproofed projection booths precede a series of examples including the Neighborhood Playhouse, Grand Street, New York City, by H.C. Ingalls and F.B. Hoffman, a general purpose hall.

69:1 HOLABIRD, JOHN AUGUR (1886-1945)

Entered United States Military Academy, 1903, resigned his commission in 1909 and entered the Ecole des Beaux Arts. Entered his father's office, Holabird and Roche.

Obituary: ARCHITECTURAL FORUM 82 (July 1945): 76.

69:2 Root, John Wellborn. "John Augur Holabird, an Appreciation." AMERICAN INSTITUTE OF ARCHITECTS' JOURNAL 4 (November 1945): 213-20.

Early career, education, partnerships, and a nonradical approach to design lead on to a discussion of philosophy and a list of his accomplishments by his last partner Root.

70:1 HOLABIRD AND ROCHE (Partnership 1883-1923)

William Holabird (1854-1923) and Martin Roche (1853-1927).

Burnham Library, Chicago, has numerous drawings of thirty-nine projects, plus two projects of Holabird and Roche, and Louis H. Sullivan.

70:2 AMERICAN ARCHITECT. "The Work of Holabird and Roche." Vol. 118 (August 11, 1920): 165-72.

Specifically minor works of the firm including some of the thirty telephone exchange buildings which they have designed, the Kildare, McKinley and Franklin Exchanges of Chicago, and the Chicago Nursery and Half Orphan Asylum.

70:3 ARCHITECTURAL REVIEWER. "Holabird and Roche." Vol. 1 (June 1897): 1-41.

This was a short-lived publication (see 49:2). Holabird and Roche biographical sketches precede a discussion of their contributions mainly in the high-rise commercial field, although other building types in a wide variety of styles are included.

70:4 Rudd, J. William. HOLABIRD AND ROCHE, CHICAGO ARCHITECTS. Vol. 2. Charlottesville: American Association of Architectural Bibliographers, 1966. Pp. 53-80.

A major architectural firm of post-fire-Chicago, named Holabird and Simmonds, 1880-81; Holabird, Simmonds and Roche, 1881-83; and Holabird and Roche thereafter, even though E.A. Renwick was a partner from 1893. Holabird died in 1923 and was replaced by his son, John, and at the death of Roche in 1927 the firm became known as Holabird (John) and Root (John Wellborn, III). Brief biographical sketches; an interview with Richard Cabeen, a member in 1963 of the firm Holabird and Root; and a list of buildings complement the bibliography.

70:5 Sturgis, Russell. "The Warehouse and the Factory in Architecture." ARCHITECTURAL RECORD 15 (January and February, 1904): 1-17, 122-33.

Achievements of simple, commercial warehouse design are emphasized and the Clow Building, Chicago, by Holabird and Roche is illustrated and compared to ancient architecture. Although brick is used and in some areas carefully moulded, Sturgis criticizes the fact that a wide overhanging cornice necessitates a change in the use of materials.

70:6 Weber, P.J. "A Review of the Work of Holabird and Roche." ARCHITECTURAL REVIEWER 1 (June 30, 1897): 1-41.

Short biographical sketches of the two architects precede descriptions of their major works in Chicago, including their important office buildings beginning with the Tacoma of 1888. Glass mosaic panels for several of their buildings are illustrated. Their work at Fort Sheridan, in addition to residential, public, and religious architecture, is well covered.

70:7 Winkler, F.K. "Some Chicago Buildings, Represented by the Work of Holabird and Roche." ARCHITECTURAL RECORD 31 (1912): 313-86.

Chicago commercial architecture is discussed at the beginning of this article prior to a consideration of the two partners of the firm and their contributions. Their commercial architecture is quite simple, but justifications are made for their more elaborate decorative treatments, especially when displayed upon high-rise club buildings, hotels, and monumental government structures.

71:1 HOLABIRD AND ROOT (Partnership 1927-)

John Augur Holabird, in succession to his father, William, joined John W. Root in partnership, 1927, after death of Martin Roche.

71:2 Simons, Kenneth W. NORTH DAKOTA'S STATE CAPITOL. Bismarck, N.D.: N. pub., 1934. 64 p.

A $2 million Capitol of 1932, essentially in the Art Deco style, well described and illustrated with plans and photographs.

71:3 Whitehead, Russell Fenimore. "Holabird and Root, Masters of Design." PENCIL POINTS 19 (February 1938): 66-97.

Background and education of the two partners precedes a discussion of their attitude to design and structures actually designed by them. They designed high-rise buildings for Chicago, especially for the Fair, "A Century of Progress." Most of their buildings, with few exceptions, would fit into the Art Deco style.

72:1 HOPKINS, JOHN HENRY (1792-1868)

First Episcopal Bishop of Vermont, 1832-68. Architect of several religious buildings mainly in Vermont.

72:2 Wodehouse, Lawrence. "John Henry Hopkins and the Gothic Revival." ANTIQUES 103 (April 1973): 776-83.

Hopkins wrote the first book on the Gothic in America. This book, AN ESSAY ON GOTHIC ARCHITECTURE, 1836, illustrated his ideas and some of his designs, including Trinity Church, Pittsburgh, 1825. He also designed St. Thomas, Brandon, Vermont, 1860-63, and Trinity, Rutland, Vermont, 1863-65.

73:1 HORNBOSTEL, HENRY FRED (1867-1961)

Educated at Columbia and the Ecole des Beaux Arts.

Avery Library, Columbia University, has design problems written by Henry Fred Hornbostel for the Department of Architecture, School of Mines, Columbia College, New York City.

Obituaries: ARCHITECTURAL FORUM 116 (January 1962): 14; PROGRESSIVE ARCHITECTURE 143 (February 1962): 50.

73:2 THE BRICKBUILDER. "As He is Known, Being Brief Sketches of Contemporary Members of the Architectural Profession." Vol. 24 (1915): 26.

> "He never permits himself to be confused or hampered or limited by masses of detailed requirements," but with his tremendous energy accomplished an enormous amount of work in a comparatively short space of time.

73:3 North, Arthur T. "Emory University, Atlanta, Georgia." AMERICAN ARCHITECTURE 118 (October 6, 1920): 429-32.

> Hornbostel researched the possibility of using Georgia marble or at least the "offal," or the first sawing waste, when the blocks were trimmed. Thus the buildings were built of concrete with a marble veneer. "Great credit is due to that master mind and skilled hand which has found a use for a waste product."

73:4 Swales, F.S. "Master Draftsman." PENCIL POINTS 7 (1926): 72-92.

> From Brooklyn High School to Columbia University for architecture was the logical choice for Hornbostel, who then worked for several firms in New York City. A Columbia classmate paid for his training at the Ecole des Beaux Arts where he became well known as a perspective artist. In 1897 he returned to the States continuing as a perspectivist but soon won fame and established a practice after winning competitions and commissions. His later career is outlined and the article is illustrated by numerous sketches, notably of bridge structures and university buildings.

74:1 HOWARD, JOHN GALEN (1864-1931)

Educated Massachusetts Institute of Technology and Ecole des Beaux Arts. Worked for Richardson, Shepley, Rutan and Coolidge, and McKim, Mead and White. Took S.M. Cauldwell into partnership in New York before moving to California to become Director of the School of Architecture at University of California and there joined in partnership with J.D. Galloway. School of Library Service, Columbia University, has five plans of the University Library, University of California.

Obituaries: ARCHITECTURAL FORUM 55 (September 1931): 19; ARCHITECTURAL RECORD 70 (October 1931): 278.

74:2 Bach, Richard F. "Hilgard Hall, University of California." ARCHITECTURAL RECORD 46 (September 1919): 203-10.

Hilgard Hall fits into the group planning concept of American University development. The applied decoration of this particular building consists of "overlaying of thin coats of plaster of differing colors and of scratching through these coats," called sgraffito.

74:3 Croly, Herbert. "The New University of California." ARCHITECTURAL RECORD 23 (April 1908): 269-93.

Public and private funds were used to finance this fast-growing institution of higher learning at the beginning of the twentieth century. Emile Bernard won the competition for the plan which, with modifications, was built by Howard, chosen by the University's Board of Trustees. Howard modified the plan according to topography and personal preference. Local stylistic prototypes were adopted in addition to those based upon European classicism, but with severe internal treatments. Completed buildings and sketches of proposed structures are illustrated.

74:4 Hays, W.C. "Some Architectural Works of John Galen Howard." ARCHITECT AND ENGINEER 40 (January 1915): 47-82.

Commercial, educational, and residential architecture and urban design by Howard is illustrated, but the major section of the article is devoted to his extensive work at the University of California, Berkeley. He revised the earlier Bernard plan and proceeded on a more or less classical theme.

75:1 HOWELLS, JOHN MEAD (1868-1959)

See Howells and Hood. He also headed a firm known as Howells and Stokes (see Isaac Newton Phelps Stokes).

Wrote: THE ARCHITECTURAL HERITAGE OF THE MERRIMACK, 1941; THE ARCHITECTURAL HERITAGE OF THE PISCATAQUA, 1937; CHARLES BULFINCH, 1908; LOST EXAMPLES OF COLONIAL ARCHITECTURE, 1931. Also wrote requirements for admission to the Ecole des Beaux Arts for the ARCHITECTURAL RECORD, January 1901.

75:2 Howells, J.M. JOHN MEAD HOWELLS. New York: Architectural Catalog Co., 193?. 44 pl.

This publication is a photographic survey of Howell's work at Harvard, Yale, Columbia, and Pratt Institute. Building types include banks, mausolea, residences, and projects including the design submitted in 1908 by Howells and Stokes for the New York Municipal Building.

75:3 Klaber, John J. "The Cobb Building, Seattle, Washington." ARCHITECTURAL RECORD 39 (February 1916): 154-60.

A specialized building for the use of doctors and dentists was a new aspect of high-rise structures in 1916. This article illustrates the special needs of the medical profession in this type of building.

75:4 Sturgis, Russell. "St. Paul's Chapel." ARCHITECTURAL RECORD 21 (February 1907): 83-95.

Sturgis admires Byzantine architecture as a style of architecture readily adapted to modern use, with St. Paul's Chapel, Columbia University a fine example. Nothing in New York City has been done as well! Even the brick and hollow tile construction techniques of Byzantium are used, as a well-known method of the late nineteenth and early twentieth-century construction technique known as Guastovino-vaulting.

76:1 **HUNT, MYRON C. (1868-1952)**

Educated at Northwestern and Massachusetts Institute of Technology.

Wrote in association with Katherine Hooker, FARMHOUSES AND PROVINCIAL BUILDINGS IN SOUTHERN ITALY, photographs by Marian Osgood Hooker, 1925.

Obituary: ARCHITECT AND ENGINEER 190 (August 1952): 35.
See Chambers (76:5).

76:2 AMERICAN ARCHITECTURE. "Work by Myron Hunt and Elmer Gray." Vol. 107 (February 10, 1915): 82-87.

"The influence of climate on design is well shown in the admirable work of Myron C. Hunt. Unusual abilities as designers with keen perceptions of the possibilities of site and environment, early marked the character of the work of these men in domestic architecture."

76:3 Boyd, John Taylor, Jr., "The Flintridge, Pasadena, California." ARCHITECTURAL RECORD 50 (July 1921): 93-101.

"The bold, rugged, vivid, colorful nature and the simple, hearty, country society - scarce two generations removed from the pioneer - are the two influences which appear in the design." Looking more like a ranch than a club, the clean cut lines and simplicity of design are described and well illustrated, including a plan.

76:4 Chambers, H.C. "Obituary." AMERICAN INSTITUTE OF ARCHITECTS JOURNAL 18 (October 1952): 165-66.

Education, partnerships, architectural expression, a listing of some of his designs, notably hospitals, and other architectural achievements are included.

76:5 Cheney, C.H. "The Work of Myron C. Hunt." AMERICAN MAGAZINE OF ART 15 (1924): 292-98.

The article describes Hunt of Los Angeles and his contribution to the improvement in art in Southern California. Simplicity, restraint, and proportion are the qualities considered typical of his work, even though today they would be considered eclectic.

76:6 Cornelius, Charles Over. "The Residence of Major J.H.H. Peshine, Santa Barbara, California." ARCHITECTURAL RECORD 45 (February 1919): 98-115.

An apology for Spanish colonial architectural styles in California and a descriptive review of this cluster of buildings picturesquely arranged. Sketches and drawings complement photographs and plans of the finished product.

76:7 McLean, R.C. "Some Late Work of Myron C. Hunt." WESTERN ARCHITECT 27 (June 1918): 49-52.

Hunt's "gathering together of different effects" are compared to the residences at Tuxedo, New York, by Bruce Price, or the St. Augustine Ponce de Leon and Alcazar by Carrere and Hastings. After Northwestern and Massachusetts Institute of Technology, Hunt traveled in Italy gathering inspiration, but he always used the styles with restraint and discrimination. Several of his projects are mentioned and illustrated.

76:8 Wight, P.B. "Two Illustrations of the Work of Myron C. Hunt." WESTERN ARCHITECT 30 (1921): 23. Pls. 1-8.

Pomona College at Claremont engaged Hunt for the Mabel Bridges Music Hall, which is briefly discussed. The plates are of the William G. Mather house at Pasadena enlarged by Hunt and Elmer Gray. It shows "the progress in residential architecture and landscape gardening in Southern California."

77:1 HUNT, RICHARD MORRIS (1827-95)

First American to study at the Ecole des Beaux Arts. Established a practice in New York City, 1855.

Avery Library, Columbia University, has two sheets of the Yorktown Monument. The American Institute of Architects Library, Washington, has drawings of eighty-two projects, many unidentified, in addition to those by either Richard Morris or Richard Howland Hunt (1862-1931).

Obituaries: AMERICAN ARCHITECT AND BUILDING NEWS 49 (1895): 45, 70; 50 (1895): 53-56.

Martha Hoppin is working on a doctoral dissertation on Hunt at Harvard.

77:2 Ames, Winslow. "The Transformation of Chateau-sur-Mer." JOURNAL OF THE SOCIETY OF ARCHITECTURAL HISTORIANS 29 (December 1970): 291-306.

Designed in 1851 for William Wetmore by Seth Bradford, Chateau-sur-Mer at Newport, Rhode Island, was considerably altered by Hunt in 1872. The result was "to bring some architectural feature out of the original impossible stone structure" according to Hunt's wife. Overlay plans and sections plus photographs clearly explain the expansion and changes of this residence.

77:3 Burnham, Alan. "The New York Architecture of Richard Morris Hunt." JOURNAL OF THE SOCIETY OF ARCHITECTURAL HISTORIANS 11 (May 1952): 9-14.

After working for Lefuel on the Bibliotheque du Louvre, Paris, and study at the Ecole des Beaux Arts, Hunt set up practice in New York. His Stuyvesant Apartments, 1869, illustrate the influence of Viollet-le-Duc and the 1879 Vanderbilt Mansion, the miniaturization of a French chateau, whereas the Ogden Mills house at Newport was as medieval as the Stuyvesant building.

77:4 Coles, W.A. "Richard Morris Hunt and His Library." ART QUARTERLY 30 (Fall-Winter 1967): 225-38.

A survey of Hunt's library - "noble and inexhaustible ...by far the richest, most comprehensive and most curious collection of books on architecture and the other fine arts" according to Van Brunt. It was the sketchbooks which were so important in the training of the architect. Hunt encouraged sketching and sketched himself. Five of his sketch books are now owned by Henry Van Brunt, Jr. The contents of these books are discussed and a list of books necessary for the architect compiled by Van Brunt in 1890 are listed.

77:5 Colton, Arthur W. "A Monograph of the William K. Vanderbilt House." ARCHITECTURAL RECORD 58 (September 1925): 295-98.

This is a book review criticism of John Vredenburg Van Pelt's monograph of one of many notable New York buildings being razed within a comparatively short time after completion.

77:6 Croly, Herbert. "The Work of Richard Morris Hunt." ARCHITECTURAL RECORD 59 (January 1926): 88-89.

The Lenox Library on Fifth Avenue by Hunt was demolished in order to build the Frick residence. At the time of this article the Astor house at 65th Street, Fifth Avenue, was in danger of demolition, to make way for a synagogue. Added to this, the Vanderbilt Mansion was to be destroyed. "The best of Mr. Hunt's many essays in domestic architecture and at the same time the most characteristic."

77:7 Hunt, Richard Morris. DESIGNS FOR THE GATEWAYS OF THE SOUTHERN ENTRANCES TO THE CENTRAL PARK. New York: D. Van Nostrand, 1866. 36 p.

Hunt exhibited sketches for entrances to Central Park at the National Academy of Design in 1865. These designs apparently did not meet with the approval of the Commissioners and thereafter a competition was held. The documents of the Commissioners, a letter to the EVENING POST and another letter from Hunt to the Commissioners are printed in full, possibly with the idea that public opinion would support Hunt's designs. There are four sets of plans accompanying five color lithographs.

77:8 Paris, William Franklyn. "Richard Morris Hunt." AMERICAN INSTITUTE OF ARCHITECTS' JOURNAL 24 (December 1955): 243-49; 25 (January 1956): 14-19; 25 (February 1956): 74-80.

At the centenary of Hunt's starting to practice, the AMERICAN INSTITUTE OF ARCHITECTS' JOURNAL republished in three parts, the article by W.F. Paris (1871-1954) for the MAGAZINE OF THE AMERICAN SOCIETY OF THE FRENCH LEGION OF HONOR 23 (Summer 1952): 117-38. Hunt was both First Secretary and Third President of the American Institute of Architects. The articles are anecdotal, chatty, and down-to-earth, even Davy Crockett gets dragged in. The one illustration in the third article is the Hunt Memorial, still extant on Fifth Avenue, by Bruce Price, architect, and Daniel Chester French, sculptor.

77:9 _____. "Richard Morris Hunt." THE HALL OF AMERICAN ARTISTS. Vol. 9. New York: New York University, 1952. Pp. 27-48.

A "pioneer and ice-breaker" in design, Hunt did not build extensively, or even a large number of commissions; he never built a skyscraper, for example. Into his office when he returned to America from the Ecole des Beaux Arts came young men, many of whom were to become leaders of the profession in the next generation. His French chateau residences, the Statue of Liberty, Chicago Columbian Exposition, and West Point buildings are touched upon.

77:10 Schuyler, Montgomery. "The Works of the Late Richard M. Hunt." ARCHITECTURAL RECORD 5 (October - December, 1895): 97-134.

After the Ecole des Beaux Arts in Paris, Hunt returned to New York where he practiced from 1855-95. Beaux Arts is the term given by Schuyler to Hunt's first projects: the Rossiter house, West 38th Street, and the Studio Building, West 10th Street. The Swiss chalet Griswold house at Newport with a Yankee mansard roof we would now call Stick style and the polychromy of Presbyterian Hospital and the Tribune Building, New York, High Victorian Gothic. Schuyler didn't have these terms but recognized and explained the sources. Monumental architecture classical (Chicago Fair Administration Building and Fogg Museum, Harvard), French Renaissance (Ochre Court, Newport; Biltmore, North Carolina), Italian Renaissance (The Breakers, Newport), are all discussed.

77:11 Van Brunt, Henry. "Richard Morris Hunt, 1828-1895." AMERICAN INSTITUTE OF ARCHITECTS' JOURNAL 8 (October 1947): 180-87.

Van Brunt was a pupil of Hunt in the early years of the New York practice after Hunt had returned from France and a six-month sojourn in Washington with Thomas U. Walter. Van Brunt, George B. Post, and Charles D. Gambrill, all to become famous in their own right, worked for Hunt from 1858. William Ware joined in 1859 to be followed by several others including Frank Furness. Many of Hunt's pupils joined him in creating the Chicago Exposition of 1893, the year of the award of the gold medal of the Royal Institute of British Architects, and two years before his death.

77:12 Van Pelt, John Vredenburgh. A MONOGRAPH OF THE WILLIAM K. VANDERBILT HOUSE, RICHARD MORRIS HUNT, ARCHITECT. New York: J.V. Van Pelt, 1928. 23 p.

The imminent removal of Hunt's Vanderbilt house following the razing of White's Madison Square Garden created sufficient concern in the profession that Van Pelt decided upon this brief monograph. The building is discussed in detail from the dark French walnut "Grindling Gibbons room," to the loveliest interior, the dining room. Names of artists and contractors were researched and listed.

77:13 Veeder, Paul L. II. "The Outbuildings and Grounds of Chateau-sur-Mer." JOURNAL OF THE SOCIETY OF ARCHITECTURAL HISTORIANS 29 (December 1970): 307-17.

The Wetmore family, as clients of Seth Bradford, the original designer of the Newport mansion, and Hunt, whose later additions created what can be seen today, are carefully considered. Plans of the property acquisition and layout are illustrated and discussed as are porter's lodge, carriage house, barn, billiard room, Chinese moon gate, gateways, stables, grapery and palm house, and tea house.

77:14 Wallis, F.E. "Richard M. Hunt, Master Architect and Man." ARCHITECTURAL REVIEW (Boston) New Series 5 (1917): 239-40.

A preeminent architect, instructor, and source of inspiration, Hunt's fame was greatest at the beginning of the Boston publication of THE ARCHITECTURAL REVIEW. The article is an anecdotal account by a one-time assistant of Hunt.

77:15 Weisman, Winston. "New York and the Problem of the First Skyscraper." JOURNAL OF THE SOCIETY OF ARCHITECTURAL HISTORIANS 12 (March 1953): 13-21.

Depending upon one's definition of a skyscraper, several structures could be considered the first, including George B. Post's Western Union Telegraph Building and Hunt's New York Tribune Building, both built between 1873 and 1875. Weisman also lists the New York [Equitable] Life Assurance Company Building by Gilman, Kendall and George B. Post, as consultant engineer, of 1868-70, a building which becomes the "first" in THE RISE OF AN AMERICAN ARCHITECTURE, Edgar Kaufmann, Jr., ed. (See).

78:1 ITTNER, WILLIAM BUTTS (1864-1936)

Educated Manual Training School, Washington University, St. Louis. Worked for Eames and Young prior to establishing a practice in St. Louis, 1887.

Wrote: THE PLANNING AND CONSTRUCTION OF MODERN SCHOOL PLANTS, St. Louis, 1922.

78:2 Study, Guy. "The Work of William Butts Ittner." ARCHITECTURAL RE-

CORD 57 (1925): 97-124.

Architect to the St. Louis, Missouri, Board of Education, Ittner has advanced school design, breaking away from traditional standards. The article illustrates plans, general views, and details of a wide range of schools in a number of states, in some historic style or another, but all having modern amenities, services, layout, and accommodations.

79:1 JENNY, WILLIAM LE BARON (1832-1907)

Educated in engineering at the Lawrence Scientific School, Cambridge, Massachusetts, and the Ecole Centrale, 1856. Opened an office in Chicago in 1866, and later practiced as Jenny, Schermerhorn and Bogart. Practiced alone and after 1891 with William H. Mundie.

Published PRINCIPLES AND PRACTICE IN ARCHITECTURE, 1869, with an earlier partner, Sanford Loring.

Burnham Library, Chicago, has letters, an autobiographical typescript, six projects by Jenny, fourteen by Jenny and Mundie, two by Jenny, Mundie and Jensen and one by Jenny and William A. Otis.

Obituaries: AMERICAN ARCHITECT AND BUILDING NEWS 91 (1907): 237-38; 92 (1907): 5-6. THE BRICKBUILDER 16 (May 1907): 93; ARCHITECTURAL RECORD 22 (August 1907): 155-57.

79:2 Huxtable, Ada Louise. "Home Insurance Building, 1883-1885." PROGRESSIVE ARCHITECTURE 38 (June 1957): 207-8.

A major landmark in the development of the skyscraper, being completely skeletal and as fireproof as possible. The frame was carefully analyzed at its demolition in 1931. Above the sixth floor were I-section steel beams, 12 inches deep, which were first being rolled at the period of its construction. Cast-iron columns were utilized throughout plus some wrought iron work.

79:3 Jenkins, Charles E. "A Review of the Work of William Le Baron Jenny." ARCHITECTURAL REVIEWER 4 (March 31, 1897): 1-45.

This was a short-lived publication devoted to "leading architects of the West, and, as far as possible gives an illustrated review of what they have done." The first issue was on Jenny and Mundie. Their careers, individual contributions, and joint works are illustrated and discussed.

79:4 Turak, Theodore. "The Ecole Centrale and Modern Architecture: The Education of William LeBaron Jenny." JOURNAL OF THE SOCIETY OF ARCHITECTURAL HISTORIANS 29 (March 1970): 40-47.

Educated at Phillips Academy and widely traveled in the Pacific, Jenny chose the Ecole Centrale in Paris after Harvard, instead of the Ecole des Beaux Arts, whose students could only produce pretty drawings, or so it was thought by some. Jenny trained as engineer and architect and practiced from 1869 in the Gothic style. His Home Insurance Building, Chicago, 1885, is mentioned at the beginning of the article, but only a discussion of the pros and cons of its being "the first skyscraper ever erected" are offered.

79:5 _____. "Jenny's Lesser Works: Prelude to the Prairie Style?" THE PRAIRIE SCHOOL REVIEW 7 (Third Quarter, 1970): 5-12, 17-20.

Jenny was trained as an engineer at the Ecole Centrale des Arts et Manufactures, but always considered himself an architect. He settled in Riverside, an early village suburb of Chicago by Olmsted, and there designed a hotel and residences, including his own, in the Swiss chalet and other similar styles. He equally practiced in the Gothic mode, was a follower of Richardson, but also read and practiced the tenets of Viollet-le-Duc.

79:6 _____. "William Le Baron Jenny: A Nineteen Century Architect." Doctoral dissertation, University of Michigan, 1966. 391 p.

An evaluation of Jenny's technical and aesthetic contributions leading to skeleton constructions catering to human need. The impact of Durand's teachings as forwarded at the Ecole Centrale, Paris, had an impact on Jenny's philosophy of design as did the ideals of Viollet-le-Duc. These influences are seen in Jenny's commercial work, but American romanticism is to be found as the basis for his domestic architecture.

80:1 KAHN, ALBERT (1869-1942)

Born Westphalia, and apprenticed in Detroit to George D. Mason. Associated with George Nettleton and Alexander Trowbridge in 1892, but later joined his three brothers, Julius, Louis, and Moritz, as Albert Kahn, Associated Architects and Engineers.

Avery Library, Columbia University, has a signed drawing by Albert Kahn of Chaumont, 1891.

Obituaries: MICHIGAN SOCIETY OF ARCHITECTS WEEKLY BULLETIN 16 (December 15, 1942): 1, 5-6; ARCHITECTURAL RECORD

93 (January 1943): 14-16; ARCHITECTURAL FORUM 78 (January 1943): 36; THE OCTAGON 15 (February 1943): 15-16.

Frank Lloyd Wright considered Kahn America's greatest architect in 1941. (See Wegg under Wright.)

80:2 ARCHITECTURAL FORUM. "Albert Kahn." Vol. 69 (August 1938): 87-142.

An architect of international repute with an impressive list of clients, Kahn has designed $800 million worth of concrete, glass, and steel. The article includes an historical section, the organization of a 400-strong workforce, questions, such as "what the manufacturer wants from his architect, 1. Functional design and 2. Business-like execution;" and a survey of more recent projects. Flow diagrams, plans, sections, photographs, and descriptions are provided of grain silos, automobile plants, aircraft factories, and general industrial plants.

80:3 Baldwin, G.C. "The Offices of Albert Kahn." ARCHITECTURAL FORUM 29 (1918): 125-30.

Literally a description of the Kahn office in the Marquette Building, Detroit. Office organization is described and the forms used for various assignments are illustrated.

80:4 THE BRICKBUILDER. "As He Is Known, Being Brief Sketches of Contemporary Members of the Architectural Profession." Vol. 24 (1915): 127.

Educated in Germany, Kahn trained in Detroit before establishing his first partnership in 1895. "Kahn was among the first to perceive the importance of improving the design of factory and industrial buildings," notably in the automobile industry.

80:5 Detroit Institute of Arts. THE LEGACY OF ALBERT KAHN. Detroit: Detroit Institute of Arts, 1970. 184 p.

W. Hawkins Ferry, a noted Detroit historian, has contributed a biographical essay on Kahn, 1869-1942. This is followed, period by period, by photographs of the firm's work, 1888 to 1943. There is a brief foreword by Willis F. Woods and an epilogue by Sol King following an essay on Albert Kahn Associates, 1942-70, and work in progress.

80:6 Fisher, Fred J. THE FISHER BUILDING, GRAND BOULEVARD AT SECOND, DETROIT, MICHIGAN. Detroit: Detroit Press, 1928. 27 p.

All aspects of this structure are illustrated with colored sketches, and are described with an introduction by Fisher who explains that the building has "the highest degree of utility with majestic beauty." Foldout plans are included in the rear cover pocket.

80:7 Hilderbrand, Grant. "New Factory for the Geo. N. Pierce Company, Buffalo, New York, 1906." JOURNAL OF THE SOCIETY OF ARCHITECTURAL HISTORIANS 29 (March 1970): 51-55.

Built for the Pierce Great Arrow car, this reinforced concrete building has spans up to sixty-one feet and roof lighting necessary for factory development. Kahn was associate architect to Lockwood, Greene and Co. of Boston, and brought to the design his experience of the Detroit Packard Factory of 1904.

80:8 _____. DESIGNING FOR INDUSTRY: THE ARCHITECTURE OF ALBERT KAHN. Cambridge, Mass.: The M.I.T. Press, 1974. 232 p.

The M.I.T. Press advertisement states: "About 100 photographs and working drawings illustrate this documentation of Albert Kahn's career. His firm, operating under a unique team practice system, designed over two thousand factories, representative examples of which are discussed in detail here. Major nonindustrial works are also included. Kahn's output is considered in the context of his contemporaries both in the United States and in Europe in order to clarify the usefulness of the contributions he made."

80:9 Huxtable, Ada Louise. "The Revolutionary Crow Grows Old Quickly." THE NEW YORK TIMES, July 26, 1970, section 2, p. 20.

Henry Ford's 1,200-acre plant at River Rouge, Detroit, by Kahn is an important structure to the architectural historian but an anathema to the workers who earn a living there. The evolution of the plant and the accomplishments of Kahn are listed.

80:10 Kahn, Albert. ARCHITECTURE BY ALBERT KAHN ASSOCIATES, ARCHITECTS AND ENGINEERS. New York: Architectural Catalog Co., 1948. 174 p.

A compilation of material from ARCHITECTURE AND DESIGN of the work of the firm from its inception until after World War II. All building types are illustrated from the most functional industrial complexes to eclectic historical buildings of a domestic sale. Sixteen pages of double and triple columns provide quite a comprehensive listing of the firm's work.

80:11 _____. INDUSTRIAL AND COMMERCIAL BUILDINGS, DETROIT. Detroit: A. Kahn, Inc., 1937. 160 p. Illus.

A well-illustrated publication devoted, as the title suggests, solely to industrial and commercial buildings, up to 1937. Eleven pages, with two columns per page, are devoted to listing projects of the firm. The remainder of the book consists of photographs of structures, including numerous interiors.

80:12 Moore, Charles J. "Some Essentials of the Modern Manufacturing Building." AMERICAN ARCHITECT AND BUILDING NEWS 99 (June 14, 1911): 219-23.

"Requirements of a modern manufacturing plant are economy of operation, freedom from fire hazard and ample light, with the most perfect system of ventilation." This is a quotation by Charles J. Moore, Operating Manager of the Packard Motor Car Company's plant at Detroit by Albert Kahn and his associate, Ernest Wilby.

80:13 Nelson, George. INDUSTRIAL ARCHITECTURE OF ALBERT KAHN, INC. New York: Architectural Book Publishing Co., Inc., 1939. 176 p.

An historical survey of industrial architecture and the work of Albert Kahn related to the technological developments. The organization of the firm which has designed structures in five continents is explained, prior to a photographic survey with notes.

80:14 Shreve, Richmond H. "Address... In Presenting a special Medal of the American Institute of Architects to Mr. Kahn, Detroit, June 24, 1942." MICHIGAN SOCIETY OF ARCHITECTS WEEKLY BULLETIN 16 (July 14, 1942): 3.

Shreve was president of the American Institute of Architects in the year that Kahn was presented with the Institute's Special Medal. The humble address by Kahn is given on p. 1.

80:15 Swales, F.S. "Master Draftsman, 19. Albert Kahn." PENCIL POINTS 6 (June 1925): 42-58, 84.

Sixteen of Kahn's pencil drawings from his European sketchbook illustrate this article on an architect who was extremely successful in designing for the automobile industry. Kahn's work is untutored, but the drawings are interesting records of French medieval architecture (with others from Italy).

80:16 Woolfenden, William E. "Architectural Drawings by Albert Kahn." DETROIT INSTITUTE OF ARTS BULLETIN 24 (1947): 11-12.

81:1 LA FARGE, CHRISTOPHER GRANT (1862-1938)

Educated Massachusetts Institute of Technology and worked for Richardson prior to setting up practice in New York, 1884, later to join George L. Heins (see).

Publications: THE CATHEDRAL OF ST. JOHN THE DIVINE, 1907; HISTORY OF THE AMERICAN ACADEMY IN ROME, 1915.

Avery Library, Columbia University, has seven facsimile letters concerning the building of the Cathedral of St. John the Divine, New York City; Princeton University has thirty-five sheets of the United States Naval Hospital Reservation, New York City, six projects by La Farge and Morris and one project by La Farge, Warren and Clark.

Obituaries: ARCHITECTURAL FORUM 70 (January 1939): 42; THE BUILDER 155 (October 21, 1938): 778.

81:2 THE BRICKBUILDER. "As He is Known, Being Brief Sketches of Contemporary Members of the Architectural Profession." Vol. 24 (1915): 261.

Sensitivity in relation to all the qualities of architecture is the forte of La Farge. Education, partnerships, and service to the profession in public speaking and offices held complement his architectural contribution.

82:1 LE BRUN, NAPOLEON EUGENE (1821-1901)

Worked for Thomas U. Walter and at first practiced with C. Runge prior to independent practice during which time a notable range of buildings were designed.

The Historical Society of Pennsylvania has twenty-two sheets of the Academy of Music, Philadelphia.

Obituary: AMERICAN ARCHITECT AND BUILDING NEWS 73 (1901): 17.

82:2 Longstreth, Richard W. "A Country House by Napoleon Le Brun." JOURNAL OF THE SOCIETY OF ARCHITECTURAL HISTORIANS 26 (December 1967): 310-11.

Little research has been done on Le Brun's domestic architecture. This design of "Chelwood," 1860, for Charles R. King, Andalusia, Pennsylvania, illustrates an unpretentious house, little altered over the years.

82:3 Peterson, Charles E., ed. "Napoleon Le Brun, 1821-1901." JOURNAL OF THE SOCIETY OF ARCHITECTURAL HISTORIANS 16 (March 1957): 30.

A paragraph-long note on Le Brun in reference to mention of him in an article entitled "Robert Cary Long, Jr.

and The Battle of the Styles," by Wilbur H. Hunter in the same issue of the JOURNAL OF THE SOCIETY OF ARCHITECTURAL HISTORIANS, pp. 28-30.

82:4 Schuyler, Montgomery. "The Work of N. Le Brun and Sons." ARCHITECTURAL RECORD 27 (April 1910): 365-81.

A pupil of Thomas U. Walter, Le Brun the Elder continues a tradition in American architecture begun at its founding. Schuyler traces the religious architecture of the Le Bruns to Romanesque, Gothic, and Italian Renaissance traditions. The architecture of New York City fire department buildings has improved by the employment of the Le Bruns whether they utilized Dutch or Italian Renaissance styles. The firm's work culminated in the Metropolitan Life Insurance Building, Madison Square, 1889-1909, a building of elegance which Schuyler admires.

83:1 LIENAU, DETLEF (1818-87)

Educated Royal Architectural College, Munich, and under Henri Labrouste in Paris, prior to emigration to the United States in 1848. Partnerships with Henri Marcotte but major works designed independently.

Avery Library, Columbia University, has approximately seventy sets of 800 drawings of projects by Lienau in addition to manuscript notes, photographs, and miscellaneous material, and a typewritten biography by J. Henry Lienau. The Georgia Historical Society has eight photostatic copies of Avery drawings of the Wayne-Gordon House.

Obituaries: AMERICAN ARCHITECT AND BUILDING NEWS 22 (1887): 129; BUILDING 7 (September 3, 1887): 80.

83:2 Bernard, Diana. "The Lockwood-Mathews Mansion: Harbinger of the Gilded Age." THE VICTORIAN SOCIETY IN AMERICA NEWSLETTER 5 (Fall 1973): 1-6.

Lienau apparently designed some twenty extensive mansions for wealthy clients. This particular mansion at Norwalk, Connecticut, is described in great detail, down to the European furnishings and paintings hung on the walls. The City of Norwalk bought the building in 1941 for $200,000 and attempted to proceed toward demolition in 1963, when some enlightened taxpayers fought for its salvation.

83:3 Kramer, Ellen W. "Detlef Lienau, An Architect of the Brown Decades."

JOURNAL OF THE SOCIETY OF ARCHITECTURAL HISTORIANS 14 (March 1955): 18-25.

Lienau's first commissions in the United States include a house for his brother in Jersey City, 1849; Grace Church, Jersey City, 1850; and the Shiff House, New York City, sometimes considered to be the first example in America of the French Second Empire style because of its Mansard roof.

83:4 _____. "The Domestic Architecture of Detlef Lienau, A Conservative Victorian." Doctoral dissertation, New York University, 1958. 429 p.

An assessment of this architect's work during the years pre and post-Civil War, after his European training, as a part of New York's contribution to Victorian architecture as a whole. Lienau studied under Henri Labrouste in Paris. Was his Shiff House, Fifth Avenue, New York City, 1850, the first Second Empire styled structure in the United States? He practiced in the Italianate, Stick, Queen Anne, and Colonial Revival styles and passed his influence on through Hardenbergh and Pelz, who trained in his office.

83:5 _____. THE DOMESTIC ARCHITECTURE OF DETLEF LIENAU, A CONSERVATIVE VICTORIAN. New York: New York University Press, 1957. 345 p.

A development of Kramer's doctoral dissertation. See previous entry.

83:6 Lawton, Alexander R. "Telfair Academy of Arts and Sciences, Savannah, Georgia." GEORGIA HISTORICAL SOCIETY, March 1917.

83:7 Schaack, Margaret Donald. "History in Houses: The Lockwood-Mathews Mansion." ANTIQUES, March 1970, pp. 378-81.

A brief and not too informative article but with interesting photographic illustrations of this Norwalk, Connecticut, house.

83:8 Snow, Barbara. "Lockwood-Mathews House, Connecticut." ANTIQUES 82 (November 1962): 552.

Built in 1863 for Le Grand Lockwood and owned after 1876 by Charles D. Mathews, this Scottish Manor house was purchased in 1941 by Norwalk, Connecticut, and was intended for demolition.

84:1 LITTLE, ARTHUR (1852-1925)

Educated at Massachusetts Institute of Technology, 1875, and after

European travel worked for Peabody and Stearns before practicing with Herbert W.C. Browne (1860-1946) from 1889.

Publication: EARLY NEW ENGLAND INTERIORS, 1878.

Obituary: AMERICAN INSTITUTE OF ARCHITECTS' JOURNAL 13 (1925): 191.

84:2 Sturges, Walter Knight. "Arthur Little and the Colonial Revival." JOURNAL OF THE SOCIETY OF ARCHITECTURAL HISTORIANS 32 (May 1973): 147-63.

In a century of ecclectic styles, the Colonial Revival was no more an archaeologically accurate representation of the original than of any other style, and Arthur Little who designed in this mode was no different from any of his contemporary architects. Biographical information is scanty but several residences are illustrated and described to show how competent the architect was in blending forms, details, color pattern, and arrangement.

85:1 LONGFELLOW, ALDEN AND HARLOW (Partnership 1887-92)

A partnership consisting of Alexander Wadsworth Longfellow (1854-1934), who was trained at Harvard and the Ecole des Beaux Arts and worked for Richardson until 1887 when he organized the firm with Alfred B. Harlow (1857-1927) and Frank E. Alden (1859-1908). In 1892 Alden and Harlow moved to Pittsburgh. Longfellow stayed in Boston and in 1895 joined in partnership with his brother, R.K. Longfellow. See also Alden and Harlow.

Obituaries: A.W. Longfellow. NEW INTERNATIONAL YEAR BOOK, 1934, p. 487; F.E. Alden. AMERICAN ARCHITECT AND BUILDING NEWS 94 (October 14, 1908): 16.

85:2 Van Trump, James D. AN AMERICAN PALACE OF CULTURE: THE CARNEGIE INSTITUTE AND CARNEGIE LIBRARY OF PITTSBURGH. Pittsburgh: Pittsburgh History and Landmarks Foundation, 1970.

Designed by Longfellow, Harlow and Alden, and won in competition 1891, built 1892-95, with additions by Alden and Harlow 1904-7. This structure is Beaux Arts, and the classical expression follows on from the work of McKim, Mead and White for whom Alfred Harlow worked. Sculptor John Massey Rhind carved sculptures depicting Shakespeare, Bach, Galileo, and Michelangelo.

86:1 LOWELL, GUY (1870-1927)

Educated Harvard in 1892, Massachusetts Institute of Technology and the Ecole des Beaux Arts prior to practice in Boston.

Publications: AMERICAN GARDENS, 1902; MORE SMALL ITALIAN VILLAS AND FARMHOUSES, 1920; SMALLER ITALIAN VILLAS AND FARMHOUSES, 1916.

Obituaries: AMERICAN ARCHITECTURE 131 (February 20, 1927): 230; THE NEW INTERNATIONAL YEARBOOK, 1927, p. 481; AMERICAN INSTITUTE OF ARCHITECTS' JOURNAL 15 (1927): 114; ARCHITECTURAL RECORD, April 1927, p. 373.

86:2 Croly, Herbert. "The Lay-Out of a Large Estate. Harbor Hill, the Country Seat of Mr. Clarence Mackay, at Roslyn, Long Island." ARCHITECTURAL RECORD 16 (December 1904): 531-55.

See under McKim, Mead and White.

86:3 Russell, Benjamin F.W. "The Works of Guy Lowell." ARCHITECTURAL REVIEW (Boston) 13 (1906): 13-40.

Lowell accepted America's reliance, in the design field, upon European precedents but felt that they should be adapted to America, a country of "strong individuality and differences." The illustrations, mainly of residences, show Lowell's adaptations of classical styles, some with colonial flavor in red brick, but many in wood and local stone set within gardens also by Lowell who was as competent in landscape architecture as in architecture. Interiors tend to follow the trend of each room or area being a style unto itself.

87:1 MAGINNIS, CHARLES DONAGH (1867-1955)

Senior partner of Maginnis and Walsh (and Sullivan)

Obituaries: MICHIGAN SOCIETY OF ARCHITECTS MONTHLY BULLETIN 28 (April 1955): 6; 29 (March 1955): 43; ARCHITECTURAL FORUM 102 (March 1955): 29; LANDSCAPE ARCHITECTURE 45 (July 1955): 226.

87:2 Baxter, Sylvester. "The National Shrine of the Immaculate Conception, Washington, D.C." ARCHITECTURAL RECORD (July 1922): 2-15.

Precedents both ancient and modern are listed as having influenced this religious structure. It is in the Byzantine style to complement the Capitol, rather than the Gothic which Maginnis felt would be out of place in Washington. Study sketches of plan developments, interior spaces, and elevational treatments are juxtaposed to final designs as seen in a model. "The design as finally achieved, is a product of gradual evolution under long and careful study by the architects."

87:3 _____. "A Selection from the Works of Maginnis and Walsh." ARCHITECTURAL RECORD 53 (February 1923): 92-115.

Roman Catholic architecture tends to be built mainly in areas settled by Spanish, French, and English Catholics, and, generally speaking, architects of that faith are employed in the construction of religious and educational buildings commissioned by Catholics. A survey of the firm's work from the Atlantic to the Pacific tends to be English Gothic, Spanish Colonial Baroque, or Early Christian in style, according to location.

87:4 THE BRICKBUILDER. "As He is Known, Being Brief Sketches of Contemporary Members of the Architectural Profession." Vol. 24 (1915): 76.

Educated in Ireland and trained in Boston, 1886-96, Maginnis then set up his first partnership. His major structures were Roman Catholic churches in which he always captured the "character of the edifice." He was a master of the art of color.

87:5 Byrne, Barry. "An Appreciation." LITURGICAL ARTS 5 (1936): 90-104.

An appreciation of the building for the Catholic Foreign Mission Society of America at Maryknoll, New York, designed with the use of Chinese detailing, foreign elements, and interesting massing producing a unified building. A plan and several photographs aids the reader in the description and criticism.

87:6 Emerson, William, and Chandler, H. Daland. "Charles Donagh Maginnis." AMERICAN INSTITUTE OF ARCHITECTS JOURNAL 23 (May 1955): 209-19.

An obituary, beginning with early life in Ireland, training, commitment, major projects, and historical precidents upon which he relied. He was awarded the gold medal and was president of the institute.

87:7 Shanley, J. Sanford. "Charles Donagh Maginnis, 1867-1955. A Tribute." LITURGICAL ARTS 23 (August 1955): 152-55.

A distinguished Catholic layman who has constructed many Catholic churches, gained the gold medal of the American Institute of Architects, and is quoted as having high praise for LITURGICAL ARTS, gains a tribute in this article. Requiem Mass was eulogized on Feburary 18, 1955. John La Farge, Chaplain of the Liturgical Arts Society, also provides a note on Maginnis, the society's first president. The speech made by Maginnis when he received the American Institute of Architects' gold medal is quoted, and there is a detailed section on biographical and bibligraphical notes.

87:8 Walsh, R.P., and Roberts, A.W., eds. CHARLES DONAGH MAGINNIS, FAIA, 1867-1955: A SELECTION OF HIS ESSAYS AND ADDRESSES. New Haven, Conn.: N. pub., 1955. 51 p.

The biographical note at the beginning of the book states that Maginnis, who was Irish by birth and English by training, came to the United States in 1885. He established the firm of Maginnis, Walsh and Sullivan in 1898, and Maginnis and Walsh in 1908. The sketch also lists awards, achievements, and accomplishments. There are six essays including topics concerned with the making of an architect, religious architecture, crisis in the profession, and architecture in relation to the American city.

88:1 MAGONIGLE, HAROLD VAN BUREN (1867-1935)

Employed by Vaux and Bradford, Charles C. Haight, and McKim, Mead and White. Began his own practice circa 1909.

Publications: MEMORIES OF RURAL FRANCE, 1932; AN ARCHITECTURAL MONOGRAPH ON ESSEX: A CONNECTICUT RIVER TOWN, 1920; ARCHITECTURAL RENDERING IN WASH, 1929; THE NATURE, PRACTICE AND HISTORY OF ART, 1924; and was editor January to May 1912 of THE NEW YORK ARCHITECT (1907 to 1912).

Avery Library, Columbia University, has more than fifty sketches of historic buildings, architectural renderings, charts, book covers, photographs, and his own architectural projects including schools, religious buildings, and competition entries for federal government and other structures.

Obituaries: AMERICAN ARCHITECTURE 147 (September 1935): 116; HERALD TRIBUNE, August 30, 1935; See Cunningham (88:4) and Sullivan (88:5).

88:2 Boyd, John Taylor. "Residence of William McNair, Esq. New York." ARCHITECTURAL RECORD 41 (May 1917): 386-402.

Family accommodations were situated on the top floors for air and view, a major feature in this plan and the contrary of urban residential architecture generally. Plans are provided and described and so too are the spacious arrangements for circulation of movement, major rooms, and details of grillwork for doors, windows, and lamps.

88:3 THE BRICKBUILDER. "As He is Known, Being Brief Sketches of Contemporary Members of the Architectural Profession." Vol. 24 (1915): 180.

"No ancestral tree could possibly offer a better combination of the qualities essential to the making of an architect than...the poetic qualities of a Celt... and the modest patience of the Dutch," since Magonigle had Scottish-Dutch ancestors. His stylistic development in offices in New York and Boston provided him with valuable training in his profession.

88:4 Cunningham, Harry Francis. "Harold Van Buren Magonigle...Portrait." ARCHITECTURE NEW YORK 72 (October 1935): 219.

That Magonigle was not a religious man but loved his wife, art, and friends and "hating sham, indecision, temporizing and such" is the poetic theme of this obituary.

88:5 Sullivan, Francis. "A Conscientious Artist." PENCIL POINTS 16 (October 1935): 512-22.

"This was a man of brilliant and varied talents, an artist with an enduring record of accomplishment, and a teacher and leader to whom a large following looked for guidance and inspiration."

88:6 Swales, Francis C. "Master Draftsmen, 10." PENCIL POINTS 6 (March 1925): 47-66.

His career and the architects for whom he worked are listed. "As with his designs, his drawing is marked by an individuality much more easily detected than explained." A large representation of a variety of his drawings, including competition entries are illustrated.

89:1 MAHER, GEORGE W. (1864-1926)

Prairie School architect who began his apprenticeship with Bauer and Hill and later worked for James Lyman Silsbee. Opened his own practice, Chicago, 1888.

Fresno County Free Library has two sheets of a Library and Water Tower for Fresno, California.

Obituaries: AMERICAN ARCHITECTURE 130 (October-December 1926): 323; AMERICAN INSTITUTE OF ARCHITECTS' JOURNAL 14 (1926): 504.

89:2 David, Arthur C. "The Architecture of Ideas." ARCHITECTURAL RECORD 15 (April 1904): 361-84.

European time-honored traditions of the eastern seaboard

were overthrown in the West by many notable architects. The article is concerned with the work of two architects, Richard Schmidt and George Maher. Numerous interiors and details are photographed.

89:3 North, Arthur T. "Engineers and Architects in Artistic Collaboration; The Shaft House at Ishpeming, Michigan." AMERICAN ARCHITECTURE 118 (December 15, 1920): 783-87, 791.

"The traveler through the mining regions of this country has undoubtedly been impressed with the sheer ugliness of [mining] shaft houses. . . ." Condron Company engineers recommended to the owners that they retain George W. Maher as architectural consultant. The results had a significant effect. "These instances also indicated the rapprochement between architects and engineers, which is sure to increase because it is natural, necessary and holds great promise for future American architecture."

89:4 Rudd, J. William. "George W. Maher." THE PRAIRIE SCHOOL REVIEW 1 (First Quarter, 1964): 5-13.

Almost the whole issue of this new publication is devoted to a summation of a master's thesis at Northwestern University, Chicago. Portrait, photographs, plans, drawings. Maher, like Wright, first worked for James Silsbee; in 1893 he became a partner of J.L. Cochran. His work was essentially residential with an occasional bank or educational building.

89:5 WESTERN ARCHITECT. "George W. Maher, A Democrat in Architecture." Vol. 20 (1914): 25-28.

Maher's philosophical attitudes as they relate to architecture are forwarded. There are fine small photographs of residences including his own.

89:6 Wight, Peter B. "The Winona Savings Bank and Winona National Bank Building, Winona, Minnesota." ARCHITECTURAL RECORD 41 (January 1917): 37-50.

"While it is in reality the result of deliberately avoiding all stylistic trends, the bank is part Egyptian, part Prairie Style with a mish-mash mixture of verticals and horizontals in massing, fenestration and architectural elements." Wight doesn't say this, but rather praises innovative qualities for their own sake. He quotes lengthily from Maher and the article is well illustrated.

90:1 MAYBECK, BERNARD RALPH (1862-1957)

Educated at the Ecole des Beaux Arts, Paris, 1886, and later worked in New York City for his classmates, Carrere and Hastings (notably on the Ponce de Leon Hotel, St. Augustine, Florida).

Published: PALACE OF FINE ARTS AND LAGOON, PANAMA PACIFIC INTERNATIONAL EXPOSITION, 1915.

Obituaries: ARCHITECTURAL FORUM 107 (December 1957): 77-79; ARCHITECTURAL RECORD 122 (November 1957): 24; HOUSE AND HOME 12 (November 1957): 69.

90:2 Bangs, Jean Murray. "Bernard Ralph Maybeck, Architect, Comes into His Own." ARCHITECTURAL RECORD 103 (January 1948): 72-79.

"Aided by the University of California and private individuals, she [Bangs] has assembled the first comprehensive record of his contribution." Outline facts of his career are provided prior to an outline of the poetic imagination and use of natural materials in his residential architecture. The numerous photographs are well explained with detailed descriptions.

90:3 _____. "Maybeck-Medalist." ARCHITECTURAL FORUM 94 (May 1951): 160-62.

Maybeck's son received the American Institute of Architecture Gold Medal for 1951 on behalf of his father. Although Maybeck was famed for his Palace of Fine Arts in San Francisco, Miss Bangs briefly surveys his contribution as architect and teacher.

90:4 Besinger, Curtis. "After 50 Years This House Is Newer Than Many Moderns." HOUSE BEAUTIFUL 104 (May 1962): 150-57, 172.

The article is concerned with the timeless quality of the Stuart Dole House which had recently been refurbished by Evelyn and George Kosmak, architects, and Ruth Dibble, interior designer. Numerous photographs, some in color, plus plans serve to illustrate the simplicity of Maybeck's architecture of good design, materials, and workmanship.

90:5 Harris, Jean. "Bernard Ralph Maybeck." AMERICAN INSTITUTE OF ARCHITECTS' JOURNAL 15 (May 1951): 221-23.

Mrs. Harris has edited a short speech by Maybeck given at Mills College, October 1917. It illustrates his interest in planning and landscape design, spectacular views, and regard for climate.

90:6 Huxtable, Ada Louise. "Lively Original Versus Dead Copy." THE NEW YORK TIMES, May 9, 1965, section 2, p. 19.

Maybeck's Palace of Fine Arts, San Francisco, 1916, was to be demolished in order that it be rebuilt. This is the theme of an article on preservation, restoration, and reconstruction.

90:7 McCoy, Esther. FIVE CALIFORNIA ARCHITECTS. New York: Reinhold Publishing Corp., 1960. Pp. 1-58.

"For him there was no dead architecture," and this eclecticism can be seen in his work whether in the English arts and crafts tradition and the Richardsonian Shingle, or the Mission style or classicism of the 1912 Panama-Pacific International Exposition where he designed the Palace of Fine Arts. In 1951 Maybeck was awarded the Gold Medal of the American Institute of Architects.

90:8 _____. "Roots of California Contemporary Architecture." ARTS AND ARCHITECTURE 73 (October 1956): 14-17, 36-39.

The Los Angeles City Art Department arranged an exhibit of seven California architects and their work, 1900-35, including Maybeck, who is briefly mentioned. "Sieved through his extraordinary personality, classical themes became legends of our times."

90:9 Morrow, Irving, F. "The Packard Building at Oakland." CALIFORNIA ARTS AND ARCHITECTURE 35 (February 1929): 55-59.

"Mr. Maybeck stands consistently as the apostle of spontaneous, even irresponsible joy in art...." Simplicity, gigantism, color, sumptiousness are combined in this rather Moorish-looking building.

90:10 Nichols, Frederick D. "A Visit with Bernard Maybeck." JOURNAL OF THE SOCIETY OF ARCHITECTURAL HISTORIANS 11 (October 1952): 30-31.

"Climate and its constant consideration were always the first study of the architect," is the theme of the article. Maybeck worked for Carrere and Hastings after study at the Ecole des Beaux Arts, and the article lists some of the projects in which he was involved.

91:1 MCARTHUR, JOHN (1823-90)

Pennsylvania Hospital, Philadelphia, has twenty-two drawings including six by McArthur and E. Collins, and the Danville State Hospital has twenty sheets of its buildings.

Obituaries: AMERICAN ARCHITECT AND BUILDING NEWS 27 (1890): 35, 129; ARCHITECT AND BUILDING 12 (January 18, 1890): 25.

91:2 Maass, John. "Philadelphia City Hall, Monster or Masterpiece." AMERI-

CAN INSTITUTE OF ARCHITECTS' JOURNAL 43 (February 1965): 23-30.

This grandiose, complex, lavish, over-decorated, huge structure is well described with an objective sensitivity. The competition, lengthy period during which it was erected, the evolving design, personages, and political involvement are all discussed. Its preservation is worthy of Philadelphia and its supporters. A similar article was published by Maass in CHARETTE 44 (January 1964): 23-26.

91:3 Philadelphia. Commissioners for the Erection of the Public Building. PROCEEDINGS OF THE LAYING OF THE CORNER STONE. Philadelphia: H.B. Ashmead, 1874.

Stonelaying July 4, 1874. Complete background information on the structure including municipal legislation, history, description, statistics, and progress of the work.

91:4 Philadelphia. Commissioners for the Erection of the Public Building. REPORT. Philadelphia: Printed for the Commissioners, 1876.

Full title of the report tells all: "Report and proceedings of the Joint Committee investigation, appointed by the Commissioners for the erection of Public Buildings, to inquire as to charges and complaints made respecting the materials, supplies and manner of construction of public buildings of the City of Philadelphia."

91:5 Wodehouse, Lawrence. "John McArthur, Jr. (1823-1890)." JOURNAL OF THE SOCIETY OF ARCHITECTURAL HISTORIANS (December 1969): 271-83.

McArthur is well known as the designer of the Philadelphia City Hall, and usually gains a good press in most histories of nineteenth-century American architecture. His other works, however, made him a leader in the profession in and around Philadelphia from the Civil War years (when he designed hospitals) to his death in 1890. He designed office buildings, schools, college buildings, churches, hotels, cast-iron commercial fronts, and residences, including his own, no longer extant at 4201 Walnut Street.

92:1 MCKIM, CHARLES FOLLEN (1847-1909)

See McKim, Mead and Bigelow; McKim, Mead and White.

Educated at Harvard and the Ecole des Beaux Arts and worked for Richardson, 1870-72, thereafter practiced on his own or with Mead until 1877 when the formal partnership was begun.

Obituaries: AMERICAN ARCHITECT AND BUILDING NEWS 96 (1909): 115, 280; ARCHITECTURAL RECORD 26 (October 1909): 308, November 1909): 381-82; ROYAL INSTITUTE OF BRITISH ARCHITECTS' JOURNAL 16 (1908-9): 748, 764.

Alexander R. Butler produced a Ph.D. dissertation at Johns Hopkins University in 1953 entitled "McKim's Renaissance: A Study in the History of the American Architectural Profession."

92:2 Andrews, Wayne. MR. MORGAN AND HIS ARCHITECT. New York: Pierpont Morgan Library, 33 East 36th Street, New York City, 1957. 12 p. plus 6 photos.

Social, cultural, and financial details of J. Pierpont Morgan and his harried architect, Charles F. McKim.

92:3 Bacon, Henry. "Charles Follen McKim - A Character Sketch." THE BRICKBUILDER 19 (February 1910): 38-47.

Bacon worked for McKim, Mead and White, thus, this is a personal recollection. Examples of McKim's early and later draftsmanship are illustrated, plus photographs of some dominant classic buildings which obviously appealed to Bacon.

92:4 Brown, Glenn. "Personal Reminiscences of Charles Follen McKim." ARCHITECTURAL RECORD 38 (November 1915): 575-82; 38 (December 1915): 681-89; 39 (January 1916): 84-88; 39 (February 1916): 178-85.

The Buffalo American Institute of Architects Convention of 1901 elected McKim president in his absence and Glenn Brown was then asked to personally notify the eminent architect. His work on the Park Commission for the planning of Washington, D.C., is considered in the second article. Staying in the nation's capital, the third article considers the White House renovations. McKim's affable persistent method of forwarding his viewpoint resulted in many positive schemes including the establishment of the American Academy in Rome.

92:5 Chicago, Art Institute. EXHIBITION OF THE WORK OF CHARLES FOLLEN MCKIM, JANUARY 18TH TO FEBRUARY 6, 1910. Chicago: The Art Institute of Chicago, 1910. 7 p.

The pamphlet lists sixty-nine schemes illustrated by photographs and pen drawings which had originally been shown at the American Institute of Architects' headquarters in Washington at the time of Mead's acceptance, on McKim's behalf, of the gold medal of the American Institute of Architects.

92:6 Cortissoz, Royal. "The Secret of the American Academy in Rome." AMERICAN MAGAZINE OF ART 13 (November 1922): 459-62.

"That Institution sprang from the genius of a great architect, Charles F. McKim. He invented the Academy; he fostered it. It is his legacy to American art. . . ." A discussion on the growth of the Academy, colleagues associated with McKim in achieving his goal, and some of the results and products of the Academy.

92:7 _____ . "Some Critical Reflections on the Architectural Genius of Charles F. McKim." THE BRICKBUILDER 19 (February 1910): 23-37.

"If ever there was a homogeneous firm in the history of the architectural profession, it was that of McKim, Mead and White." McKim was a genius but only as one of a trio. A survey of his life and work is provided with complementary photographs.

92:8 Granger, Alfred Hoyt. CHARLES FOLLEN MCKIM: A STUDY OF HIS LIFE AND WORK. Boston and New York: Houghton Mifflin Co., 1913. 145 p.

After admitting that, "Never before has there been such a complete unity in trinity in human practice as in the work of" McKim, Mead and White, Granger states that he wants "to point out certain buildings and parts of buildings which may be said to belong personally to McKim" and his influence upon American architecture. A history of McKim's life and work is attempted even though one or two works are acknowledged to be designs of White (the Gorham Building) or B.L. Fenner (the New York Municipal Building) a partner of the firm, whose design won the competition.

92:9 Hill, Frederick Parsell. CHARLES F. MCKIM, THE MAN. Francestown, N.H.: M. Jones Co., 1950. 44 p. (limited edition, 250 copies).

Hill adds "many interesting, intimate, amusing incidents," to the already well-known biography of McKim by Charles Moore.

92:10 Moore, Charles. THE LIFE AND TIMES OF CHARLES FOLLEN MCKIM. Boston and New York: Houghton, Mifflin Co., 1929. 356 p.

Includes an early autobiographical study by William Rutherford Mead. Also includes McKim at Harvard, in the office of Russell Sturgis, at the Ecole des Beaux Arts, Paris, travels in Europe, apprenticeship to Richardson, marriage, partnerships, divorce, remarriage and success at gaining commissions in Boston and Cambridge, including the Boston Public Library, and the association of major American and European painters and sculptors.

The establishment of the American Academy at Rome was a lifetime ambition of McKim which he saw through to fruition. His appointment to the Senate Parks Commission for Washington and the award of the Gold Medal of the Royal Institute of British Architects were highlights of McKim's successful career.

92:11 Paris, W. Franklyn. "Charles Follen McKim." NEW YORK UNIVERSITY HALL OF AMERICAN ARTISTS 10 (1955): 81-94.

The McKim tablet at the American Academy in Rome begins: "Founder of the American Academy in Rome, Eminent Architect, Distinguished by life-long and unselfish public service for the cause of the Arts in his native land...." The author of this article considers McKim leader of the profession after the death of Richardson. An extremely complimentary article, the author attempts to analyze McKim's overall career in addition to his notable architectural achievements.

92:12 Peabody, Robert Swain. "A Tribute to Charles Follen McKim." THE BRICKBUILDER 19 (1910): 55-56.

Reminiscences of early days in the Louis Napoleon Paris where Peabody and McKim were fellow students. McKim was the athletic, hard-working, earnest student, as Alberti of Renaissance Florence. Later, "coupled with his persuasive charm of manner, he had brought many loyal clients to build better than they knew or had dreamed of."

92:13 Sloane, William Milligan. "Commemorative Tributes to McKim, Norton, Ward, Aldrich and Jefferson." AMERICAN ACADEMY OF ARTS AND LETTERS 11 (1922): 1-25.

"His life began in a heroic epoch of tumult...and ended in an age of struggle for emancipation from materialism." His qualities are enumerated.

92:14 Swales, F.S. "Charles Follen McKim, 1847-1909." ARCHITECTURAL REVIEW (London) 26 (October 1909): 183-91.

A memorial, listing his background and major architectural attainments, styles and major collaborators, both in partnership and in association on collaborative design projects.

92:15 Walker, Charles Howard. "The Influence of McKim." THE BRICKBUILDER 19 (1910): 48-53.

Experimental and novel to begin with, McKim became a serious student of classical architecture. His classicism was passed on to others in the firm, the profession, and ultimately to the country. Several interior photographs of the White House are included.

93:1 **MCKIM, MEAD AND BIGELOW (Partnership 1877-78)**

A short-lived partnership of Charles Follen McKim (1847-1909), William Rutherford Mead (1846-1928), and William B. Bigelow. The partnership reformed as McKim, Mead and White. McKim, Mead and Bigelow designed a rectory for Christ Church, Rye, 1877; house for Mrs. A.C. Alden, Fort Hill, Lloyd's Neck, Long Island, 1879; and Union League Club, New York City, 1879.

94:1 **MCKIM, MEAD AND WHITE (Partnership 1878-)**

(See also under individual listings)

Partnership began 1878 and continued beyond the death of Stanford White (1853-1906) and the death of Charles Follen McKim (1847-1909). William Rutherford Mead (1846-1928) ceased to be a partner after 1919 but was never an actual designer. Thus all structures designed after those by White and McKim were completed by partners brought into the firm on January 1, 1906, and later. They include William M. Kendall (who won in competition the design for the New York Municipal Building), Burt L. Fenner, William S. Richardson, and Teunis J. Van Der Bent. Stanford's son, Lawrence Grant White, joined the firm in 1914 and became a partner in 1920.

The New York Historical Society has drawings of 386 projects by the firm as do the following repositories: Burnham Library, Chicago, thirty-five sheets of Lathrop House; University of Virginia Alderman Library, eight projects; Avery Library, Columbia University, two sheets; Pierpont Morgan Library, two sheets; Syracuse University, two sheets of the Rhode Island State House. Leland Roth is working on a doctoral dissertation at Yale on the firm's work.

94:2 Andrews, Wayne. "McKim, Mead and White: New York's Own Architects." THE NEW YORK HISTORICAL SOCIETY QUARTERLY 35 (January 1951): 87-96.

> "McKim, Mead and White, the founders of that infinitely influential architectural firm which now, at the beginning of its seventy-second year in business, has deposited its archives in The New York Historical Society." The article surveys the work and achievement of the firm up to the deaths of White and McKim.

94:3 _____. "McKim, Mead, White: Their Mark Remains." THE NEW YORK TIMES, Sunday, January 7, 1951, Magazine Section, pp. 81-21.

> An announcement that the firm, after seventy-two years, and with the original partners long since dead, had presented its records to the New York Historical Society,

including four tons of glass negatives, plans, specifications, and correspondence. The New York Historical Society put on an exhibition of McKim, Mead and White's Manhattan landmarks. Many are illustrated in a small scale and several discussed in relation to the philosophy of the original partners. "New York City minus McKim, Mead and White would be as poor a thing as a parade without banners."

94:4 Barber, Donn. "The Work of McKim, Mead and White." ARCHITECTURAL RECORD 40 (October 1916): 395-96.

Announcement of McKim, Mead and White monograph (see below 94:19) covering the years 1879 to 1915, illustrating 150 projects. The article presents a general appreciation of the firm's work.

94:5 Boyd, John Taylor, Jr. "The Addition to the New York Harvard Club." ARCHITECTURAL RECORD 38 (December 1916): 615-30.

This addition doubles the facilities of the Club and has allowed a rearrangement of space. All aspects of the new building are described with numerous drawings, plans of various floor levels and photographs.

94:6 Cooney, John P., Jr. THE RHODE ISLAND STATE HOUSE. Providence, R.I.: State Bureau of Information, 1933. 36 p.

This tiny pocket-sized book provides more information on Providence, the governors and speakers of Rhode Island, the memorials incorporated into the building, and dimensions of rooms than on the architecture.

94:7 Croly, Herbert D. "The Harmonie Clubhouse." ARCHITECTURAL RECORD 19 (April 1906): 236-43.

Built in a residential area of almost uniform row houses, Herbert Croly, the architectural critic, justifies the clubhouse as being "showy," renaissance revival, and faced with marble. The entrance hall has a copy of Cellini's Perseus.

94:8 _____. "The Layout of a Large Estate. Harbor Hill, the Country Seat of Mr. Clarence Mackay, at Roslyn, Long Island." ARCHITECTURAL RECORD 16 (December 1904): 531-55.

Harbor Hill, the house and the gate lodge were by White, although all other structures, including stables and farm buildings were by Warren and Wetmore. The article emphasizes the importance of landscape architecture as part of the total design of an estate. White was a competent landscape architect, but in the case of Harbor Hill, the well-known Boston architect Guy Lowell was retained as landscape architect.

94:9 _____. "The New Harvard Clubhouse." ARCHITECTURAL RECORD 19 (March 1906): 194-98, 206.

The new Georgian Harvard Club, New York, replaces an earlier, simpler colonial version by the same firm. The grand new dining hall is illustrated and given prominence in the accompanying description.

94:10 David, A.C. "An Architectural Oasis." ARCHITECTURAL RECORD 19 (February 1906): 135-44.

The firm designed and built at least seven structures at the small town of Naugatuck, Connecticut, and although each building was in a different style, they all betrayed the unifying qualities of the firm's products. The Naugatuck National Bank was completed in 1893, and was complemented by two other buildings on the Town Square: the Public School, 1894, and Congregational Church, 1905. White is known to have designed the high school, 1905, high on a hill above the square. All were built for J.H. Whittemore who also commissioned a house, 1890; farmhouse and stables, 1896; and another house for Harris Whittemore in 1903.

94:11 _____. "The Finest Store in the World." ARCHITECTURAL RECORD 17 (January 1905): 42-49.

The Havana Tobacco Co. in the St. James Building, New York City, "did wish to create the impression that the man who bought his box of cigars in the finest store in the World was in good company." One hundred thousand dollars were spent in rugs, tapestries, mural landscapes of Cuba by Willard Metcalfe, palms, tropical plants, glass cigar cases on marble bases, with marble tables, floors, walls, and columns. This was store design for the age of affluence.

94:12 _____. "A Modern Instance of Colonial Architecture. The House of Mr. B.W. Arnold at Albany, New York." ARCHITECTURAL RECORD 17 (April 1905): 305-17.

Georgian rather than "Colonial," this house has certain characteristics reminiscent of those on Beacon Street, Boston. Marble trimmings enhance the red brick on the exterior whereas interiors range in style from Jacobean, as in the mahogany paneled dining room, to white woodwork and silver grey colonial color schemes in the hall.

94:13 Desmond, Henry W., and Croly, Herbert. "The Work of Messrs. McKim, Mead and White." ARCHITECTURAL RECORD 20 (September 1906): 153-246.

A second survey of the work of McKim, Mead and White, fifteen years after the first, by ARCHITECTURAL RECORD (see 94:33), and coincidentally at the time of the death of Stanford White. The years 1880-95, are classified as experimental whereas the economic conditions in the United States changed between 1895 and 1906. The renaissance and classical styles used by the firm are justified as being more akin to America than the medieval styles of militant Catholicism. "They have established a tradition...they have a loyal following among the younger architects all over the country... by the force of compelling example."

94:14 Dorr, Charles H. "A Study of Church Decoration. The Paulist Fathers Church in New York City and Notes on the Work of W.L. Harris." ARCHITECTURAL RECORD 33 (March 1913): 187-203.

Inaugurated by Father Isaac Thomas Hecker of Brook Farm fame, Stanford White was employed to beautify the interior of the church of the Paulist Fathers, Columbus Ave. at 59th Street, built as St. Paul the Apostle by Jeremiah O'Rourke, 1876-85. John La Farge painted the ceiling and designed the windows; Frederick MacMonnies, the three adoring angels with musical instruments; Philip Martiny, the sanctuary lamp; and White the altar and ciborium of the chancel, 1890.

94:15 Farrand, Beatrix. "Dumbarton Oaks...." LANDSCAPE ARCHITECTURE 34 (July 1944): 131-35.

Subtitled "An Historic Setting for the Making of History" this article is concerned with the 1801 Georgetown, D.C., residence to which Lawrence Grant White (son of Stanford White) added the music room and the surrounding terraces, loggias, and gardens in association with Beatrix Farrand, landscape gardener.

94:16 Goldsmith, Goldwin. "I Remember McKim, Mead and White." AMERICAN INSTITUTE OF ARCHITECTS' JOURNAL 13 (April 1950): 168-72.

Goldsmith worked at first as a stenographer for McKim, Mead and White, later setting up practice as Van Vleck and Goldsmith. He reminisces on members of the firm comparing one partner with another: "Where Mr. White dashed from one place to another about the building, Mr. Mead made a systematic and careful survey."

94:17 Goodyear, William H. "Horizontal Curves in Columbia University." ARCHITECTURAL RECORD 9 (July-September 1899): 82-93.

"Columbia University buildings are absolutely the first modern structures to which the Greek horizontal curves are applied." That is, the upward curve of the steps in front of the Butler Library, for example, which are eight inches higher in the center to draw one's eye toward the library. The idea came originally from the Parthenon to prevent the illusion of a horizontal line sagging.

94:18 Huxtable, Ada Louise. "The Plot Thickens." THE NEW YORK TIMES, Sunday, February 14, 1971, section 2, p. 25.

A synopsis of the owners of Villard houses and their attitudes towards preservation, plus the wheeling and dealing that seems to have been perpetuated during 1971 to sell the properties for maximum financial gain, irrespective of the significance of the group of houses as a nationally famed contribution to late nineteenth-century American architecture.

94:19 McKim, Mead and White. A MONOGRAPH OF THE WORK OF MCKIM, MEAD AND WHITE 1879-1915. 4 vols. New York: The Architectural Book Publishing Co., 1914.

Each volume of this monograph has approximately 100 plates. Several plates are devoted to major projects and in all cases, plans, elevations, details, and photographs are used.

94:20 _____. RECENT WORK BY THE PRESENT PARTNERS OF MCKIM, MEAD AND WHITE, ARCHITECTS. New York: Vogue La Galere, 1952. 47 p.

"The Present Partners" were Lawrence Grant White, son of Stanford White, and James Kellum Smith. A list of all their works in almost every building type is provided, after which a selected few are illustrated.

94:21 _____. RECENT BUILDINGS DESIGNED FOR EDUCATIONAL INSTITUTIONS BY MCKIM, MEAD AND WHITE. Philadelphia: Beck Engraving Co., 1936. 12 p. 76 pl.

Illustrations with a general introductory foreword of university buildings mainly of the 1920's and 1930's, but listed as being those designed after the publication of the major four-volume monograph of the firm, 1915. The plates are arranged by building types of college buildings after general plans of six colleges. At the end of the book is a chronological list of educational institutions by the firm, 1890-1935.

94:22 _____. RESTORATION OF THE WHITE HOUSE. Washington, D.C.: Government Printing Office, 1903. 51 p.

Includes message of the President and a report by the architects in addition to historical notes on the building by Charles Moore. Photographs of the 1902 restoration complement plans of the White House.

94:23 Moses, Lionel. "McKim, Mead and White: a History." AMERICAN

ARCHITECTURE 121 (May 24, 1922): 413-24.

Lists the partners who joined the firm on January 1, 1906: William M. Kendall, Harvard, 1876; Bert L. Fenner, Rochester and Massachusetts Institute of Technology, 1887-91; William S. Richardson, from practice in San Francisco; Teunis Van der Bent, architectural engineer from University of Delft, Holland; Daniel T. Webster; Lawrence Grant White, Harvard, 1907, and Ecole des Beaux Arts, entered the office in 1914 and became a partner in 1920, one year after Mead retired.

94:24 Phillips, McCandlish. "City Seeks a Way to Save Harlem Enclave." THE NEW YORK TIMES, March 30, 1972, section L, p. 39.

Striver's Row built for D.W. King in Harlem, 1891, was a speculative development which was designated as an historic landmark in 1967. White designed the north side of 139th Street between Seventh and Eighth Avenues in the Italianate style; James Lord Brown, the south side of 138th Street, Georgian Revival; and those in between by Bruce Price and Clarence Luce in a more exuberant Georgian.

94:25 Price, C. Matleck. "The Design of the Avery Architectural Library." ARCHITECTURAL RECORD 33 (June 1913): 535-49.

In praise of an architectural design problem for a repository for architectural literary works. Pros and cons of stack room plan and alcove plan are presented, the latter winning out as an arrangement for the perusal of an architectural collection of books. Plans, sections, elevations, and numerous details are illustrated for this library topped by the School of Architecture.

94:26 Ramsey, Stanley C. "The Work of McKim, Mead and White." ROYAL INSTITUTE OF BRITISH ARCHITECTS' JOURNAL 25 (November 5, 1917): 25-29.

Descriptive poetic verbiage of the Washington Arch, New York City, 1892; Cullum Memorial, West Point, 1898, both by White; and St. Gabriel's Branch Library, New York City, 1907.

94:27 Reilly, C.H. MCKIM, MEAD AND WHITE. London: Benn, 1924. 23 p. 5 pls.

A brief essay by an English architect who headed the School of Architecture at Liverpool University. McKim, Mead and White produced an architecture for their country, day and age. Thus, even the Italian Renaissance revival had a "great freshness and ingenuity."

94:28 Schuyler, Montgomery. "Cullum Memorial, West Point." ARCHITECTUR-

AL RECORD 15: 431-44.

Inspiration for this structure came from the Basilica of the Giants at Agrigentum, a Greek building, and the Romantic-Classical Faculty of Medicine in Paris.

94:29 _____. "A Modern Classic." ARCHITECTURAL RECORD 15 (May 1904): 431-44.

White's Knickerbocker Trust Co. Building, New York, was designed having giant Corinthian columns as its dominant emphasis. Schuyler justifies this approach quoting Viollet-le-Duc, who reasoned that the columns are structural with screens between and were not used solely as an external, expressive ornamentation.

94:30 _____. "The New White House." ARCHITECTURAL RECORD 13 (April 1903): 358-88.

"Congress has never been given to pampering the President of the day, nor his womankind." The White House was Irish in its design aesthetic and a Virginia planter's mansion in concept until McKim created a veritable palace for social functions, "promiscuous hospitality and a return to the original elegance."

94:31 Sturgis, Russell. "The Carnegie Libraries in New York City." ARCHITECTURAL RECORD 17 (March 1905): 237-46.

Includes Tompkins Square Branch, No. 224, East 125th Street, and a branch on East Broadway. They are considered to be too over-studied and classical on rather small sites. Sturgis complains of the Paris-oriented front facades compared to the functional rear facades which are not seen.

94:32 _____. "A Fine Work of American Architectural Sculpture." ARCHITECTURAL RECORD 15 (April 1908): 293-311.

The fine work is the porch of St. Bartholomew's Church, now at the west end of Bertram Goodhue's church on Park Avenue between 50th and 51st Streets of 1919, but originally designed to fit the second St. Bartholomew's by Renwick and Sands of 1872 at 44th Street and Madison Avenue. The porch was a memorial to Commodore Vanderbilt and four sculptors contributed to Stanford White's porch based upon the Romanesque Church of St. Gilles du Gard, France: Herbert Adams, Philip Martiny, Daniel Chester French, and Andrew O'Connor, 1903.

94:33 _____. "Great American Architects Series: McKim, Mead and White." ARCHITECTURAL RECORD 4 (May 1895, supplement): 1-111.

Almost all the major works by McKim, Mead and White

from the beginning of the partnership in 1878 to 1895 are described, illustrated, discussed, and criticized. Russell Sturgis was one of the major architectural critics of the late nineteenth century and at times was dogmatic in his remarks. For example, he described Madison Square Garden as "seriously disfigured by the ornament in terra cotta thickly spread over the surfaces. . . well modeled but how badly it is put together." (p.15)

94:34 _____. "The Warehouse and the Factory in Architecture." ARCHITECTURAL RECORD 15 (January 1904): 1-17; 15 (February 1904): 122-33.

The Judge Building, 1890, West 16th Street and Fifth Avenue, New York City, by McKim, Mead and White is discussed in relation to the Chicago style buildings by Babb, Cook and Willard. Sturgis felt that the Judge Building was too architectural with its system of decoration and thus out of context as a factory-warehouse building. Sturgis questioned the lion-headed gargoyles and ornamental cornices.

95:1 MEAD, WILLIAM RUTHERFORD (1846-1928)

See McKim, Mead and White.

Educated at Norwich University, Vermont, and Amherst College, Mead entered the office of Russell Sturgis and later joined in partnership with McKim and Bigelow in 1877, a partnership which was dissolved to reform in 1878 as McKim, Mead and White. There are only three illustrations of Mead's own early work: 1. Cayuga Lake Hotel, NEW YORK SKETCH BOOK, April 1875; 2. Dwight S. Herrick House, Peekskill-on-Hudson, AMERICAN ARCHITECT AND BUILDING NEWS, June 3, 1877; 3. Thomas Dunn House, Newport, Rhode Island, AMERICAN ARCHITECT AND BUILDING NEWS, July 28, 1877.

The American Academy of Arts and Letters Library, New York has 100 items of correspondence relating to the National Institute of Arts and Letters and the American Academy of Arts and Letters.

Obituaries: AMERICAN ART ANNUAL 25 (1928): 371; AMERICAN ARCHITECTURE 134 (July-September 1928): 12; ARCHITECTURAL RECORD 64 (1928): 254; AMERICAN INSTITUTE OF ARCHITECTS' JOURNAL 16 (1928): 280; ARCHITECTURAL FORUM 49 (July 1928): 37.

95:2 ARCHITECTURAL RECORD. "William Rutherford Mead." Vol. 64 (September 1928): 254.

Brief obituary listing Mead's achievements and a recital

of the main facts and landmarks in his life.

95:3 THE BRICKBUILDER. "As He Is Known, Being Brief Sketches of Contemporary Members of the Architectural Profession." Vol. 24 (December 1915): 315.

Brief synopsis of the life and achievements of Mead.

95:4 Cortissoz, Royal. "William Rutherford Mead, FAIA. 1846-1928." AMERICAN ARCHITECTURE 134 (July 5, 1928): 12.

An obituary and appreciation of the life and work of Mead in relation to the firm of McKim, Mead and White. "Thanks largely to his steadfast wisdom, there never was more effective teamwork than that of these three."

95:5 PENCIL POINTS. "William Rutherford Mead, 1846-1928." Vol. 9 (August 1928): 529.

Obituary of Mead who died in Rome, the reins of the American Academy in his hands. He had retired from the firm in 1919.

96:1 MEIGS, MONTGOMERY CUNNINGHAM (1816-92)

Educated Franklin Institute, University of Pennsylvania, and United States Military Academy. The Library of Congress, Manuscripts Division, has 3800 items, 1849-92. National Archives, Washington, has sixteen projects and the Metropolitan Museum of Art, New York City, one sheet of the United States Capitol.

Obituary: AMERICAN ARCHITECT AND BUILDING NEWS. 35 (January 9, 1892): 17.

96:2 Cox, Warren. "Washington's Forgotten Architect." ARCHITECTURAL FORUM 118 (January 1963): 71-78.

The Pension Building, 1883, "Washington's version of the Palazzo Farnese...was the scene of inaugural balls... [and] for the dispensing of pensions to widows and orphans of Union Veterans." The pension's service moved out in 1926, and the building was taken over by the Civil Service Commission. Other buildings in Washington threatened with destruction in 1963 are illustrated.

96:3 East, Sherrar E. "The Banishment of Captain Meigs." COLUMBIA HISTORIC SOCIETY 40-41 (1940): 97-143.

Honest Captain Meigs didn't fit too well in the Washington of the late 1850's and early 1860's. He would have nothing to do with the corrupt contractors' lobby in Congress and was thus banished to the Dry Tortugas. President Lincoln soon brought him back, however, and Meigs became Quartermaster General of the Army until 1885.

96:4 [Lehman, Donald H.] HISTORICAL STUDY NO.1: PENSION BUILDING. Washington, D.C.: General Services Administration, 1964. (16) p.

Meigs, who was Lincoln's Quartermaster General, designed this million dollar structure, built 1882 to 1885, in the Italian Renaissance Revival style of Michelangelo's Farnese Palace, Rome. A 1200-foot-long frieze, three-feet high, runs around the building at second floor level. This was a memorial to Civil War sailors and soldiers by the Bohemian-American sculptor, Caspar Buberl.

96:5 Meigs, M.C. REPORT ON THE CONSTRUCTION OF THE NEW PENSION BUILDING MADE TO THE SECRETARY OF THE INTERIOR. Washington, D.C.: Government Printing Office, 1887. 7 p.

This is the 1887 annual report in the form of a letter by Meigs listing appropriations, state, and progress of the construction of the building, materials, contracts, services related to the structure, heating and ventilation, and works still to be completed. Contractors for the year are listed.

96:6 Skramstad, Harold K. "The Engineer as Architect in Washington. The Contribution of Montgomery Meigs." RECORDS OF THE COLUMBIA HISTORICAL SOCIETY, 1969-1970 (actually 1971), pp. 266-84.

Meigs combined ability with political know-how in his work as an engineer, in the United States Corps of Engineers, working on architectural and engineering projects for the federal government.

96:7 Weigley, Russell Frank. QUARTERMASTER GENERAL OF THE UNION ARMY. New York: Columbia University Press, 1959. 396 p.

This is a biography of the whole career of Meigs as an Army officer. Chapters 4 and 5 are most pertinent to his architectural and engineering contribution to the construction of the United States Capitol and acqueduct at Washington. His honesty in the disbursement of funds and contracts (an area of building construction prone to corruption) against Secretary of War John B. Floyd is a noteworthy account.

97:1 MELLOR, WALTER (1880-1940)

University of Pennsylvania, 1904, B.S. Partnership with Arthur Meigs, 1906-40.

Obituaries: ARCHITECTURAL FORUM 72 (February 1940): 48, 60; THE FEDERAL ARCHITECT 10 (January 1940): 35-37; ARCHITECTURAL RECORD 87 (February 1940): 118.

97:2 THE BRICKBUILDER. "As He is Known, Being Brief Sketches of Contemporary Members of the Architectural Profession." Vol. 24 (1915): 208.

Education, influences, training, and partnerships led to an informal personal architectural expression, "free of academic tendencies, but always sane and not at all bizarre. It is frank, sincere and straightforward."

98:1 MELLOR, MEIGS (and HOWE) (Partnership 1906-40)

Walter Mellor (1880-1940) (see) and Arthur Meigs.

University of Pennsylvania has twenty-nine sheets of Gamma Phi Delta Fraternity.

98:2 Cret, Paul P. "A Hillside House, the Property of George Howe, Chestnut Hill, Philadelphia." ARCHITECTURAL RECORD 48 (August 1920): 83-106.

"A mixture of pure art in a garden scene," combining the formality of European landscape architecture is the setting for this moderate-sized residence. Interiors are diverse and of different styles, all of which are illustrated, showing the relationship of interior to exterior through paving and landscaping.

98:3 Eberlein, Harold D. "Examples of the Work of Mellor, Meigs and Howe." ARCHITECTURAL RECORD 39 (March 1916): 212-46.

"Informal, comfortable, well mannered, interesting, sincere" are five adjectives associated most in the work of this firm, whose residences span all styles of architecture, classic and romantic, in addition to the innovations of the arts and crafts movement and the American Shingle style.

98:4 Gilchrist, Edmund B. "The Residence of Heatly C. Dulles, Villa Nova, Pennsylvania." ARCHITECTURAL RECORD 49 (January 1921): 3-17.

Although a cottage in the arts and crafts medieval revival style, Gilchrist praises the house on the basic grounds of function, internal-external expression, and as a place of shelter. Each portion of the house and its surrounding landscape is analyzed, described, and praised.

98:5 Meigs, Arthur Ingersoll. AN AMERICAN COUNTRY HOUSE, THE PRO-

PERTY OF ARTHUR E. NEWBOLD, JR., ESQ., LAVEROCK, PA. New York: The Architectural Book Publishing Co. Inc., 1925. 30 p. 99 pl.

"This book is written and arranged primarily for the student of architecture, either technical or lay. With this end in view great care has been taken to present the photographs and drawings in a logical sequence, and in such a way as to make the reference from the photographs to the drawings as easy and convenient as possible," wrote Arthur I. Meigs in his introduction to his book on a residence based upon French medieval vernacular forms.

98:6 _____. "Goodhart Hall, Bryn Mawr College, Pennsylvania." ARCHITECTURAL RECORD 65 (February 1929): 105-56, 167-274.

"All buildings have a function to fulfill but architecture is the aesthetic fulfillment of that function." Bryn Mawr Gothic dictated the aesthetics, and Meigs gives the precidents of the medieval period upon which he has based his design. There are about 100 pages of illustrations of every conceivable detail, however minute.

98:7 Sexton, R.W. "A Winter Retreat in the Grand Manner." ARTS AND DECORATION 48 (March 1938): 16-18, 35.

Built on the foundations of an old house, the residence looks almost as it must have done originally in 1798. The new residence was intended as a winter retreat in the south, thus rooms are exposed to the attraction of winter sunlight; it is constructed of wood and clapboard.

98:8 Wister, Owen. Preface, and articles by others. A MONOGRAPH OF THE WORK OF MELLOR, MEIGS AND HOWE. New York: The Architectural Book Publishing Co., 1923. 212 p.

Thirty-four residences, all in the Medieval Revival Arts and Crafts inspired tradition are presented, well-illustrated with plans, general and detailed photographs with essays on each by members of the firm and close architectural associates.

99:1 MILBURN, FRANK PIERCE (1868-1926)

99:2 Wodehouse, Lawrence. "Frank Pierce Milburn (1868-1926), A Major Southern Architect." THE NORTH CAROLINA HISTORICAL REVIEW 50 (Summer 1973): 289-303.

A southern practitionery for thirty-five years, Milburn designed 250 major structures in addition to residential architecture. High-rise buildings were designed by him for Washington, D.C., in addition to court houses, university halls, and alterations to state capitols. The article emphasizes his contribution in North Carolina where he paralleled the eclecticisms of the New York stylists and in some of his work, captured the spirit of Richardson, Sullivan, and Wright.

100:1 MILLER, WILLIAM HENRY (d. 1921)

1892-97 associated with Samuel H. Hillyer.

Obituary: AMERICAN ARCHITECTURE 121 (March 1, 1922): 168.

Edgar Raymond Dethlefson produced a master's thesis on Miller at Cornell University in 1957. It is well illustrated and relies heavily upon newspaper articles of the period. As in any first attempt at a catalogue raisonne, several buildings have been overlooked including W.H. Wells residence at 2931 E. Jefferson Avenue, Detroit (DETROIT EVENING NEWS, September 15, 1889), now the University of Detroit Dental Library, and those buildings illustrated in the AMERICAN ARCHITECT AND BUILDING NEWS (See AVERY PERIODICALS INDEX for listings).

100:2 Cantor, Jay E. "Living with Antiques." ANTIQUES, December 1972, pp. 1052-59.

The Finch-Guerlac House at Ithaca, New York, began as an 1840's Greek Revival cottage, with a Gothic addition of 1851, and was renovated in 1874-75 by Miller. This early commission by Miller resulted in a cottage, completely changed in external appearance although with a plan little different from the original. Well illustrated and with color reproductions.

101:1 MOSER, JOHN (1832-1904)

Supervising Architect of the Treasury Department in 1890, and designer of a controversial, yet unbuilt, New York Chapter, American Institute of Architects Building.

Obituaries: AMERICAN ARCHITECT AND BUILDING NEWS 86 (October 1, 1904): 1; INLAND ARCHITECT AND NEWS RECORD 44 (September 1904): 9.

101:2 Gordon, F.C. "The Skyscraper." AMERICAN ARCHITECT AND BUILDING NEWS 46 (December 8, 1894): 100-101.

Moser "is an enthusiast in his profession and one who believes religiously that its high and noble functions should, first and always, be consecrated to the cause of truth, in which alone lasting beauty may be achieved." The skyscraper is analyzed as a structure from this viewpoint. Utility, decoration, and unity of facade treatment all combine toward functional beauty.

102:1 MOULD, JACOB WREY (1825-86)

Studied under Owen Jones in England. Set up practice in New York, 1853, assisted Calvert Vaux in 1867, and succeeded him as architect of the public parks in 1870.

Obituaries: AMERICAN ARCHITECT AND BUILDING NEWS 19 (1886): 301-2; BUILDING 4 (June 19, 1886): 290.

102:2 Van Zanten, David T. "Jacob Wrey Mould: Echoes of Owen Jones and the High Victorian Styles in New York, 1853-1865." JOURNAL OF THE SOCIETY OF ARCHITECTURAL HISTORIANS 28 (March 1969): 41-57.

An appendix lists buildings and projects 1848 to 1886, and although the article begins in 1853, there are several schemes dating from after 1860. They include Holy Trinity Chapel, 1865; West Presbyterian Church, 1863-65; bandstands, terraces, gateways, and telegraph poles for the New York parks system.

103:1 MULLETT, ALFRED BULT (1834-90)

Associated with Isaiah Rogers before the Civil War and became Supervising Architect of the Treasury Department, 1865-74. Thereafter he practiced with his sons in Washington, D.C. The National Archives, Washington, D.C., has files and drawings of all of his sixteen projects. Avery Library, Columbia University, has four sheets on the State, War and Navy Building, Washington, D.C., and the St. Louis Public Library five sheets of the local post office and custom house.

Obituaries: ARCHITECTURE AND BUILDING 13 (October 25, 1890): 235; AMERICAN ARCHITECT AND BUILDING NEWS 30 (1890): 45.

103:2 Brooks, George R. "The Old Post Office." MISSOURI HISTORICAL SOCIETY BULLETIN, July 1964, pp. 307-9.

The solution to the preservation of Mullett's post office, St. Louis, relies upon finding a suitable use for the building. Brooks argues for the structure as a stylistic example of architecture of its period, which encountered difficulties in construction in the 1870's as would any structure of comparable size today.

103:3 Burchard, Marshall. "Will Rebuilding Save This Landmark?" ARCHITECTURAL FORUM, July 1961, pp. 116-18.

"When Grandpa's face is dirty you don't shoot him" begins this article on Mullett's St. Louis post office, a building with the grime and pollution of almost a century, which should not be demolished. The article discusses and illustrates a proposal by St. Louis architect Joseph D. Murphy for refurbishing the building.

103:4 Haney, Thomas V. "Year of Decision for Old Mint." THE NEW YORK TIMES, Sunday, February 1, 1970, section 2, p. 39.

The San Francisco Mint was declared government surplus, leading the San Francisco State College to make application for its use and for the Smithsonian Institute to request it as a western branch of its organization. The building is a significant one for preservationists and numismatists alike. The article's subject is that of coins produced at the mint. It is the only Greek Revival (although extremely late) example of architecture on the West Coast and the only example of that style by Mullett.

103:5 Huxtable, Ada Louise. "No Canoeing Allowed Here." THE NEW YORK TIMES, Sunday, August 2, 1970, section 2, p. 18.

"The Old St. Louis Post Office has been running for its life since 1959." It is government surplus standing on expensive downtown real estate. Huxtable shows how forces of city government and the "Feds," both with ulterior motives, have forwarded the demolition of the building. Letters are quoted that "are either terribly stupid or terribly clever...to make preservation difficult and horsetrading easy."

103:6 [Lehman, Donald H.] HISTORICAL STUDY NO. 3: EXECUTIVE OFFICE BUILDING. Washington, D.C.: General Services Administration, 1964. 100 p.

This is a detailed study of Mullett's largest, most expensive ($10 million), and famous structure. The State, War and Navy Building, on the west side of the White House, is now known as the Executive Office Building. The early history of projects by Mills, Young and Walter are mentioned prior to a discussion of Mullett the "reluctant designer." Thomas Lincoln Casey and Richard von Ezdorf followed Mullett after his resignation of the post of Supervising Architect of the Treasury Department in 1874.

103:7 Pickens, Buford. "Progress, Preservation, St. Louis' Old Palais." HIS-

TORIC PRESERVATION 12 (1960): 60-63.

The subject was the post office at St. Louis, which, in 1960, was threatened with destruction. The article briefly describes the building, its importance as part of America's heritage, and the innovations involved in its construction, notably the railroad tunnel along Eighth Street from one of the bridges over the Mississippi.

103:8 Wodehouse, Lawrence. "Alfred B. Mullett and his French Style Government Buildings." JOURNAL OF THE SOCIETY OF ARCHITECTURAL HISTORIANS 31 (March 1972): 22-37.

Alfred Mullett held the post of Supervising Architect of the Treasury Department from 1865 to 1874, during which time he erected $50 million worth of governmental buildings. But his claim to fame should not be attributed to the quantity of his structures, rather, he, with John Mc Arthur, Jr., were the two most noteworthy architects of the Second Empire or General Grant style of architecture, a style which was as popular as General Grant in the late 1860's, and as unpopular at the end of the President's second term, and has remained so ever since.

103:9 _____. "Alfred B. Mullett's Court Room and Post Office at Raleigh, North Carolina." JOURNAL OF THE SOCIETY OF ARCHITECTURAL HISTORIANS 26 (December 1967): 301-5.

An introductory article on Mullett exploring a minor work in detail in what was, during the 1870's a small southern town. Local problems and the usual chicanery in the construction of federal buildings are discussed.

103:10 _____. "General Grant Architecture in Jeopardy." HISTORIC PRESERVATION 22 (January-March 1970): 20-26.

The theme of the article is that America's architectural heritage is a significant part of her history and that the preservation of structures by Mullett is as significant as the preservation of earlier structures. A brief outline of Mullett's career and works are provided with especial emphasis on the St. Louis post office.

104:1 MULLGARDT, LOUIS CHRISTIAN (1866-1942)

Educated Washington University, St. Louis, and practiced in that city from 1893 after working for several firms in Boston. Wrote the introduction to THE ARCHITECTURE AND LANDSCAPE GARDENING...OF THE PANAMA-PACIFIC INTERNATIONAL EXPOSITION, 1915.

Obituary: ARCHITECT AND ENGINEER 148 (January 1942): 41;

148 (February 1942): 42-43.

104:2 ARCHITECT AND ENGINEER. "Who's Who in Pacific Coast Architecture." Vol. 35 (1913): 47-48.

Background and training in Boston, work in Chicago, practice in St. Louis and in San Francisco after 1905 are the major points of this one-page article.

104:3 ARCHITECTURAL FORUM. "Some Recent California Architecture, the Work of Louis Christian Mullgardt." Vol. 33 (1920): 51-54.

The Spanish style of various expositions influenced California architects to use this colonial style for museums and other public buildings and in residential architecture as the president's house at Stanford University.

104:4 ARCHITECTURAL RECORD. "An Architectural Innovator. Some Houses by Louis Christian Mullgardt." Vol. 30 (August 1911): 117-34.

Mullgardt was educated at Harvard and trained under Richardson in Boston and Henry Ives Cobb in Chicago, his work in private practice is individualistic. Although he worked in England, personal reasons brought him back to the States and particularly to California. His residences are sited with care to landscape detailing, a statement backed up by descriptions and illustrations.

104:5 THE BRICKBUILDER. "As He Is Known, Being Brief Sketches of Contemporary Members of the Architectural Profession." Vol. 24 (1915): 179.

"An original designer [with] freshness of vision [and] technical expedients," are the qualities of his work. Born in St. Louis, he traveled for experience and even built in Scotland before returning to the States where his fame in exhibition architecture is well known.

104:6 Clark, Robert Judson. LOUIS CHRISTIAN MULLGARDT, 1866-1942; AN EXHIBITION MARKING THE CENTENNIAL YEAR OF THE ARCHITECT'S BIRTH. Santa Barbara: University of California Art Gallery, 1966. 39 p.

The exhibit was held in the M.H. de Young Memorial Museum, San Francisco, April 5, through May 8, 1966, and David Gebhard wrote the introduction. Mullgardt worked in Chicago, St. Louis, England, and finally San Francisco. His contribution to residential architecture, his position on the Architectural Board of the Panama-Pacific International Exposition, his projects, and stylistic developments are described and illustrated. There is a bibliography of articles by and on Mullgardt and a chronology of buildings and projects.

104:7 _____. "Louis Christian Mullgardt and the Court of Ages." JOURNAL

OF THE SOCIETY OF ARCHITECTURAL HISTORIANS 21 (December 1962): 171-78.

The East Court of the Panama-Pacific International Exposition at San Francisco of 1915 was designed by Mullgardt. The whole was to have been exceedingly rich and elaborate in detailing but economy measures curtailed this over-abundance of ornamentation. The style was Spanish-Renaissance-Moorish-Gothic.

104:8 Croly, H.D. "Some of the California Work of Louis Christian Mullgardt." ARCHITECT AND ENGINEER 36 (March 1914): 47-88.

Original, fresh, novel, and innovative are the adjectives used to describe Mullgardt. His houses, varying in size as well as in historical style, are well illustrated as are his commercial, educational, religious, and exhibition (Panama-Pacific) buildings.

104:9 Newcomb, Rexford. "The Work of Louis Christian Mullgardt in Honolulu." WESTERN ARCHITECT 31 (1922): 123-26.

"Honolulu's character is in essence an epitome of traditionally good Renaissance Europe. . . . " Ten plates support this contention.

104:10 Phillips, W.B. "Recent Work of Louis Christian Mullgardt." AMERICAN ARCHITECT AND BUILDING NEWS 100 (August 9, 1911): 49-53.

A justification of the Spanish Colonial style of Mullgardt with descriptions of a select number of residences.

104:11 Swales, F.S. "Master Draftsmen." PENCIL POINTS 5 (August 1924): 51-57, 65.

Personal reminiscences by Swales who seems to have known Mullgardt more intimately than other architects about whom he wrote. Most of the anecdotes concern construction limitations. All sketches illustrated are free and lively.

105:1 NIMMONS, GEORGE C. (1865-1947)

Worked for Burnham and Root and formed a partnership with William K. Fellows, 1897-1910, thereafter practicing alone until 1933, when he became senior partner in Nimmons, Carr and Wright.

105:2 Carr, George Wallace. "Four Stores for Sears, Demonstrate Trend in Commercial Building Design." ARCHITECTURAL CONCRETE 4, no. 2 (1938): 2-6.

Four Sears at Glendale, California; Highland Park,

Michigan; Baltimore, Maryland; and Chicago, Illinois: all designed in concrete for the sake of economy but providing a "beautiful, appropriate structure." Speed, care in formwork are the practical considerations, but aesthetics, proportion, and "the relation of parts to the whole" were not sacrificed in so doing. The firm made a conscious effort to design against weathering and staining.

105:3 Nimmons, George C. "The New Renaissance in Architecture, As Seen in the Design of Buildings for Mail Order Houses." AMERICAN ARCHITECTURE 134 (August 5, 1928): 141-48.

A glorification of the mail order house and notably those designed by Nimmons for Sears, Roebuck and Co., for eleven million customers. Illustrated are stores at Minneapolis, Los Angeles, Milwaukee, Detroit, Boston, and Memphis.

105:4 Starrett, Theodore. "The Building of a Great Mercantile Plant. ARCHITECTURAL RECORD 19 (April 1906): 265-74.

The plant is Sears, Roebuck and Co., a gigantic mail order city in itself, having a volume of mail comparable to a city the size of Milwaukee (300,000 inhabitants) and sending out forty tons of catalogs per day. The Merchandising Building of extensive proportions was constructed from January 1905 to January 1906. Statistics of materials, space-use, and of the 7000 employees are provided.

105:5 Sturgis, Russell. "Some Recent Warehouses." ARCHITECTURAL RECORD 23 (May 1908): 373-86.

The Carter & Holmes Warehouse, Chicago (discussed pp. 383-84 and illustrated at figure 5) "is very simple in conception - making but little pretense to architectural effect; but the esentials, the obvious necessities of the case are well met."

105:6 Wight, Peter B. "The Ravisloe Country Club, Homewood, Illinois." ARCHITECTURAL RECORD 43 (May 1918): 404-12.

Wight describes this California Spanish Mission style building built twenty-three miles south of Chicago, but does not in any way attempt to critically evaluate it. This is a pity, since Wight was quite an outstanding, if little known, architect, whose opinions would have been valued. Plans and photographs provided.

106:1 PALMER AND HORNBOSTEL (n.d.)

106:2 Schuyler, Montgomery. "A Question of Public Architecture, The Education Building at Albany." ARCHITECTURAL RECORD 26 (December 1909): 389-92.

Schuyler praises the exhibition architecture of the 1893 Chicago World's Fair as being pompous, theatrical, and scenic - the sort of architecture needed at a fair - but he abhors the continued use of the style in architecture of permanence. The Education Building at Albany "is without doubt a brilliant academic study, however irrelevant it may be to any needs of modern man." The building is also of a gigantic scale and has the world's record for the height of a colonnade.

106:3 Western University of Pennsylvania. INSTRUCTIONS AND REGULATIONS OF A COMPETITION FOR THE SELECTION OF AN ARCHITECT. . .FOR THE WESTERN UNIVERSITY OF PENNSYLVANIA. . . PITTSBURGH, PENNSYLVANIA, 1908. 25 p. 7 pl.

Contains the premiated designs by Palmer and Hornbostel selected from sixty-one submissions, in addition to providing the rules and regulations of the competition.

107:1 PEABODY, ROBERT SWAIN (1845-1917)

Educated Harvard, 1866, and Ecole des Beaux Arts, Paris. Trained and apprenticed to Gridley J.F. Bryant and Ware and Van Brunt. Entered into partnership with John Goddard Stearns, Jr. (1843-1917), in 1870, and practiced in the Boston area.

Publications: AMERICAN ARCHITECT'S SKETCHBOOK, 1912; A HOLIDAY STUDY OF CITIES AND PORTS, 1908; NOTE BOOK SKETCHES, 1873.

Obituaries: AMERICAN ARCHITECTURE 112 (1917): 272; 130 (July-September 1926): 181-91; AMERICAN INSTITUTE OF ARCHITECT'S JOURNAL 5 (1917): 517.

107:2 Holden, Wheaton Arnold. "Robert Swain Peabody of Peabody and Stearns in Boston - The Early Years (1870-1886)." Doctoral dissertation, Boston University, 1969. 417 p.

Such a wealth of architectural material exists on the firm that this dissertation limits its scope to the first sixteen years: "1870-74, English Victorian Gothic; 1874-76, Broadening Eclecticism in Commercial Structures; 1876-79, Queen Anne and Georgian; 1879-82, Neo-Renaissance; 1882-86, Triumph of the Eclectic."

107:3 _____. "The Peabody Touch: Peabody and Stearns of Boston, 1870-1917." JOURNAL OF THE SOCIETY OF ARCHITECTURAL HISTORIANS 32 (May 1973): 114-31.

An outstanding architect of the generation after Richardson, Peabody is little remembered today but was admired as man and architect by his own generation. The article describes and illustrates examples of the work of the firm in the varying styles and building types and ends with a checklist of designs, selected competitions entered, and a list of prominent architects who at one time worked for the firm.

107:4 Schweinfurth, J.A. "Robert Swain Peabody, Tower Builder, 1845-1917." AMERICAN ARCHITECTURE 130 (September 5, 1926): 181-91.

The Boston Society of Architects held a dinner in honor of Peabody after forty years of practice. This article is an appreciation of the architect and illustrates some of his work with his partner Stearns.

108:1 PEABODY AND STEARNS (1870-1917)

See also Robert Swain Peabody (1845-1917), and John Goddard Stearns (1843-1917).

The Society for the Preservation of New England Antiquities has seventeen sheets of the W.S. Appleton House and nine of the A.L. Williston House.

108:2 Sturgis, Russell. "Great American Architects Series." ARCHITECTURAL RECORD, supplement to the July 1896 Issue, pp. 53-97.

"The work of this firm is scattered over a great extent of country," and is in any one of many styles: renaissance sometimes with quasi-Romanesque sculpture, Tudor, German Renaissance (Union League Club, Fifth Avenue, New York City) to the eighteenth-century revival classicism of the Machinery Building at the Chicago World's Fair, 1893. Their domestic architecture encompassed an even greater series of styles than their other building types.

109:1 PERKINS, DWIGHT HEALD (1867-1941)

Educated at Massachusetts Institute of Technology where he taught for a short period before practicing in Chicago for Wheelock and Clay and Burnham and Root. Practiced with William K. Fellows and John L. Hamilton from 1894.

Publication: REPORT OF THE SPECIAL PARK COMMISSION TO THE CITY COUNCIL OF CHICAGO ON THE SUBJECT OF A

METROPOLITAN PARK SYSTEM, 1905. Joint author with Fellows and Hamilton of EDUCATIONAL BUILDINGS, 1925.

Obituaries: ARCHITECTURAL FORUM 75 (December 1941): 78; PENCIL POINTS 22 (December 1941): 60; ARCHITECTURAL RECORD 90 (December 1941): 14.

109:2 ARCHITECTURAL FORUM. "Dwight H. Perkins, Father of Today's New School Ideas." Vol. 97 (October 1952): 119-25.

Father of Lawrence Perkins, this early pioneer in modern school design created an uninstitutional architecture of the Prairie style. He forwarded the idea of a one-story school, and of gymnasiums on upper floors for good lighting. The trials and tribulations of practice and a brief survey of his life are included in this well-illustrated monograph.

109:3 THE BRICKBUILDER. "As He Is Known, Being a Brief Sketch of Contemporary Members of the Architectural Profession." Vol. 24 (1915): 46.

Citizen and patriot in addition to being an architect and city planner, interested in park systems and playgrounds. Education and training are mentioned and so too are his innovative school designs.

109:4 Minot, Addison. "The Office of Perkins, Fellows and Hamilton." ARCHITECTURAL FORUM 29 (1918): 61-66.

This Chicago firm designed their own office building which, according to Minot, is contrary to usual practice. Most architects rent space in a commercial building. The workings of the building and the way in which the firm operates administratively and otherwise are described.

109:5 Wight, Peter B. "Public School Architecture at Chicago: The Work of Dwight H. Perkins." ARCHITECTURAL RECORD 27 (June 1910): 495-511.

Chicago's Board of Education chooses its architects with care, according to their ability in planning and designing schools. An innovator in play parks, Perkins has provided well-constructed schools (which, when over three stories in height, are fireproofed by law). Planning, construction, detailing, functional buildings for a specific purpose and straightforward aesthetics instead of applied historic decoration are the qualities of Perkins' work. A sad note to end the article: Perkins had been (apparently falsely) found guilty of extravagance and insubordination and dismissed by the Board!

110:1 PETERSON, FREDERICK R. (1808-85)

Born in Germany.

110:2 Horsley, Carter B. "A New Cooper Union Emerging." THE NEW YORK TIMES, Sunday, November 18, 1973, section 8, p. 1, 10.

The Cooper Union Building is an historic landmark which was modernized in 1973 at a cost of $15 million. The whole inside was completely removed leaving a five-story high shell into which new and expanded accommodations were added. In demolishing the old interiors, interesting construction techniques and detailing of early cast-iron (and later additions) were discussed.

110:3 Huxtable, Ada Louise. "That Was No Lady in Hoopskirts." THE NEW YORK TIMES, Sunday, February 25, 1973, section D, pp. 23, 25.

Cooper Union's main building at Astor Place, New York City, 1853-58 by the Prussian architect Peterson. He used some of the first-known examples of wrought iron beams of I-section in the structure. The building was restored and renovated at the time of the article.

111:1 PLATT, CHARLES ADAMS (1861-1933)

Educated at the New York Academy of Design, studied in France and Italy until setting up practice in 1916.

Publications: ITALIAN GARDENS, 1894. Avery Library, Columbia University, has a letter from Platt to Stanford White, and the Detroit Institute of Arts has nine sheets of the R.A. Alger Jr. House, Grosse Pointe, Michigan.

Obituaries: AMERICAN ARCHITECTURE 143 (November 1933): 125; ARCHITECTURAL FORUM 59 (October 1933): 17.

111:2 Clement, S. Merrell. "Charles A. Platt, an Appreciation." ARCHITECTURAL RECORD 74 (October 1933): 338.

A very general assessment of "the true artist, fired with conviction and endowed with the ability to express it with strength and beauty."

111:3 Cortissoz, Royal. CATALOGUE EXHIBITION OF THE WORKS OF CHARLES ADAMS PLATT. No. 94. New York: American Academy of Arts and Letters, 1938. 34 p. and plates.

Platt was an etcher and painter as well as architect. The catalogue lists and illustrates oil paintings in addition to photographs mainly of college buildings which he designed.

111:4 _____. MONOGRAPH OF THE WORK OF CHARLES ADAMS PLATT. New York: The Architectural Book Publishing Co., 1913. 10 p. and 183 pl.

Platt's talents as architect and landscape gardener as well as artist are discussed by Cortissoz in a seven-page introduction to a survey of thirty-six designs of residences. Each house is illustrated by site plan, general and detailed photographs of exteriors and interiors, including the landscaping of the grounds, working-drawing plans, and elevations and dimensioned working details.

111:5 Croly, Herbert. "The Architectural Work of Charles A. Platt." ARCHITECTURAL RECORD 15 (March 1904): 181-244.

The younger generation of American architects were, at the time of this article, experimenting within narrower limits than earlier generations. Platt fitted into the new mould notably in the design of residence, a major consideration in the article. All are of a colonial or some variety of classicism, some palatial, but others such as that for Platt himself, and another for Croly at the artists colony at Cornish, New Hampshire, are smaller and far more "original."

111:6 _____. "English Renaissance at Its Best: The House of James Parmalee at Washington, D.C." ARCHITECTURAL RECORD 36 (August 1914): 81-97.

"Like all successful works of art, it [the house] is born complete. It was matured on the day that it was finished." Platt apparently always endowed his buildings with a sense of maturity even though he was not copying Georgian architecture in this stylistic residence. The library, for example, has an Adam fireplace, and the freely adapted detailing by the architect of the remainder of the room marries into perfection.

111:7 _____. "Pidgeon Hill, Residence of Meredith Hare, Huntington, Long Island." ARCHITECTURAL RECORD 48 (September 1920): 178-91.

Pidgeon Hill has the intended appearance of an old Long Island farmhouse which has been enlarged for modern living. It fits quite well into the landscape as seen from a series of photographs, in addition to the plans and interior shots.

111:8 _____. "A Waterfront Villa: The House of Russell A. Alger, Jr." ARCHITECTURAL RECORD 36 (December 1914): 481-86.

The article considers residences in relation to water, whether on rivers, oceans, or lakes and the legal problems of such sites. The Alger House is at Grosse Pointe, Michigan, and has been sited high above the shoreline of the lake with the skill of a landscape architect, as only Platt could provide.

111:9 David, A.C. "Cooperative Apartment House in New York." ARCHITECTURAL RECORD 24 (July 1908): 1-18.

The general idea of cooperative buildings and their costs are enumerated prior to a discussion of the studio building at 66th Street and Lexington Avenue. Numerous illustrations of apartments of varying types show a lavish way of life with double-story studio spaces usually measuring about twenty-four by twenty-eight feet.

111:10 Howe, Samuel. "The Garden Work of Charles Adams Platt." AMERICAN ARCHITECTURE 101 (May 1, 1912): 198-201.

Platt's contribution was the humanization of the landscape even though he was not too ready to discuss his methods.

111:11 Illinois University. THE LIBRARY BUILDING.... Urbana: University of Illinois Press, 1929. 16 p.

Dedicated on October 18, 1929, the library was designed in 1921, in the Georgian style, a style which was chosen because it had "withstood the test of time." The reinforced concrete stacks area was constructed first as a bracing for the whole building. The library was planned to be easily extended, as expansion necessitated.

111:12 Lay, Charles Downing. "An Interview with Charles Adams Platt." LANDSCAPE ARCHITECTURE 2 (1911-12): 127-31.

"He is said to have entered architecture through the garden gate," of Italian landscape architecture. Platt's method of evolving a program of client's needs resulted from interviews, client's needs, their particular site, costs, through to the finalized design which was the result of a marriage between architecture and the surrounding landscape.

111:13 Smith, Hugh A. THE UNIVERSITY OF ROCHESTER: A STORY OF EXPANSION AND ITS BACKGROUND. Rochester, N.Y.: University of Rochester, 1930. 30 p.

George Eastman contributed $2-1/2 million to build a new the Men's College of Rochester on eighty-seven acres of Genesee River Valley land. Academic buildings of the main quadrangle are in the Greek Revival style and those of the lower campus in the Georgian Colonial. Many buildings are illustrated including an art gallery for community and university, and the School of Medicine.

111:14 Tilton, Leon Deming, and O'Donnell, Thomas E. HISTORY OF THE GROWTH AND DEVELOPMENT OF THE CAMPUS OF THE UNIVERSITY OF ILLINOIS. Urbana, Ill.: University of Illinois Press, 1930. 245 p.

Plans of the university's development from 1872 are illustrated in addition to all subsequent plans by various local and nationally famed architects, including a study of the ultimate development by Platt, who was architect of numerous halls on the campus in the Georgian style. A tabulated list of buildings, year of completion, cost, and name of the architects is provided. So too are relevant letters between architects and administrators in relation to the growth of the campus.

112:1 POLK, WILLIS JEFFERSON (1867-1924)

Studied in France, 1900-02, thereafter worked for Daniel H. Burnham in Chicago, returning to his native San Francisco to begin practice in 1904.

San Mateo County Historical Association has eighty-nine sheets of three residential projects.

Obituary: AMERICAN ARCHITECTURE 126 (November 5, 1924): 422 (written by Bernard Maybeck).

112:2 Dills, Keith W. "The Hallidie Building." JOURNAL OF THE SOCIETY OF ARCHITECTURAL HISTORIANS 30 (December 1971): 323-29.

The article lists earlier European and American examples of the glass curtain wall, notably Beman's Studebaker Building, Chicago, 1895, or John Elliot's May Company Department Store, Cleveland, 1899. Polk is discussed in relation to architects of the California School and his contribution is assessed. The Hallidie Building is considered by Dills to be San Francisco's most famous building of the present century even though the building over the years has been both reviled and praised.

112:3 Price, C. Matlack. "Notes on the Varied Work of Willis Polk." ARCHITECTURAL RECORD 34 (December 1913): 566-83.

"We find Willis Polk the designer of Banks, Churches, Country Houses, Power Plants, Stables and Gardens, with a blithe facility which must be enviously admired by many less versatile." Various designs are illustrated and briefly mentioned to forward this viewpoint.

112:4 Scott, MacDonald W. "A Glass-Front Building." ARCHITECTURAL RE-

CORD 44 (October 1918): 381-84.

The Hallidie Building is briefly described and illustrated with a detailed drawing of the glass and metal facade in relation to the reinforced concrete structure.

112:5 Solon, Leon V. "The Residence of Mrs. Andrew Welch, San Francisco, California." ARCHITECTURAL RECORD 45 (March 1919): 194-209.

The architecture of Spain has been literally adapted to this particular residence, where architect and sculptor have worked in close association. "Climatic conditions have always been a prime and controlling factor in architectural design," and, apparently, noticeably so in this row house type, incorporating a courtyard.

113:1 POND AND POND (Partnership 1886-1926)

Irving Kane Pond (1857-1939). Degree in Civil Engineering, University of Michigan. Worked for Jenny in Chicago and practiced with his brother, Allen Bartlit Pond, (1858-1929) after 1886 and until 1926. Thereafter, I.K. Pond associated with a number of different architects.

Irving K. Pond published BIG TOP RHYTHMS, A STUDY OF LIFE AND ART, 1937; THE MEANING OF ARCHITECTURE, 1918; A STRANGE FELLOW AND OTHER CLUB PAPERS, 1938.

National Archives, Washington, has twenty-four sheets of the United States Post Office, Kankakee, Illinois.

Obituary of Allen B. Pond: AMERICAN ARCHITECTURE 135 (April 20, 1929): 534; of Irving K. Pond: MICHIGAN SOCIETY OF ARCHITECTS WEEKLY BULLETIN 13 (October 10, 1939): 3; ARCHITECTURAL RECORD 86 (October 1939): 12; THE OCTAGON 11 (November 1939): 12.

113:2 Pond, Irving K. "The Life of Architecture." ARCHITECTURAL RECORD 18 (August 1905): 146-60.

Not intended to be a survey of the firm's work but rather a sampling to illustrate the philosophy of the firm that architecture is the expression of life; a rationalistic rather than stylistic approach. "Architecture is a personal art. . . shown in the composing and balancing of masses of solid and void, ornament and surface, color and texture, line and form which make a work of architecture instinct with life. . . ."

113:3 ______. "The [New York] Telephone Exchange." ARCHITECTURAL RECORD 24 (October 1908): 259-76.

A telephone exchange is not a building type to excite the profession or the public, it is nevertheless one that has to be carefully considered. Structure and fire-proofing are important in a building storing wires and engineering equipment in addition to catering to telephone operators.

113:4 Sturgis, Russell. "A Chicago Factory. The Kent Building." ARCHITECTURAL RECORD 17 (January 1905): 66-67.

A column and a half criticism of a commercial building in Chicago, which Sturgis considers simple and dignified. "Historical nor ethnological in its genesis, because it has grown up from a momentary need."

113:5 _____. "Factories and Warehouses." ARCHITECTURAL RECORD 19 (May 1906): 369-75.

Utilitarian and economically functional, the Chicago Telephone Building has a few pieces of applied decoration which do not seem to be justifiable according to Russell Sturgis.

114:1 **POPE, JOHN RUSSELL (1874-1937)**

Educated City College of New York, Columbia University, the American Academy in Rome, and the Ecole des Beaux Arts. Worked for Bruce Price until he set up practice for himself. National Archives, Washington, D.C., has 133 sheets of The National Archives Building.

Obituaries: AMERICAN ARCHITECT AND BUILDING NEWS 151 (September 3, 1937): 270; ARCHITECTURAL FORUM 67 (October 1937): 18; ARCHITECTURAL RECORD 82 (October 1937): 37; AMERICAN ARCHITECTURE 151 (October 1937): 87; ROYAL INSTITUTE OF BRITISH ARCHITECTS' JOURNAL 45 (November 22, 1937): 102; AMERICAN INSTITUTE OF IRANIAN ART AND ARCHAEOLOGY BULLETIN 5 (June 1937): 56 (by Arthur Upham Pope).

114:2 Boyd, John Taylor. "The Residence of Honorable Henry White, Washington, D.C." ARCHITECTURAL RECORD 42 (November 1917): 402-19.

White was former Ambassador to France. "Everything about Mr. White's residence expresses its fitness for its purpose of a diplomat's residence." Built on a high ridge, this Georgian design is described and illustrated with numerous interiors and plans.

114:3 Brown, Glenn. "The Lincoln Memorial in Washington, D.C." AMERICAN ARCHITECTURE 118 (October 20, 1920): 489-99, 503-6; 118

(October 27, 1920): 523-33.

The whole question of siting, legislation, and attitudes of the Fine Arts Commission are discussed in relation to the design of Pope on the North Capitol Street axis site and the Bacon design (see) which was built.

114:4 Childs, Marquis W. "Mr. Pope's Memorial." MAGAZINE OF ART 30 (April 1937): 200-202.

The Jefferson Memorial, for Washington's Tidal Basin, is considered by the author as another Victorian gewgaw, totally empty of significance. The article is also a diatribe against a congressman from New York City, a member of Tammany Hall and a real estate appraiser. What on earth would Jefferson's view have been concerning the Memorial?

114:5 Croly, Herbert. "A New Use of Old Forms. Two Houses by John Russell Pope." ARCHITECTURAL RECORD 17 (April 1905): 271-93.

In praise of flexibility, initiative, and independence derived from Beaux Arts training and wide European travel, in the design of two houses. Both houses are in the Beaux Arts style with a suggestion of the Italianate. Dignity, propriety, and acoustics, from a technical viewpoint, are the qualities of Pope's architecture as seen by his critic.

114:6 ______. "Recent Works of John Russell Pope." ARCHITECTURAL RECORD 29 (June 1911): 441-511.

Articles on Pope's residential architecture are always popular. Thus this lengthy well-illustrated essay emphasizes Pope's reliance upon McKim, but also shows how he caters to the tremendous variety in taste in this country. Added to that is his versatility and adventurousness which is not to be confused with superficial eclecticism. Rural residences predominate in a variety of historic styles reflective of the attitudes of his clients, but urban residences are also discussed.

114:7 Grief, James. "New Sculpture Halls for the National Gallery." (Tate Gallery, England). LONDON STUDIO 14 (September 1937): 139-41.

The tremendous scale, even in the details such as "screen-columns," tend to miniaturize even the most gigantic sculptures which the galleries of the Tate were designed to contain.

114:8 Higgins, Daniel P. "Business and Management in the practice of Architecture." AMERICAN ARCHITECTURE 133 (April 20, 1928): 491-502.

Subtitled "Their Application in Coordinating Office and Field Forces in the Development of the Estate of Mrs.

Marshall Field," the article discusses the emphasis of this approach by McKim upon Pope. Budgets, unit price records, and a general high level competence in organization were all brought into play in this particular project of such a large estate at Lloyd Neck, Huntington, Long Island. The article is accompanied by numerous interior and exterior preliminary sketches by Otto R. Eggers.

114:9 Hooper, Parker Morse. "Office Procedure. Office Manual of John Russell Pope." ARCHITECTURAL RECORD 69 (February 1931): 177-82; 69 (March 1931): 261-72; 69 (April 1931): 359-62.

Architecture as a business cannot be divorced from aesthetic considerations. Pope, as a well-known aesthetician, combines also the qualities of efficiency in office organization. The chain of command is diagrammed and explained in detail, providing checklists of items related to trades and thus to working drawings as a communication aid. An actual residence is provided as an example in the third article as the design develops from preliminary sketch to square footage and cost.

114:10 Hudnut, Joseph. "The Last of the Romans: Comment on the Building of the National Gallery of Art." MAGAZINE OF ART 34 (April 1941): 169-73.

Since Thomas Jefferson, "we have been trying to create an American Architecture by the imitation of European masterpieces. Today after ten thousand experiments, the futility of this process is not yet amply demonstrated; one more effort was needed, it appears, if only to prove the hardiness of the neo-classic thesis," and that "one more effort" was Pope's National Gallery, Washington. The article is a condemnation of classical prototypes for building uses of the twentieth century. Hudnut analyzes the museum as a building. Surely it is "not an opportunity merely for the virtuosity of architects."

114:11 _____. "Twilight of the Gods." MAGAZINE OF ART 30 (August 1937): 480-84, 522-24.

"No quality in architecture is more treacherous than symbolism." The article concerns the Jefferson Memorial and the extended layout of Washington emphasizing that, "Conspicuous and expensive discomfort is, for most people, the equivalent of beauty in public buildings....A deeper and truer expressiveness is felt everywhere in America, and must soon be sovereign in Washington. Our architects, if there are to be architects - will attend that quiet imperious voice. The Gods hear it and tremble."

114:12 Kimball, Fiske. "John Russell Pope, 1874-1937." AMERICAN ARCHITECTURE 151 (October 1937): 87.

An obituary of an architect whose "mind and heart were directed to an activity purely artistic."

114:13 Paris, W. Franklyn. "John Russell Pope." AMERICAN SOCIETY LEGION OF HONOR MAGAZINE 22 (Summer 1951): 119-34.

His attitudes, architecture, and achievements were based upon a classical education in Rome and practice in that mode on returning to the United States. The article discusses mainly his achievements in the classical idiom, most notably mausolea and memorials. A similar article was published by Paris in THE HALL OF AMERICAN ARTISTS, vol. 6, 1951.

114:14 Roosevelt Memorial Association. PLAN AND DESIGN FOR THE ROOSEVELT MEMORIAL. New York: Pynson Printer, 1925. 19 p.

"At the center of an island of white granite...a living shaft of water rises....From the base of the fountain symbolical ships carry the message of Roosevelt's life to the four corners of the compass." There are plates by Pope drawn by Otto R. Eggers and submitted to the Congress and approved by the President.

114:15 Saylor, Henry Hodgman. THE NATIONAL GALLERY OF ART, WASHINGTON, D.C. New York: Saylor, 1941. 16 p.

Architectural philosophy, gallery space, scale, lighting, and all services, including air conditioning, are described and illustrated with a plan.

114:16 Smith, Howard Dwight. "The Relation of the House to the Landscape Illustrated by Examples of the Work of John Russell Pope." AMERICAN ARCHITECTURE 113 (April 3, 1918): 397-404.

Landscape is the setting for architecture, as a backdrop for a home. Historic precedents are given as an introduction to the work of Pope for one particular client.

114:17 _____. "The Residence of Allan S. Lehman, Tarrytown, New York." ARCHITECTURAL RECORD 44 (December 1918): 483-501.

The reason for the Tudor style in America: "The Problems to be met and solved in England are probably more nearly similar to our own than are any others." Philanglicism demands the Tudor and other English styles! Boldness of design, detailed surface textures, and the landscape setting all created the atmosphere of a sixteenth-century residence. It "is a decided step forward in the progress of a peaceful art of domestic architecture in America." Numerous interior and exterior views, plus plans are provided.

114:18 Swales, F.S. "Master Draftsmen, 8: John Russell Pope." PENCIL POINTS 5 (December 1924): 64-80, 90.

Even as a student Pope's draftsmanship was scholarly in illustrating his severely classical design which won him two architectural prizes. The watercolor sketches, measured sketches, and drawings are mainly from his European sketchbook although there are one or two of his own designs including that for a bank which won him two student prizes.

114:19 Wood, W.B. "A House of Unusual Architectural Merit: The Hill Residence, Washington, D.C." THE BRICKBUILDER 22 (1913): 27-32.

Some buildings are more charming because they cater to humans, while other pieces may be more architecturally correct. Pope combines both qualities according to Wood in this Washington residence. It is well illustrated with plans, internal and external elevations, and photographs.

115:1 POST, GEORGE BROWNE (1837-1913)

Education in engineering at New York University and worked for R.M. Hunt. Practiced from 1860 with Charles D. Gambrill and in 1867, after the Civil War, under his own name.

New York Historical Society has drawings of thirty-two projects (additional drawings and acount book have recently been given) and Princeton University has seven sheets of Reunion Hall, Princeton. New York Historical Society also has one sheet of a church by Post and Gambrill.

Obituaries: AMERICAN ARCHITECTURE 104 (December 3, 1913): 3; ARCHITECTURAL RECORD 35 (January 1914): 94-96 (by Montgomery Schuyler); ROYAL INSTITUTE OF BRITISH ARCHITECTS' JOURNAL 21 (1913-14): 107; NEW INTERNATIONAL YEARBOOK, 1913, p. 568.

115:2 Hastings, Thomas. COMMEMORATIVE TRIBUTES TO GEORGE BROWNE POST. New York: American Academy of Arts and Letters, Proceedings of the Academy, vol. 10, no. 17, 1922. Pp. 11-16.

"Mr. Post was perhaps the most active and successful architect in finding a solution which would best meet the construction difficulties." An innovator and pioneer in architecture and engineering.

115:3 Mikkesen, Michael A. "The Wisconsin State Capitol, Madison, Wisconsin." ARCHITECTURAL RECORD 42 (September 1917): 194-233.

The state of Wisconsin is briefly described in relation to Madison where the earlier Capitol burned in 1904. Five architectural firms were invited to submit designs, and the winner's scheme was built from 1907 to 1917. "In some of its features, it is undoubtedly the most beautiful public building in America. Sumptuous after the Roman Renaissance manner, yet of an economy of means . . . good taste . . . in plan a daring and unusual solution." Numerous photographs of interiors, external details, and plan.

115:4 Paris, W. Franklyn. "George B. Post." NEW YORK UNIVERSITY HALL OF AMERICAN ARTISTS 10 (1955): 33-46.

Background, contribution, works, honors, and achievements of this architect are listed.

115:5 Post, George B. THE COLLEGE OF THE CITY OF NEW YORK. New York. 190 p. 10 pl.

The ten plates include plan, aerial and other perspectives by the office of Post for halls at the college in a freely adapted, secular medieval style of architecture.

115:6 Post, J.O. RECENT AND CURRENT WORK OF GEORGE BROWNE POST. New York: The Harwell-Evans Co., 1909. 10 p.

Ten pages of description cover the Wisconsin State Capitol, and college buildings for City College, New York. Additionally, there are some five plates on a selection of the firm's work, with interiors and plans.

115:7 Schuyler, Montgomery. "The New York Stock Exchange." ARCHITECTURAL RECORD 12 (September 1902): 413-20.

"Decidedly the most important and perhaps the most interesting piece of construction in New York is. . . ." Harmoniously arranged and with a large central hall lighted from both sides, the colonnaded screen provides a Roman facade as well as a functional way of dividing and supporting huge areas of glass window. The pediment and its sculptures by J.Q.A. Ward are equally praised.

115:8 Stuart, Percy C. "The New York Stock Exchange." ARCHITECTURAL RECORD 11 (July 1901): 525-52.

An historic background to the New York Stock Exchange precedes considerations of foundations, safe deposit vault, services such as lighting and ventilation, architectural expression of the interiors, planning, and facade treatment. Plans, sections, and elevations are provided, and on pp. 553-55 there is a supplemental technical report on "The Builder's Responsibility for the construction of the New York Stock Exchange."

115:9 Sturgis, Russell. "Facade of the New York Stock Exchange." ARCHITECTURAL RECORD 16 (November 1904): 464-82.

Sturgis questions the propriety of a classical facade for the Stock Exchange, but having accepted that a colonnade of Corinthian columns supporting a pediment has been utilized by the architect, praises the bold three-dimensional pedimental sculptures by J.Q.A. Ward.

115:10 _____. "Great American Architects Series." ARCHITECTURAL RECORD (Supplement), May 1895, pp. 1-111.

The article begins with a biographical sketch of Post's life, before evaluating his major contributions. "He, indeed, is one of the two or three [architects] for whom is claimed something of the inception of the steel frame construction which has made lofty buildings practicable." Most of the structures illustrated and discussed are high-rise. When Post designed other structures such as the extensive Vanderbilt Mansion, southwest corner Fifth Avenue and 57th Street, which was as elaborate, in its early French Renaissance and Louis XVI style, he was as decorative as in the skyscrapers.

115:11 Wagner, W. Sydney. "The Hotel Statler in Detroit." ARCHITECTURAL RECORD 37 (April 1915): 320-39.

Comfort and convenience of guests, flexibility, location and arrangement of services, and economy of materials and constructure are aspects of this Adam-Italianate Hotel being discussed. Plans and details of the building accompany a detailed description.

115:12 Warner, Ralph F. "A Wage Earners' Community Development at Beloit, Wisconsin." AMERICAN ARCHITECTURE 113 (May 22, 1918): 657-66.

This is company housing for 1000 employees. A site plan of fifty acres is provided in addition to the wide variety of house plans accompanying pen and ink perspectives of residences constructed mainly of wood with Mansard or Swiss chalet roofs, and with an occasional one of stucco.

115:13 Weisman, Winston. "The Commercial Architecture of George B. Post." JOURNAL OF THE SOCIETY OF ARCHITECTURAL HISTORIANS 31 (October 1972): 176-203.

Post is viewed in the context of his period and the article is an assessment of his contribution, countering Hitchcock's published remarks inferring Post's insignificance. Weismann begins with the Equitable Life Assurance Co. Building of 1868-70, "the first commercial building to be designed with the elevator in mind" and thus the first skyscraper. In the Long Island Historical Society Building, 1878-79, an Albertian-Schinkelesque structure, Weisman sees a prototype for the Boston Public Library by McKim, Mead and White. Post's engineering ability is seen at Chicago, 1893, and the essay concludes with a consideration of skyscrapers and bank buildings. There are two appendices listing drawings of projects held by the Map and Print Room of the New York Historical Society.

115:14 ______. "New York and the Problem of the First Skyscraper." JOURNAL OF THE SOCIETY OF ARCHITECTURAL HISTORIANS 12 (March 1953): 13-21.

See Richard M. Hunt.

115:15 Willauer, Arthur Ebbs. "A College of the City of New York." AMERICAN ARCHITECT AND BUILDING NEWS 93 (May 13, 1908): 155-60; 93 (May 20, 1908): 163-68.

"Perhaps there is no class of building which so appeals to men as that devoted to higher education," and in these particular buildings "Post may be said to have been successful." A history of the college and a comparative analysis of it and those colleges at Oxford and Cambridge provide subject matter for the text.

116:1 POTTER, EDWARD TUCKERMAN (1831-1904)

Educated Union College and apprenticed to Richard Upjohn until opening his own office.

Publications: THE AERATION OF CITIES AND THEIR BUILDINGS, 1871; NOTES RELATING TO CONCENTRATED RESIDENCES IN VARIOUS COUNTRIES, 1888; URBAN HOUSING IN NEW YORK, 1904; WORLD PICTURES IN CAPITALS, 1869.

Avery Library, Columbia University, has memorabilia, ledger, cash book, and photographs.

Obituary: AMERICAN ARCHITECT AND BUILDING NEWS 86 (1904): 106.

Sarah Landau is working toward a doctoral dissertation at New York University on E.T. and W.A. Potter.

116:2 Bloor, A.J. "The Late Edward T. Potter." AMERICAN ARCHITECT AND BUILDING NEWS 87 (January 21, 1905): 21-22.

This is a lengthy quotation of an obituary in THE NEW

YORK TRIBUNE by Bloor. It is essentially concerned with Potter's study, research, and recommendations regarding tenement houses in New York City.

116:3 _____. "The Late E.T. Potter's Varied Activities." ARCHITECTS AND BUILDERS' MAGAZINE (New Series) 6 (February 1905): 237-38.

Bloor wrote this letter explaining Potter's work including his humanitarian buildings, which had apparently been overlooked in an earlier obituary of the magazine.

116:4 Chafee, Richard. "Edward Tuckerman Potter and Samuel L. Clemens (Mark Twain)." M.A. thesis, Yale University, 1963. 110 p.

Rewritten and copyrighted in 1966, Avery Library, Columbia University, New York City, has a copy of this thesis. Chapter headings include: 1. Mark Twain as a Client, 2. Edward Tuckerman Potter, Richard Upjohn and Churches, 3. Houses by E.T. Potter, 4. Epilogue. There is also a catalogue raisonne.

116:5 Potter, Frank Hunter. THE ALONZO POTTER FAMILY. Concord, N.H.: Rumford Press, 1923. Pp. 29-31.

Quotes Schuyler in describing E.T. Potter as an "athlete of the Gothic Revival" style in its most Victorian phase, but equally a lover of music. Interested in functional design, he seems to have concerned himself with the portable house, in addition to Darwinian theories, prison reform, and movies.

116:6 Tunnard, Christopher. "A Deviation by the Brothers Potter." ARCHITECTURAL REVIEW 103 (February 1948): 67.

E.T. Potter designed Memorial Hall at Union College in the Ruskinian Venetian Gothic Revival style, c. 1856. It fitted into the Joseph Ramee plan of 1812, but was equally complemented by W.A. Potter's proposed though unexecuted additional wings.

117:1 POTTER, WILLIAM APPLETON (1842-1909)

Educated Union College and practiced with Robert H. Robertson (see) in New York City.

Princeton University Department of Buildings and Grounds has five sheets of Alexander Hall and ten of Ryne Administration Building.

Sarah Landau is working toward a doctoral dissertation at New York University on E.T. and W.A. Potter.

117:2 Potter, Frank Hunter. THE ALONOZO POTTER FAMILY. Concord, N.H.:

Rumford Press, 1923. Pp. 58-60.

Mentions early buildings and Potter's position as Supervising Architect to the Treasury Department under Grant's second administration when scandal and corruption was rife. Thereafter Potter again practiced architecture privately entering the competition for the Cathedral of St. John the Divine, New York City, but was forced to disqualify himself for fear of accusations of nepotism since his brother was Bishop of New York.

117:3 Schuyler, Montgomery. "The Work of William Appleton Potter." ARCHITECTURAL RECORD 26 (September 1909): 176-96.

Potter's work in the High Victorian Gothic, Romanesque Revival, Shingle style and Queen Anne variations verging on the classical are analyzed and criticized, but the building types discussed are almost wholly limited to religious, collegiate, and domestic types.

117:4 Tunnard, Christopher. "A Deviation by the Brothers Potter." ARCHITECTURAL REVIEW 103 (February 1948): 67.

Joseph Ramee planned Union College, Schenectady, in 1812; E.T. Potter added Memorial Hall in the Venetian Gothic Revival style, in 1856, and W.A. Potter, developing from English architects William Burges and Henry Vaughan, added Washburn Hall, 1885, and proposed additional wings (perspective illustration) which were not executed.

117:5 Wodehouse, Lawrence. "William Appleton Potter, Principal Pasticheur of Henry Hobson Richardson." JOURNAL OF THE SOCIETY OF ARCHITECTURAL HISTORIANS 32 (May 1973): 175-92.

Some architects who followed Richardson, such as Sullivan and Wright, captured the spirit of his work. Others, such as Potter, merely copied Richardson, and thus could be termed "pasticheurs." Potter was well-connected socially, and because of this and his political affiliations to the Republican party became Supervising Architect of the Treasury Department. Potter developed away from Richardson into a slightly classical vein, paralleling and possibly influencing McKim, Mead and White. However, having begun in the High Victorian Gothic, he returned to a collegiate Gothic re-revival with Tudor flourishes at the end of the century.

118:1 PRICE, BRUCE (1843-1903)

Worked for Niemsee and Nelson. Studied in Paris and opened an office at Wilkes-Barre, Pennsylvania, 1873, and from 1877, in New York City.

Contributed to HOMES IN CITY AND COUNTRY, 1893.

National Archives, Washington, has drawings of seven projects by Bruce Price, DeSibour and John Russell Pope.

Obituaries: AMERICAN ARCHITECT AND BUILDING NEWS 80 (1903): 81; THE BRICKBUILDER 12 (June 1903); THE INLAND ARCHITECT AND NEWS RECORD 41 (June 1903); ARCHITECT AND BUILDERS JOURNAL 4 (July 1903); THE WESTERN ARCHITECT 2 (June 1903): 18; AMERICAN INSTITUTE OF ARCHITECTS' QUARTERLY BULLETIN 4 (July 1903): 96-97.

118:2 THE BRICKBUILDER. "Bruce Price, 1845-1903." Vol. 12 (1903): 112.

Price worked in the architectural office of Niernsee and Nelson after self-education, but ultimately became a well-known architect in New York and throughout New England with structures at Yale University. He died in Paris, France.

118:3 THE KING MODEL DWELLINGS. New York: S. Leos, 1891. 23 p.

Price was one of four firms of architects who designed houses at 138 and 139th Streets between Seventh and Eighth Avenues, New York City, for David H. King, Jr. This brochure has a sketch on the cover by B.L Fenner of McKim, Mead and White and five sketches of interiors of the houses by N. Hutchins for James Lord Brown. (There are two other sketches, house plans, and a plan of the area). The brochure is essentially an advertisement stating the advantages of the buildings, their disposition, attraction, terms of purchase, planning, and "novel features."

118:4 Sturgis, Russell. "Great American Architects Series." ARCHITECTURAL RECORD, Supplement to the June 1899 issue, pp. 1-112.

An architect who had "an equal regard for the refinements of a Greek order, for the logical sincerity of Gothic design, and for the picturesque dash of the French Renaissance." Sturgis appreciates the four-sided unity in architectural design of the American Surety Building on the southeast corner of Broadway and Pine Street, New York City, and the same quality in all of the tall structures by Price. His work at Yale and the Chateau Frontenac, Quebec, Canada, illustrate different stylistic trends, but Price's most original contribution is in his residential architecture in shingles and boulders.

119:1 PURCELL, WILLIAM GRAY (1880- ?)

See also Purcell and Elmslie.

Purcell was educated at Cornell University, 1899, and later set up a partnership with a classmate, George Feick, 1906-09. Elmslie was taken into the partnership in 1909 and Feick dropped out in 1913. The firm was known as Purcell, Feick and Elmslie, 1909-1913. Earlier he worked for Adler and Sullivan and later for Sullivan as chief draftsman. Burnham Library has five sheets of the Charles A. Purcell House, River Forest, Illinois, and fifteen sheets of the Third Church of Christ Scientist, Portland, Oregon.

120:1 PURCELL AND ELMSLIE (Partnership 1909-21)

See also William Gray Purcell (1880- ?) and George Grant Elmslie (1871-1952).

Purcell has written several articles including one on Sullivan, another on Viollet Le Duc, and there is a colloquy between Ralph Waldo Emerson and Purcell. Purcell and Elmslie published THE AMERICAN RENAISSANCE, 1912.

Burnham Library, Chicago, has drawings of thirty-two projects, additionally, one project of the Edison Shop, San Francisco, by Purcell and Elmslie with Walter H. Ratcliffe, Jr., six projects by Purcell, six projects by Purcell and Feick, and twenty-five projects of Purcell, Feick and Elmslie.

120:2 Architectural Forum. "Early Modern in the Middle West." ARCHITECTURAL FORUM 71 (Supplement, December 1931): 12-13.

Eight of their buildings are illustrated to show the change of direction toward an American modern architecture. Eclecticism is behind us!

120:3 Gebhard, David. "A Guide to the Architecture of Purcell and Elmslie." THE PRAIRIE SCHOOL REVIEW 2 (First Quarter, 1965.)

Catalogue raisonne of sixty-five of their works, including photographs, plans, and drawings.

120:4 _____. A GUIDE TO THE EXISTING BUILDINGS OF PURCELL AND ELMSLIE, 1910-1920. Rosewell, N.Mex.: Rosewell Museum and Art Center, 1960. Unpaged.

Two hundred copies of this report were published. Therein, Gebhard wrote a three-page essay and produced a directory of Purcell and Elmslie's buildings standing in 1960, eighty-six in all. These buildings are also listed by type, state, and town.

120:5 _____. "Purcell and Elmslie, Architects." THE PRAIRIE SCHOOL REVIEW 2 (First Quarter, 1965): 5-15.

Their work in relation to that of the Viennese Secessionist Movement, Louis Sullivan, and Frank Lloyd Wright. Portraits, plans, elevations, sketches, and photographs.

120:6 _____. "William Gray Purcell and George Grant Elmslie and the Early Progressive Movement in American Architecture from 1900 to 1920." Doctoral dissertation, University of Minnesota, 1957. 471 p.

The research for this dissertation is based upon the firm's records and correspondence, conversations with Elmsie up to 1952 and Purcell to 1957, when the dissertation was written. Their work is linked to Sullivan, the arts and crafts movement, and the California school, resulting in open planning in domestic work and functionalism and decoration in the commercial field. Avery Library, Columbia University, has a microfilm copy.

120:7 Gebhard, David, ed. "The Work of Purcell and Elmslie." THE WESTERN ARCHITECT, January 1913, January 1915, and July 1915. Reprinted as one volume by The Prairie School Press, Park Forest, Ill., 1965. 92 p. Illus.

The three issues of THE WESTERN ARCHITECT were devoted to the work of Purcell and Elmslie, centered at Minneapolis, following closely in the tradition of Louis Sullivan and on many occasions paralleling the work of Wright. Purcell and Elmslie were responsible for the writing and layout of the issues; Gebhard adds notes, captions, and an introduction.

121:1 **REED AND STEM (Partnership 1884-1911)**

Charles Reed (d.1911) and Allen H. Stem (1856-1931). A.H. Stem practiced with (his father?), J.H. Stem, 1878-84, and with Reed, 1884-1911. They were essentially railroad architects sometimes in association with Warren and Wetmore (see).

121:2 Eberlein, Harold D. "Recent Railway Stations in American Cities." ARCHITECTURAL RECORD 36 (August 1914): 98-121.

See same article under Warren and Wetmore.

122:1 **REID, JOHN, JR. (n.d.)**

122:2 Henderson, V.H. "The Phi Delta Theta Chapter House at the University of California." ARCHITECTURAL RECORD 43 (May 1918): 413-19.

Football players choose this fraternity house to be used as their training quarters prior to the big game because "they regarded it as far more conveniently and agreeably arranged for student life than any other of the houses possessed by the seventy different fraternities and houseclubs at the University of California." Plans, interior and exterior photographs provided.

122:3 Morrow, I.F. "The Work of John Reid, Jr." ARCHITECT AND ENGINEER 60 (February 1920): 43-85.

"Mr. Reid is one of the architects of French training who has zealously eschewed the easy French superficiality, and who exemplifies this trait of order." Reid apparently combined form and elements in his architecture. "The union of both capacities to the fullest degree is reserved for real genius." Numerous examples of his work in all styles are illustrated and some briefly mentioned.

123:1 RENWICK, JAMES, JR. (1818-95)

Educated Columbia College, began practice in 1843, and joined partnership with Joseph Sands in the 1870's. Sands died in 1880, and was replaced by James L. Aspinwall (1854-1936). Renwick's nephew, William W. (1864-1933), joined the firm known as Renwick, Aspinwall and Renwick. Later the partnership of Aspinwall, Renwick and Russell was formed. Other combinations consisted of Renwick (James), Aspinwall and Guard; Renwick, Aspinwall, and Tucker; Renwick, Aspinwall, and Owen; and a very early association, Renwick, Auchmuty, and Sands (Vassar College, 1860).

Avery Library, Columbia University, has thirty-three drawings and nineteen sketches of St. Patrick's Cathedral, New York City, three sheets of Columbia University; Smithsonian Institute, two sheets; Burnham Library, Chicago, nine sheets of the Second Presbyterian Church, Chicago.

Obituary: AMERICAN ARCHITECT AND BUILDING NEWS 48 (1895): 125. Effingham P. Humphrey submitted a master's thesis at New York University in 1942 on "The Churches of James Renwick, Jr."

123:2 Aspinwall, J. Lawrence. "'Applegarth' Residence of Charles W. Wetmore, Esq., Center Island, Oyster Bay, Long Island." ARCHITECTURAL RECORD 13 (March 1903): 279-91.

Tudor in style but "spacious, warm and dignified," the house is described in detail with plan, exterior and interior photographs.

123:3 Conroy, Sarah Booth. "The Restoration of James Renwick." POTOMAC

(THE WASHINGTON POST), January 30, 1972, p. 9 ff.

123:4 Huxtable, Ada Louise. "There but for the Grace . . ." THE NEW YORK TIMES, Sunday, February 17, 1974, section 2, p. 29.

Renwick built Grace Church, New York City, 1843-46, and added clergy houses and other accommodations in the 1880's. They faced on to 4th Avenue at the rear of the church. The group is a total entity in the Gothic Revival style, but the need for additional and change-of-use facilities has led the church toward the inevitable idea of demolition of part of the 4th Avenue buildings. To preserve and refurbish them would be expensive but not as expensive as the proposed new structures at present day costs.

123:5 _____. "Renwick Gallery Wins Survival Battle." THE NEW YORK TIMES, January 28, 1972, p. 24.

Scheduled for demolition in 1958, the Corcoran Gallery, Washington, D.C., commissioned in 1858 and opened as a gallery in 1871, has been restored at a cost of $2.8 million. The spirit of Renwick's day and age seems to have been recaptured - "a jewel setting for the arts of design."

123:6 McKenna, Rosalie Thorne. "James Renwick, Jr., and the Second Empire Style in the United States." MAGAZINE OF ART 44 (March 1951): 97-101.

The General Grant style as it was known in the United States began with the John A.C. Gray House, Newport, Rhode Island, 1857, by Vaux and Withers, but the style soon caught the imagination of Renwick. His Corcoran Gallery, Washington, 1859; the Charity Hospital, New York, 1858-61; and the Administration Building at Vassar College, Poughkeepsie, New York, 1860, by Renwick, Auchmuty and Sands were early exponents of the style. The article traces the historic French prototypes of the Second Empire style in France and the United States.

123:7 Price, C. Matlack. "Lawyers' Mortgage Company Building, New York City." ARCHITECTURAL RECORD 52 (July 1922): 52-62.

This article has nothing but praise for the structure at 56 Nassau Street. It is a good advertisement to the banking world as well as a work of art, which like so much architecture is limited to "specific and essential requirements." Photographs, plan, and architectural details.

123:8 Schuyler, Montgomery. "Recent Church Building in New York." ARCHITECTURAL RECORD 15 (June 1903): 508-34.

Renwick and Sands were responsible for St. Bartholomew's Church, 1872, southwest corner Madison Avenue and 44th Street, to which Stanford White added the Vanderbilt Memorial porch, later removed to the new St. Bartholomew on Park Avenue.

124:1 RICHARDSON, HENRY HOBSON (1838-86)

Educated Harvard, class of 1859, and Ecole des Beaux Arts, Paris, where he worked for Theodore Labrouste. Practiced from 1866 with Emlyn Littel and later Charles D. Gambrill (see Gambrill and Richardson) until 1878, thereafter independently.

Houghton Library, Harvard University, has about 5,000 drawings of 117 projects. Harvard's Fine Arts Library has one sheet of the Harvard Yard and Harvard Archives has eighteen sheets on Sever Hall.

Obituaries: ARCHITECT 35 (1886): 306-7; AMERICAN ARCHITECT AND BUILDING NEWS 19 (1886): 205; ROYAL INSTITUTE OF BRITISH ARCHITECT'S JOURNAL 3 (November 4, 1886): 21; BUILDING 4 (May 1, 1886): 204.

Ticknor of Boston published eighteen plates of Austin Hall, Harvard, 1886, and twenty-three plates of the Ames Memorial Building, North Easton, 1886, in their Monographs of American Architecture Series.

124:2 AMERICAN INSTITUTE OF ARCHITECT'S JOURNAL. "A Solid Base for Chicago School." Vol. 49 (February 1968): 76.

Richardson's Glessner House, Chicago, was willed to the Chicago Chapter of the American Institute of Architects, an organization unable to accept the gift during the period of the depression. It was thus given to the Armour Institute of Technology and is now used as a resource center of the Illinois Institute of Technology School of Architecture.

124:3 Bosworth, Welles. "I Knew H.H. Richardson." AMERICAN INSTITUTE OF ARCHITECT'S JOURNAL 16 (September 1951): 115-27.

"His personality was so overpowering that the atmosphere was charged with it, and we all held our breaths when he came round for his morning visits. . . ." Mr. Bosworth should have held his pen as well as his breath.

124:4 Brown, Robert F. THE ARCHITECTURE OF HENRY HOBSON RICHARDSON IN NORTH EASTON, MASSACHUSETTS. The Oakes Ames Memorial Hall Association and The Easton Historical Society, 1969. N.p.

An introduction on the Ames family, their fortune, interests in the arts, and employment of Richardson precedes a chronology of structures designed by the architect at North Easton for the Ames family. All five structures: library, memorial hall, gate lodge, railroad station, and gardener's cottage on the Ames estate are illustrated with contemporary photographs and plans from publications of the period.

124:5 Comes, John Theodore. "The Allegheny County Court House." INTERNATIONAL STUDIO 28 (1906): iii-vii.

The courthouse needed to expand in 1906, and since surrounding land was so expensive, it was proposed to increase the height of this famed Richardson structure. The Romanesque period is analyzed as a logical style for a nineteenth-century building, and the courthouse is studied in detail for composition, planning, structure, and decoration. The "edifice marks one of the most interesting epochs of American architectural history, and is the work of one of America's greatest men," and thus should not be tampered with.

124:6 Eaton, Leonard K. "Richardson and Sullivan in Scandinavia." PROGRESSIVE ARCHITECTURE, March 1966, pp. 168-71.

"It is quite clearly a mistake to date European awareness of American architecture from the publication of Wright's work by the Wasmuth Verlag," of 1910. Rather, Richardson's influence can be found in garden suburbs generally and in the urban architecture of Sweden. Sullivan had an impact in Sweden and Denmark.

124:7 Friedlaender, Marc. "Henry Hobson Richardson, Henry Adams and John Hay." JOURNAL OF THE SOCIETY OF ARCHITECTURAL HISTORIANS 29 (October 1970): 231-46.

Adams and Hay were Washington clients of Richardson who built adjoining houses on Lafayette Square. Friedlaender, working with the Adam Papers, adds to earlier articles on this subject (see Scheyer) because of closer documentation both in the Adams Papers and allied collections.

124:8 Hill, Leroy Draper. THE CRANE LIBRARY. Quincy, Mass.: The Trustees of the Thomas Crane Public Library, 1962. 32 p.

Introduction by Walter Muir Whitehill. Quincy Library was a gift in memory of Thomas Crane (1803-75). The essays contained in the book show the need for a library in Quincy during the nineteenth century, the choosing of a distinguished architect, and the development of the library in the hands of that architect. There are plans, sketches, and details of the third project for the building and portraits of the men associated with the library.

124:9 Hitchcock, Henry Russell. THE ARCHITECTURE OF H.H. RICHARDSON AND HIS TIMES. New York: Museum of Modern Art, 1936. 311 p. Reprint. Hamden, Conn.: Archon Books, 1961.

Education, travel, and early beginnings in practice lead into a discussion of commissions, through Harvard friends, such as the Church of Unity at Springfield, 1866. Grace Episcopal, West Medford, was inferior to the work of Vaux and Withers, Ware and Van Brunt and Worcester High School inferior to the polychromacists in England, but with the Brattle Street Church, Boston, 1870, he was "no longer French or English,...but Richardson," or rather Richardsonian in the Romanesque sense. All of his major works are discussed in detail.

124:10 _____. "Richardson's American Express Building: A Note." JOURNAL OF THE SOCIETY OF ARCHITECTURAL HISTORIANS 9 (March and May 1950): 25-30.

A general discussion of Richardson's work in the late 1860's and early 1870's: The Dorsheimer House, Buffalo, 1868; an urban church and parsonage at Columbus, Ohio, 1872; neither buildings in the spirit of the High Victorian Gothic of Butterfield, Street, Burges or Bodley, but of the lesser known lower church architects as Bassett Keeling, F.T. Palkington, or "Victorian Harris." But the American Express Building, Chicago, was High Victorian Gothic in the articulation of the wall surface and modeling of the facade.

124:11 _____. RICHARDSON AS A VICTORIAN ARCHITECT. Baltimore: Smith College, 1966. 53 p.

The material of this publication developed from the Katherine Asher Engel Lecture at Smith College for 1965, and essentially extends and updates the ideas presented in THE ARCHITECTURE OF H.H. RICHARDSON AND HIS TIMES.

124:12 Homolka, Larry J. "Richardson's North Easton." ARCHITECTURAL FORUM, May 1966, pp. 72-77.

North Easton, Massachusetts, was a factory town of the Ames family which commissioned five buildings from Richardson: a library, town hall, railroad station, gate lodge, and gardener's cottage.

124:13 Huxtable, Ada Louise. "Keeping the There There." THE NEW YORK TIMES, Sunday, May 16, 1971, section 2, p. 21.

The Chicago Chapter of the American Institute of Architects leased the Glessner House, Chicago, and thus ensured that the structure would not be demolished. The article lists the Glessner house as one of many successful preservation projects.

124:14 _____. "A Lot Happens in Ten Years." THE NEW YORK TIMES, Sunday, May 9, 1971, section 2, p. 21.

Laments the possible passing of Union Station, New London, Connecticut, 1885, as scheduled for demolition in the 1961 urban renewal plan for a view of the river! According to Hitchcock, this station was "the best of its type."

124:15 Knight, Michael. "Station (Landmark or Eyesore) Nears End." THE NEW YORK TIMES, Friday, September 28, 1973, p. 35.

After a ten-year battle between the New London, Connecticut, City Council (which wants to use federal funds for redevelopment, before they run out in June 1974), and preservationists, the New London station appears to be doomed for destruction.

124:16 McKee, Harley J. "Building for the State of New York, 1790-1890." EMPIRE STATE ARCHITECT 16 (January-February 1956): 27; 16 (March-April 1956): 19; 16 (May-June 1956): 23; 16 (November-December 1956): 33-34; 17 (January-February 1957): 23; 17 (March-April 1957): 20-29; 17 (May-June 1957): 33, 50; 17 (July-August 1957): 17, 27; 17 (September-October 1957): 55, 81.

This survey begins with Government House at Bowling Green, New York City, and the transfer of the state government to Albany in 1797 (May-June 1956 article). The seventh article introduces the topic of the choice of site and competition (1867 - Thomas Fuller and Augustus Laver), and thereafter a detailed chronology including Richardson's advisory role of 1875. The eighth article considers changes in the design, and the last article the chambers for Assembly and Senate.

124:17 Mumford, Lewis. "The Regionalism of Richardson." ROOTS OF CONTEMPORARY AMERICAN ARCHITECTURE. New York: Reinhold Publishing Corp., 1952. Pp. 117-31. (The article was first prepared for the Dancy Lectures, Alabama College, 1941, and published in THE SOUTH IN ARCHITECTURE. New York: Harcourt, Brace and Co., 1941. 147 p.)

Richardson was the second American to attend the Ecole des Beaux Arts, Paris, and, although some of his houses had mansard roofs, his inspiration came not from the French Second Empire style, but from medieval sources. "His Romanticism was a matter of ingrained temperament, based on a rich and copious emotional nature...."

124:18 Newman, M.W. "Granite Hut." ARCHITECTURAL FORUM (November

1972): 34, 41.

Richardson's Glessner House, Chicago, completed at the time of his death, has undergone considerable restoration; it is now in use albeit not as a residence. Its preservation and innovative features are described. Photographs of the period and of the re-used areas are provided in addition to four floor plans.

124:19 O'Gorman, J.F. "Henry Hobson Richardson and Frank Lloyd Wright." ART QUARTERLY 32 (Autumn 1969): 292-315.

The article is as much about Sullivan as Richardson and Wright even though stylistic similarities are illustrated. The Glessner House arch inspired numerous arched openings by Wright including that of the V.C. Morris Shop, San Francisco, 1948-49, but other similarities are tenuous especially the Boston and Albany railroad station at Woodland, Massachusetts, 1884, or the plan of the Glessner house.

124:20 _____. "O.W. Norcross, Richardson's 'Master Builder': A Preliminary Report." JOURNAL OF THE SOCIETY OF ARCHITECTURAL HISTORIANS 32 (May 1973): 104-13.

"Without question it [Norcross Brothers] was among the most important construction companies in the country in the late Nineteenth and early Twentieth Century." Notably in the construction of designs from the hand of Richardson and some of his notable successors, also giants in the field; the builder is the executor of the design of the artist. At least half of Richardson's designs were constructed by J.A. Norcross, the office manager, and O.W. Norcross, the field manager, with whom Richardson had greatest contact and admiration. The article emphasizes architect-builder collaboration and the general workings of the contractor.

124:21 Paris, W. Franklyn. "H.H. Richardson, 1838-86." NEW YORK UNIVERSITY HALL OF AMERICAN ARTISTS 10 (1955): 49-59.

"Richardson burst upon a world which sorely needed his great talents. . . . [Prior to his time] the approach to architecture was entirely haphazard. . . . Into this architectural degradation and chaos, Richardson came. . . . He attacked America's problems joyfully, lustily as he faced everything in life. He was given less than twenty years to accomplish his task." Only a few of his projects are mentioned.

124:22 Price, Charles. "Henry Hobson Richardson: Some Unpublished Drawings." PERSPECTA 9-10 (1965): 199, 210.

In 1942 Henry R. Shepley deposited numerous Richardson

drawings in the Houghton Library of Harvard University. An inventory was made in 1963, and subsequently all drawings were microfilmed. Interesting discoveries were made in the collection and many of Richardson's projects, works, and drawings are discussed in that light. Freehand sketches, drawings, and plans by Richardson are used to illustrate the article.

124:23 Randall, Richard H. THE FURNITURE OF H.H. RICHARDSON. Boston: Boston Museum of Fine Arts, 1962. 4 p.

Exhibition January 9, to February 18, 1962. Although many of Richardson's furniture designs are in oak and heavy in appearance, they are quite original for their period. Chairs for the Woburn, North Easton, and Malden Public Libraries, the Unity Church, Springfield, and sketch of a clock for the Court of Appeals, New York, accompany the one-page descriptive essay.

124:24 Reinink, A.W. "American Influences on Late Nineteenth Century Architecture in the Netherlands." JOURNAL OF THE SOCIETY OF ARCHITECTURAL HISTORIANS 29 (May 1970).

Major portion of the article devoted to Richardson's influence upon H.P. Berlage (1856-1934). Sever and Austin Halls at Harvard and Trinity Parsonage, Boston, seem to have had greatest influence as is clearly illustrated.

124:25 Richardson, H.H. THE BILLINGS LIBRARY, THE GIFT TO THE UNIVERSITY OF VERMONT OF FREDERICK BILLINGS. Boston: Heliotype Printing Co., 1895. 21 pl.

Consists of plates including a portrait of Frederick Billings, general and detailed views of the library.

124:26 Roseberry, Cecil R. CAPITOL STORY. Albany, N.Y.: State of New York, 1964. 128 p.

A thorough discourse on all of the architects, sculptors, and designers concerned with the New York State Capitol. Well illustrated but no plans.

124:27 Rudd, J. William. "The Cincinnati Chamber of Commerce Building." JOURNAL OF THE SOCIETY OF ARCHITECTURAL HISTORIANS 27 (May 1968): 115-23.

Enumerates and illustrates some of the thirteen 1885 competition entries for the building, including two by Richardson. The building began in 1886, after the architect's death, was badly damaged by fire in 1911, and demolished the following year. At first materials from the building were to have been used in constructing the Cincinnati Astronomical Society Building, but due to wars and the depression, were not.

124:28 Scheyer, Ernst. "Henry Adams and Henry Hobson Richardson." JOURNAL OF THE SOCIETY OF ARCHITECTURAL HISTORIANS 12 (March 1953): 7-12.

Henry Adams of MONT-SAINT-MICHEL AND CHARTRES fame, a fellow student of Richardson at Harvard, and John Hay, a Secretary of State, commissioned a pair of houses built on Lafayette Square from the architect. This article is a discussion of the relationships of the two clients, their architect, and a closely-knit group of common friends.

124:29 Shepherd, Walter. "Von Herkomer's Folly." COUNTRY LIFE 86 (December 16, 1939): 636.

Von Herkomer was the Victorian artist who built "Lululaund," a Bavarian-styled castle in England at a cost of 80,000 pounds, completed in 1894. It was named after Von Herkomer's second wife, Lulu Griffiths. No mention is made in the article of Richardson, who had a hand in the design.

124:30 Stebbins, Theodore E., Jr. "Richardson and Trinity Church: The Evolution of a Building." JOURNAL OF THE SOCIETY OF ARCHITECTURAL HISTORIANS 27 (December 1968): 281-98.

Every aspect of the church is reconsidered in the light of latest research material including the Richardson drawings collection at the Widener Library, Harvard University. An early Richardson sketch for the tower, dated April 1874, based upon a similar massing at Salamanca Cathedral Spain, dispels the usual attribution of the design to that "diabolically clever" assistant Stanford White. The article is thorough and well illustrated.

124:31 Tselos, Dimitri. "Richardson's Influence on European Architecture." JOURNAL OF THE SOCIETY OF ARCHITECTURAL HISTORIANS 29 (May 1970): 156-62.

A general discussion which includes influences in Germany, Finland (Eliel Saarinen), Holland (Berlage), and Sweden after Richardson's death in 1886. Most examples are of the 1890's and early years of the twentieth century. Richardson was the first American architect to have an international impact.

124:32 Van Rensselaer, Mariana (Griswold). HENRY HOBSON RICHARDSON AND HIS WORKS. Boston and New York: Houghton, Mifflin and Co., 1888. 152 p. (1st ed. 500 copies). Reprint. Park Forest, Ill.: The Prairie School Press, 1967, introduction by James Van Trump; and again by New York: Dover Publications, Inc., 1969, introduction by William Morgan.

Mrs. Van Rensselaer (1851-1934), knew Richardson well and wrote this famed biography, the second biography of an American architect, only two years after his premature death at the age of forty-eight. On the whole, the book is well researched and documented with sketches by Richardson's pupils, even though Will Morgan's 1969 introduction states that Mrs. Van Rensselaer was "neither an outstanding scholar nor a brilliant researcher." A reasonably complete and accurate list of Richardson's works are provided in an appendix.

124:33 Van Trump, James D. "Project H.H. Richardson." CHARETTE 42 (May 1962): 4-5, 20.

During the summers of 1960 through 1963, students of the School of Architecture at the Carnegie Institute of Technology began measured drawings of the Allegheny Court House and Jail sponsored by the Historic American Building Survey. Van Trump explains the workings of Historic American Building Survey and some of its notable achievements.

124:34 Van Zanten, David T. "H.H. Richardson's Glessner House." JOURNAL OF THE SOCIETY OF ARCHITECTURAL HISTORIANS 23 (May 1964): 106-11.

Glessner chose Richardson as his architect after considering Stanford White and William Appleton Potter. Van Zanten traces the design developments of the house being one of the last of Richardson's projects, completed, notably the interiors, by his successors, Shepley, Rutan and Coolidge.

124:35 Webster, J. Carson. "Richardson's American Express Building." JOURNAL OF THE SOCIETY OF ARCHITECTURAL HISTORIANS 9 (March and May 1950): 20-24.

Gothic in roof details, the windows and furnishings of the main office provides a medieval flavoring albeit not Romanesque. The building was a well-planned, functional commercial structure.

124:36 Wodehouse, Lawrence. "William Appleton Potter, Principal Pasticheur of Henry Hobson Richardson." JOURNAL OF THE SOCIETY OF ARCHITECTURAL HISTORIANS 32 (May 1973): 175-92.

See Potter.

124:37 Zaitzevsky, Cynthia. "A New Richardson Building." JOURNAL OF THE SOCIETY OF ARCHITECTURAL HISTORIANS 32 (May 1973): 164-66.

A previously unknown work by Richardson at 681 Washington Street, Boston, for John C. Hayden "a family connection." Similar to the Cheney Building at Hartford of 1875, this building was constructed in 1869.

125:1 RICKER, NATHAN CLIFFORD (1843-1924)

125:2 Bannister, Turpin C. "Pioneering in Architectural Education." AMERICAN INSTITUTE OF ARCHITECT'S JOURNAL 20 (July 1953): 3-8; 20 (August 1953): 76-81.

"Recalling the first collegiate graduate in architecture in the United States - Nathan Clifford Ricker," is the subtitle, by the head of the Department of Architecture at the University of Illinois. The first article begins with a brief survey of European and American architectural education and particularly that at Illinois. Ricker also studied in Berlin. Returning to the United States, Ricker taught and designed buildings for the Illinois Industrial University (later to become the University of Illinois). He initiated a program in architectural engineering and promoted architectural education generally. Several notable graduates are listed.

125:3 Laing, Alan K. NATHAN CLIFFORD RICKER 1843-1924. PIONEER IN AMERICAN ARCHITECTURAL EDUCATION. Urbana, Ill.: University of Illinois, 1973. 32 p.

This recent publication marks the centenary of the first graduate in architecture from an American school.

126:1 ROBERTS, EBEN EZRA (1866-1943)

Studied architecture at Tilton Seminary and was employed 1890-93 by S.S. Beman. Practiced privately 1893-1922 when he took his son, Elmer, into partnership, 1922-26, after which he went into semi-retirement.

126:2 Steiner, Frances. "E.E. Roberts: Popularizing the Prairie School." THE PRAIRIE SCHOOL REVIEW 10 (Second Quarter, 1973): 5-20. With a catalog raisonne by Steiner, pp. 21-24.

Many of his residences designed between 1895-1900 are in the Queen Anne style, but Roberts soon came under the influence of Wright and other Prairie architects. "He did not copy their styles but slowly altered his own in such a way that it became more acceptable to the local population than was that of the more radical architects." The catalog lists 103 structures.

127:1 ROBERTSON, ROBERT HENDERSON (1849-1919)

Educated at Rutgers and worked for George B. Post prior to association with William Appleton Potter (see).

Princeton University has twelve sheets of Witherspoon Hall, Princeton.

Obituary: ARCHITECTURAL RECORD 6 (1896-97): 184-219.

127:2 Ferree, Barr. "The Art of High Building." ARCHITECTURAL RECORD 15 (May 1904): 445-66.

"High building of today - the typical and most noteworthy architectural creation of our time." Robertson's Corn Exchange Bank Building on William Street, New York City, is illustrated.

127:3 Schuyler, Montgomery. "The Works of Robert Henderson Robertson." ARCHITECTURAL RECORD 6 (October-December 1896): 184-219.

Essentially Romanesque until 1890, his work thereafter became classical with Queen Anne flourishes in urban structures and picturesquely rustic in rural dwellings. Schuyler felt that he did not contribute distinctly to the solution of the speicific problem of the tall building.

128:1 ROBINSON, ARGYLE E. (n.d.)

128:2 Sturgis, Russell. "Some Recent Warehouses." ARCHITECTURAL RECORD 23 (May 1908): 375-86.

Washington Park Warehouse, Chicago, a fireproof building where the architect "has treated the flat surface nearly as a designer of rock cut tomb fronts would have proceeded in Asia Minor about three hundred years B.C."

129:1 ROEBLING, JOHN AUGUSTUS (1806-69)

129:2 Fitch, James Marston. "The Palace, the Bridge and the Tower." ARCHITECTURAL FORUM 87 (October 1947): 88-95.

This is a chapter from Fitch's book AMERICAN BUILDING, glorifying the structural aspects of nineteenth-century design. The Palace is Paxton's Crystal Palace, the tower is the Eiffel Tower, both exposition buildings and the bridge is the Brooklyn Bridge, "a tension structure never surpassed and seldom equaled."

129:3 McCullough, David G. THE GREAT BRIDGE. New York: Simon and Schuster, 1972. 636 p.

The most complete and up-to-date account of the building of the bridge but linked to political, economic, social, and cultural aspects of the period.

129:4 Steinman, David Barnard. THE BUILDERS OF THE BRIDGE: THE STORY OF JOHN ROEBLING AND HIS SON. New York: Harcourt, Brace and Co., 1945. 457 p.

This is a biography of the Roeblings, father and son, from the immigration of John, the father, through his early works to the Brooklyn Bridge completed by Washington A. Roebling, the son. Stages in the construction of the Brooklyn Bridge are carefully described, together with a limited supplement of woodcuts and photographs.

129:5 Trachtenberg, Alan. BROOKLYN BRIDGE, FACT AND SYMBOL. New York: Oxford University Press, 1965. 182 p.

Technology, cultural history, and imagination patterns merge with the fact and symbol of this major nineteenth-century engineering feat. The economics, politics, and architecture of the bridge are as carefully explored as are the two men, father and son, John and Washington Roebling, who designed and built the bridge.

129:6 Vogel, Robert M. ROEBLING'S DELAWARE AND HUDSON CANAL AQUEDUCTS. Washington, D.C.: Smithsonian Institute Press, 1971. 45 p.

130:1 ROGERS, ISAIAH (1800-69)

Trained in Boston under Solomon Willard prior to practice alone in 1826. Supervising Architect to the Treasury Department 1862-65 where he completed buildings designed prior to 1862 by Ammi Burnham Young.

Avery Library, Columbia University, has his diaries, 1838-56, 1861, 1867.

130:2 Cummings, Abbott Lowell. "The Ohio State Capitol Competition." JOURNAL OF THE SOCIETY OF ARCHITECTURAL HISTORIANS 12 (May 1957): 15-18.

Henry Walter won the competition for the Ohio State House in 1839, but other architects were involved in its final construction including Rogers in 1859. Competition drawings are illustrated.

130:3 Myers, Denys Peter. "The Recently Discovered Diaries." COLUMBIA

LIBRARY COLUMNS 16 (November 1966): 25-31.

This issue of COLUMBIA LIBRARY COLUMNS published by the Friends of the Columbia University Libraries was devoted to American architectural topics. Myers had discovered the diaries of Rogers owned by a descendant in Atlanta. The diaries cover the period 1838-67 and are full of trivia in addition to information on work by Rogers. They are now deposited at Avery Library, Columbia University, New York City, and there is also a typewritten copy.

131:1 **ROOT, JOHN WELLBORN (1850-91)**

Studied Oxford, England, and City College, New York, entered office of James Renwick, Jr., and worked with John B. Snook. Joined Carter, Drake and Wight of Chicago, 1871-73. Until his death formed a partnership with Daniel Hudson Burnham (see).

Contributed to HOMES IN CITY AND COUNTRY, 1893.

Obituaries: AMERICAN ARCHITECT AND BUILDING NEWS 31 (1891): 49; ROYAL INSTITUTE OF BRITISH ARCHITECT'S JOURNAL 7 (1890-91): 191; INLAND ARCHITECT AND NEWS RECORD 16 (January 1891): 83-84.

131:2 Eaton, Leonard K. "John Wellborn Root and the Julian M. Case House." THE PRAIRIE SCHOOL REVIEW 9 (Third Quarter, 1972): 18-22.

This house at Marquette, Michigan, of 1886-87, illustrates Root's interest in residential architecture and his attitudes in design related to domestic architecture. "Root chose to design the Case house in his own highly individual version of the Shingle style."

131:3 Hoffmann, Donald. "John Root's Monadnock Building." JOURNAL OF THE SOCIETY OF ARCHITECTURAL HISTORIANS 26 (December 1967): 269-77.

Harriet Monroe's 1896 biography of Root related the circumstances of constructing the Monadnock Building. Mumford, Giedion and Condit all relied upon Monroe, but in this article Hoffmann sets the facts straight notably after careful research, including the letter books of Aldis and Co., the Chicago agents for the client of the Monadnock, Peter Brooks.

131:4 _____, ed. THE MEANING OF ARCHITECTURE: BUILDINGS AND WRITINGS BY JOHN WELLBORN ROOT. New York: Horizon Press, 1967. 238 p.

Functionalism and expression were the two major qualities of architectural designers, notably in the Chicago area, in the closing years of the nineteenth century. These attitudes were held as much by Root as any other, and came through both in his writings and his architecture. Illustrations are both of the period (photographs and drawings) and those taken of extant works by Hoffmann.

131:5 Monroe, Harriet. JOHN WELLBORN ROOT: A STUDY OF HIS LIFE AND WORK. New York: Houghton, Mifflin and Co., 1896. 291 p. (Facsimilie edition: Park Forest, Ill.: The Prairie School Press, 1966. Reyner Banham, ed.)

Root was in many respects a pioneer in building the first ten-story and later twenty-story block for Chicago and the first high blocks in the financial district. Harriet Monroe was a sister-in-law of Root, but except for misinterpretations and errors in the catalog of buildings, her book is a creditable early architectural biography.

131:6 Mumford, Lewis. ROOTS OF CONTEMPORARY AMERICAN ARCHITECTURE. New York: Reinhold Publishing Corp., 1952. Pp. 429-30.

Steeped in traditional architectural eclecticisms and decoration, Root soon became a major designer of the Chicago School "and created a masterpiece of clean masonry and glass, the Monadnock Building."

131:7 Paris, W. Franklyn. "John Wellborn Root." AMERICAN SOCIETY LEGION OF HONOR MAGAZINE 23 (Summer 1952): 139-52.

The success story of an architect over a twenty-year period from the great fire of Chicago in 1871 to his death in 1891. His education, training, partnership, and achievements are detailed.

131:8 _____. "John Wellborn Root." THE HALL OF AMERICAN ARTISTS. Vol. 9. New York: New York University, 1952. Pp. 51-64.

Root's career in Chicago spans twenty years from 1871, and the Chicago Fire, to 1891, when plans were being made for the 1893 Chicago Columbian Exposition. After a brief period in New York City and Chicago offices, Root partnered with Burnham. They weathered the 1873 panic, gained famed in their residential work and success as designers and innovators in skyscraper construction. He died in 1891, and the fair "was poorer without the enthusiasm and talents of John Root," said his equally famed partner.

131:9 Starrett, Theodore. "John Wellborn Root." ARCHITECTS' AND BUILDERS' MAGAZINE 44 (1912): 429-31.

Early education, training, apprenticeship in both New

York and Chicago, his partnership with Burnham and several anecdotes are the sum total of these three pages.

132:1 SCHEIBLER, FREDERICK GUSTAVUS, JR. (1872-1958)

Worked for Henry Moser.

132:2 Shear, John Knox. "Pittsburgh Rediscovers an Architect Pioneer." ARCHITECTURAL RECORD 106 (July 1949): 98-100.

Scheibler was a pioneer of modern design who taught at Carnegie Institute of Technology in Pittsburgh, the town in which he was born. His work consisted mainly of residential accommodations, individual as well as apartment towers. He utilized new materials and new techniques and was influenced by Japanese design.

132:3 Van Trump, James D. "A Prophet of Modern Architecture in Pittsburgh." CHARETTE 42 (October 1962): 10-15.

Van Trump and a photographer, James H. Cook, organized an exhibition on Scheibler's work at the Department of Fine Arts, Carnegie Institute, 1962. He was an individualist who emulated the late arts and crafts architects of Britian. A brief background of his life, work, and achievements is discussed.

133:1 SCHMIDT, RICHARD ERNEST (1865-1958)

Studied Massachusetts Institute of Technology, began practice in in Chicago 1887, and founded firm of Schmidt, Garden and Martin.

Publications: THE MODERN HOSPITAL, 1914; PAMPHLET ON HOSPITAL CONSTRUCTION, 1914-1920, 1920.

Burnham Library, Chicago, has drawings of seven projects.

133:2 David, Arthur C. "The Architecture of Ideas." ARCHITECTURAL RECORD 15 (April 1904): 361-84.

European time-honored traditions of the eastern seaboard were overthrown in the west by many notable architects. The article is concerned with the work of two architects, Richard Schmidt and George Maher. Numerous interiors and details are photographed.

133:3 Herbert, William. "An American Architecture." ARCHITECTURAL RECORD 23 (February 1908): 111-22.

A condemnation of stylistic expression in architecture precedes a glorification of the new technologies of the twentieth century and particularly as seen in the work of Richard E. Schmidt, who has attempted to express function, a sincere use of materials and structure. Such modern treatments are illustrated in commercial, residential, health, and entertainment buildings in Chicago.

133:4 Sturgis, Russell. "The Chapin and Gore Building, Chicago." ARCHITECTURAL RECORD 19 (February 1906): 154-57.

Structural expression, function, decoration, and materials are discussed and the building is illustrated with particular attention being paid to the Nepeenauk Bar.

133:5 _____. "The Madlever House in Chicago." ARCHITECTURAL RECORD 17 (June 1905): 491-98.

A meritorious residence in composition, window arrangement, and interiors, according to the reviewer.

133:6 _____. "The Schoenhofen Brewery." ARCHITECTURAL RECORD 17 (March 1905): 201-7.

"The best hope for our architectural future lies in our nonarchitectural buildings." By this, Sturgis means building types not usually used as projects in the learning process of architectural schools. Sturgis admires this Chicago Brewery design, its plan, materials, elements, details, and wall surfaces.

134:1 **SCWARZMANN, HERMAN J. (1843-91)**

German by birth and became Chief Engineer of the Fairmount Park, Philadelphia, and Architect-in-Chief of the 1876 Philadelphia Exposition.

Avery Library, Columbia University, has seven photostats (of original drawings in New York City Hall) of Store No. 628 and 630 Broadway, New York City, 1882.

Obituary: ARCHITECTURE AND BUILDING 15 (July-December 1891): 163.

134:2 Maass, John. THE GLORIOUS ENTERPRISE: THE CENTENNIAL EXHIBITION OF 1876 IN PHILADELPHIA AND H.J. SCHWARZMANN, ARCHITECT-IN-CHARGE. Watkins Glen, N.Y.: American Life Foundation, 1973. 200 p.

The sixth volume in a series devoted to "History in the Arts: A Monograph Series," John Maass points out the importance of the fair in relation to the spread of ideas, and especially so in 1876 when influences spread from the United States to other countries. Little was known of Schwarzmann until this publication. Now his contribution can be evaluated.

134:3 Sturges, Walter Knight. "Cast Iron in New York." ARCHITECTURAL REVIEW 114 (October 1953): 232-37.

Schwarzmann's Mercantile Exchange Building, New York, of 1882 uses "decorative motifs" (which in English usage would range from Batty Langley to Papworth, Loudon, and beyond" to give a stiff and sprightly sense of structure and a sensitive feeling of scale.

135:1 SCHWEINFURTH, CHARLES FREDERICK (1856-1919)

Obituaries: AMERICAN ARCHITECTURE 116 (1919): 729; AMERICAN INSTITUTE OF ARCHITECTS' JOURNAL 8 (1920): 139.

135:2 Frary, I.T. "The Rebuilding of Longwood, Residence of John L. Severance, Esq., Cleveland, Ohio." ARCHITECTURAL RECORD 41 (June 1917): 483-503.

A Gothicization of an older structure represents a perfect marriage between the client's wishes and the architect's design ability. All work is of a high quality and is well illustrated in numerous photographs. Plans are provided to differentiate between new work and that of the existing building. Landscaping and external sculptures enhance this elaborate residence.

135:3 Jenkins, Charles E. "A Review of the Works of Charles Frederick Schweinfurth." ARCHITECTURAL REVIEWER 1 (September 30, 1897): 81-115.

Schweinfurth worked in New York City 1874-83 and thereafter practiced with his brother for two years until his brother's retirement. His commissions were in all the major building types and stylistically he borrowed from all of the late nineteenth-century eclectic modes: Gothic, classical and all the Richardsonianisms, as can be seen in the illustrations (forty-three of them).

135:4 Perry, Regina Alfreda. "The Life and Works of Charles Frederick Schweinfurth - Cleveland Architect, 1856-1919." Doctoral dissertation, Case Western Reserve University, 1967. 311 p.

German by birth, Schweinfurth practiced at the end of the nineteenth and beginning of the twentieth century in the Romanesque style notably in the realm of domestic architecture. He was equally picturesque and romantic, using polychromy, elements of the Stick style, and was influenced by C.F.A. Voysey. He was a twentieth-century Gothicist in collegiate architecture for Western Reserve University, Kenyon College (Supervising Architect 1905-15), and Bexley School of Divinity.

136:1 SHEPLEY, RUTAN AND COOLIDGE (Partnership 1886-1914)

George Foster Shepley, (1860-1903), Charles Hercules Rutan, (1851-1914), and Charles Allerton Coolidge (1858-1936).

Houghton Library, Harvard University, has drawings of five projects; Avery Library, Columbia University, one; Burnham Library, Chicago, one; and the National Archives, Washington, eighteeen.

136:2 Fischer, John Baptiste. "A Jaunt to Wychwood, Geneva Lake, Wisconsin." ARCHITECTURAL RECORD 17 (February 1905): 126-36.

Situated in a beautiful area of country beside a lake, the reviewer admires the rusticity of this Elizabethan mansion and its outbuildings.

136:3 Sturgis, Russell. "Great American Architects Series." ARCHITECTURAL RECORD, Supplement to the July 1896 issue, pp. 1-52.

Heirs of H.H. Richardson, Shepley, Rutan, and Coolidge designed independently of the master. In several of their residences, they developed a semi-Byzantine Romanesque, for example in the fireplace of the Nickerson House, Dedham, Massachusetts.

Other residences were Tudorbethan and of the Richardson Shingle style while other urban houses and college buildings tended toward the Georgian. Many of their religious buildings and railroad stations were Richardsonian, but their Art Institute of Chicago is Roman in the sixteenth-century Venetian Renaissance sense. Their most recent work was the Leyland Stanford, Jr. University, California.

137:1 SILSBEE, JAMES LYMAN (1845-1913)

Educated Harvard and Massachusetts Institute of Technology, and practiced in upstate New York, 1872-82, before moving to Chicago where he practiced with Edward A. Kent. Silsbee became the first employer of Frank Lloyd Wright.

137:2 Sorell, Susan Karr. "The Evolution of a Personal Architectural Style." THE PRAIRIE SCHOOL REVIEW 7 (Fourth Quarter, 1970): 5-13. Catalogue raisonne, pp. 17-21.

The catalogue of Silsbee's work covers the years during which he practiced in Chicago c. 1882-97, (c. 1872-82 he practiced in upstate New York, with offices in Albany, Buffalo, and Syracuse. See 137:3). All 107 projects in the list were illustrated in magazines and publications so that the list is not definitive. Silsbee is perhaps best known as the first employer of Frank Lloyd Wright (and incidentally George W. Maher), but he was a competent architect in his own right, practically, chronologically, in the American eastern seaboard, Queen Anne, Shingle, Colonial Revival and 1890's eclectic styles.

137:3 Wodehouse, Lawrence. "Letter to the Editors Concerning Silsbee." THE PRAIRIE SCHOOL REVIEW 8 (Second Quarter, 1971): 30.

Commenting upon Miss Sorell's article and catalog on Silsbee in the Fourth Quarter, 1970, issue of THE PRAIRIE SCHOOL REVIEW, this letter provides a few clues and references to Silsbee's ten years of practice in New York State prior to his fifteen years in Chicago beginning c. 1882. Miss Sorell's article is exclusively on the Chicago years.

138:1 SLOAN, SAMUEL (1815-84)

Publications: AMERICAN HOUSES: A VARIETY OF ORIGINAL DESIGNS FOR RURAL BUILDINGS, 1861; CITY AND SUBURBAN ARCHITECTURE, 1859; THE MODEL ARCHITECT, 1852; SLOAN'S CONSTRUCTIVE ARCHITECTURE, 1859; SLOAN'S HOMESTEAD ARCHITECTURE, 1867; illustrated part of Peter Nicholson's THE CARPENTER'S NEW GUIDE, 1854; edited SLOAN'S ARCHITECTURAL REVIEW AND BUILDER'S JOURNAL, July 1869-October 1870.

Obituaries: AMERICAN ARCHITECT AND BUILDING NEWS 18 (1884): 49; BUILDING 2 (September 1884): 143.

138:2 Cooledge, Harold Nosman, Jr. "Samuel Sloan (1815-84), Architect." Doctoral dissertation, University of Pennsylvania, 1963. 213 p.

The life and career of Sloan is assessed in relation to American architectural history. Since no personal papers remain, the strength of the dissertation is in the architectural contribution of Sloan as architect.

138:3 _____. "A Sloan Check List, 1849-84." JOURNAL OF THE SOCIETY OF ARCHITECTURAL HISTORIANS 19 (March 1960): 34-38.

Cooledge is preparing a monograph on Sloan, but a major hinderance is the lack of any personal or professional papers. Here he presents ten illustrations and a checklist of 135 structures.

138:4 _____. "Samuel Sloan and the Philadelphia Plan." JOURNAL OF THE SOCIETY OF ARCHITECTURAL HISTORIANS 23 (October 1964): 151-54.

By Philadelphia Plan, Mr. Cooledge is referring to Sloan's improved plan for public school buildings of the 1850's. The designs internally were plain for the sake of economy, but were convenient in circulation, well-lighted, and flexible in use.

138:5 Hersey, George L. "Godey's Choice." JOURNAL OF THE SOCIETY OF ARCHITECTURAL HISTORIANS 18 (October 1959): 104-11.

GODEY'S LADY'S BOOK AND LADY'S MAGAZINE published 450 house designs between 1846 and 1892. Some were of English derivation and from American copybooks, but after 1859, Sloan designed houses expressly for the magazine. Characteristics and styles of various villas are defined and several plans and engravings used as illustrations.

139:1 SMITHMEYER, J.L. (1832-1908)

After working in the office of the Supervising Architect of the Treasury Department, Smithmeyer formed a partnership in 1872 with Paul Pelz (1841-1918) to prepare for the competition for the Library of Congress Building, Washington.

Obituaries: ARCHITECTURAL RECORD 24 (July 1908): 77-78; AMERICAN ARCHITECT AND BUILDING NEWS 93 (March 25, 1908): 15-16.

MONOGRAPHS OF AMERICAN ARCHITECTS has twenty plates of the Library of Congress, Washington, D.C., 1898.

139:2 Cole, John Y. "Smithmeyer and Pelz. Embattled Architects of the Library of Congress." QUARTERLY JOURNAL OF THE LIBRARY OF CONGRESS 29 (October 1972): 282-307.

The competition entries for the Library of Congress are illustrated and evaluated. Librarians and congressmen questioned the design and planning of the building during the period after construction had begun and even refused the payment of the architect's fees. Pages 267-70 list "A chronology," 1871-1965, prepared by the same author followed by eleven pages of a photographic "Albumn."

139:3 Hilker, Helen-Anne. "Monument to Civilization. Diary of a Building." QUARTERLY JOURNAL OF THE LIBRARY OF CONGRESS 29 (October 1972): 234-66.

An analysis of the men who built and contributed to the various designs of the library, including interior decorations and sculptures.

139:4 Hopkins, Archibald. "Smithmeyer and Pelz vs. The United States." AMERICAN ARCHITECT AND BUILDING NEWS 90 (July 28, 1906): 27-29.

This was a claim made by the architects against the government for payment of fees in the design of the Library of Congress. A bill was referred to the United States Court of Claims on March 3, 1905, resolving to pay the claim. It was passed as the Tucker Act, March 3, 1887.

139:5 Sturgis, Russell. "The New Library of Congress: A Study in Decorative Architecture." ARCHITECTURAL RECORD 7 (January-March 1898): 295-332.

Plans for the building were accepted in 1888 and General Casey was put in charge of the work with his son designing portions of the ornamentation. Decoration, detailing, and additional sculptures (with credit given to the individual sculptors, mosaicists, painters, and artisans) are critically assessed as to the spaces into which they fit. "The new Library of Congress is a model for our future proceedings, and the men who have organized it and carried it out, deserve the quite unbounded thanks of the whole community."

140:1 SNOOK, JONATHAN B. (1815-1901)

Born in England and studied in New York under Joseph Trench.

Obituary: AMERICAN ARCHITECT AND BUILDING NEWS 74 (1901): 41.

Mary Ann Smith [Clegg] of Pennsylvania State University is working toward a doctoral dissertation on Snook's commercial architecture.

140:2 Huxtable, Ada Louise. "Grand Central Depot, 1869-1871." PROGRESSIVE ARCHITECTURE 37 (October 1956): 135-38.

Constructed by Commodore Vanderbilt and costing $3 million, it had the largest single span train-shed in the United States at the time and thus set a precedent for later structures. The engineer was R.G. Hadfield. It represented two American Victorian qualities: progress and pretentious display.

140:3 Smith, Mary Ann [Clegg]. "John Snook and the Design for A.T. Stewart's

Store." THE NEW YORK HISTORICAL SOCIETY QUARTERLY 58 (January 1974): 18-33.

One of the first examples of the Italianate style in America. Until the publication of this article, historians were not sure of the architect's identity. Research in ledger and account books at the New York Historical Society has established that Snook of the firm Trench and Snook (Joseph Trench, 1815-79), was the designer of this complex which expanded along Reade and Chambers Streets and Broadway in five extensions. Plan and elevations.

141:1 SPENCER, ROBERT CLOSSON (1864-1953)

Spencer and Powers.

Educated University of Wisconsin in mechanical engineering and worked for Shepley, Rutan and Coolidge (Chicago office).

Republished THE WORK OF FRANK LLOYD WRIGHT FROM 1893 To 1900, 1965 [from THE ARCHITECTURAL REVIEW (Boston), 1900]. (See Spencer under Wright.)

141:2 Purcell, William Gray. "Spencer and Powers, Architects." THE WESTERN ARCHITECT 20 (April 1914): 33, 35-39.

Spencer set up practice in Chicago with Powers in 1905. Powers, born 1872, graduated from Armour Institute of Technology, 1899.

141:3 Rudd, J. William. "The Edward J. McCready House, Spencer and Powers, Architects." THE PRAIRIE SCHOOL REVIEW, 4 (First Quarter, 1967): 18-19.

Completed in June, 1908, the McCready house seems to be attributed to Wright on most occasions. Mr. Rudd explains the house with plans and photographs from THE BRICKBUILDER.

142:1 STEVENS, JOHN CALVIN (1855-1940)

Practiced with Francis H. Fassett and after 1891, Albert W. Cobb.

Avery Library, Columbia University, has 125 sheets of architectural drawings, perspectives, elevations, and plans of ninety-two projects, nine projects of Stevens and Cobb and ten projects of John Calvin and John Howard Stevens.

Publication: joint author with Albert Winslow Cobb of EXAMPLES

OF AMERICAN DOMESTIC ARCHITECTURE, 1889.

Obituary: ARCHITECTURAL FORUM 72 (April 1940): 112.

142:2 Stevens, John Calvin. "The Stevens Architectural Tour." AMERICAN ARCHITECT AND BUILDING NEWS 36 (May 14, 1892): 105-6.

A list of members and the cost involved in a bicycle tour of France!

143:1 STEWARDSON, JOHN (1859-96)

Educated Harvard and Ecole des Beaux Arts. Entered office of T.P. Chandler. He and his brother Emlyn Lamar Stewardson joined Walter Cope to form the partnership Cope and Stewardson (see). After the death of Cope, Stewardson took George Bispham Page into partnership.

Obituary: AMERICAN ARCHITECT AND BUILDING NEWS 51 (1896): 125.

143:2 Stewardson, John. "Architecture in America: A Forecast." AMERICAN ARCHITECT AND BUILDING NEWS 51 (Feburary 1, 1896): 51-52.

"Through the courtesy of the editors of LIPPINCOTT'S MONTHLY MAGAZINE, we are enabled to lay before our readers what in all probability is the last contribution that the late John Stewardson made to the literature of architecture." Stewardson did not, in 1896, view the immediate future as a cheering outlook. He views America's past and hopes for an American architecture of the future.

143:3 Van Pelt, John V[redenburg]. "John Stewardson, a Portrait Sketch." AMERICAN INSTITUTE OF ARCHITECTS' JOURNAL 3 (March 1945): 107-13.

A chatty annectotal account of Stewardson's days in Paris. He died of a skating accident on the Schuylkill at Philadelphia.

144:1 STICKLEY, GUSTAV (1857-1942)

Publications: CRAFTSMAN HOMES, 190?; MORE CRAFTSMAN HOMES, 1912.

144:2 Freeman, John Crosby. THE FORGOTTEN REBEL: GUSTAV STICKLEY AND HIS CRAFTSMEN MISSION FURNITURE. Watkins Glen, N.Y.: Century House, 1965. 112 p.

Stickley was editor of THE CRAFTSMAN and designer of

bold mission furniture in an age of male dominance c. 1900-15. His decline in success and impact after 1915 seems to have been due to an upsurge in the effeminate "colonial" vogue.

144:3 Mumford, Lewis. ROOTS OF CONTEMPORARY AMERICAN ARCHITECTURE. New York: Reinhold Publishing Corp., 1952. Pp. 431-32.

Stickley lived in Binghamton, New York. He forwarded the arts and crafts movement in the United States in his designs after 1900. He also forwarded the revival of the Windsor chair, and the idea of bungalow living.

145:1 STOKES, ISAAC NEWTON PHELPS (1867-1944)

Educated Harvard, 1891, Columbia and the Ecole des Beaux Arts, 1896-97. Formed partnership with John Mead Howells. Most famed for his publications THE ICONOGRAPHY OF MANHATTAN ISLAND, 6 vols., 1915-26; NEW YORK PAST AND PRESENT, 1939; RANDOM RECOLLECTIONS OF A HAPPY LIFE, 1941; AMERICAN HISTORICAL PRINTS, 1932.

145:2 Huxtable, Ada Louise. "Icnography of Manhattan, Being Reissued Soon." THE NEW YORK TIMES, March 3, 1967, p. 37.

I.N. Phelps Stokes' 5,000-page, six-volume iconography, 1498 through 1909, originally published from 1915 to 1928, is being reissued at $795. Facsimile publishing generally is touched upon and so too is the life of Stokes.

145:3 _____. "The New York That Was." THE NEW YORK TIMES, May 14, 1967, section 7, p. 7.

Another review (see March 3, 1967) of Stokes' ICONOGRAPHY..., emphasizing its value as a research document.

145:4 Lubove, Roy. "I.N. Phelps Stokes: Tenement Architect, Economist, Planner." JOURNAL OF THE SOCIETY OF ARCHITECTURAL HISTORIANS 23 (May 1964): 75-87.

Interested in low-cost, economically-planned housing in a day and age not accustomed to such architectural expressions, Stokes and the commissions which he served attempted to alleviate widespread slum conditions. Stokes' projects summed up the best of European and American precedents without being innovative, but based upon sociological considerations. His philosophical attitudes are considered notable in his anti-utopian stand. Practical and down-to-earth, Stokes wanted economics, redevelopment, and slum planning to complement each other.

146:1 **STURGIS, RUSSELL (1838-1909)**

Educated City College of New York and practiced in New York City, 1865-78. Architectural critic and historian.

Avery Library, Columbia University, has fourteen sheets of Battell Chapel and two sheets of Durfee Hall, both at Yale University, a Scrapbook of 186?, and typescripts.

Publications: "On aesthetics, art appreciation, etchings of Piranesi, European and French architecture," DICTIONARY OF ARCHITECTURE, 1901-2.

Obituaries: ARCHITECTURAL RECORD 25 (1908); 26 (1909): 125-31; NEW INTERNATIONAL YEARBOOK, 1909, p. 678.

146:2 ARCHITECTURAL RECORD. "Russell Sturgis' Architecture." Vol. 25 (June 1909): 404-10.

"Very likely the majority of the professional readers of the ARCHITECTURAL RECORD are unaware...that the late Russell Sturgis ever did any architectural work at all," begins this article and then attempts to put the matter right. His three halls and Battell Chapel at Yale, row houses on West 57th Street, New York City, and the Mechanics' National Bank, Albany, 1876, are illustrated.

146:3 Dickason, D.H. "The American Pre-Raphaelites." ART IN AMERICA 30 (July 1942): 157-65.

This article is not specifically on Sturgis but upon the American Pre-Raphaelite Brotherhood and its magazine NEW PATH. Sturgis was one of the seven brothers. Dickason later published a book on the subject, THE DARING YOUNG MEN, Bloomington, Indiana: Indiana University Press, 1953.

146:4 Schuyler, Montgomery. "Russell Sturgis." ARCHITECTURAL RECORD 25 (March 1909): 146, 220.

Obituary with portrait of this architect who "would always rather discuss than design." He provided the profession with the DICTIONARY OF ARCHITECTURE.

146:5 Wight, Peter B[onnett]. "Reminiscences of Russell Sturgis." ARCHITECTURAL RECORD 26 (August 1909): 123-31.

Publication of ideas by Sturgis in private letters to Wight

from the time of their student days at City College of New York. Wight enumerates the career and early contacts and draftsmen of Sturgis from George Fletcher Babb and William R. Mead up to 1868, the literary and critical career of Sturgis until 1894, when he resumed architectural practice with his son, and the advice to his son in architectural design. Sturgis had negative criticisms of Carrere and Hastings and McKim, Mead and White in his correspondence which seems to have been motivated as much by professional jealousy or romantic vs. classical attitudes, as architectural design criticism.

147:1 STURGIS AND BRIGHAM (Partnership early 1870s-86)

John H. Sturgis (1834-88) and Charles Brigham (d.1925).

Sturgis was British in training and worked for Gridley Bryant in Boston before setting up practice with Brigham. Their partnership lasted until Sturgis returned to Britain in 1886.

Avery Library, Columbia University, has pencil drawings of architectural details and furniture, plus photographs.

147:2 Floyd, Margaret Henderson. "A Terra-Cotta Cornerstone for Copley Square: Museum of Fine Arts, Boston: 1870-76, by Sturgis and Brigham." JOURNAL OF THE SOCIETY OF ARCHITECTURAL HISTORIANS 32 (May 1973): 83-103.

The first major structure on Copley Square until its destruction in 1906; the museum had a predominance of architectural terra-cotta, a new material in the 1870's in the United States. The South Kensington Museum in London had considerable influence upon Sturgis, and this is described at considerable length, as is the material used in both cases.

148:1 · SULLIVAN, LOUIS HENRI (1856-1924)

Studied briefly at Massachusetts Institute of Technology and the Ecole des Beaux Arts and worked for Furness and Hewitt in Philadelphia and Jenny in Chicago. Joined Dankmar Adler in 1879, became a partner 1881, and withdrew in 1895, thereafter practicing alone or occasionally with Elmslie.

Publications: THE AUTOBIOGRAPHY OF AN IDEA, 1926; CONCERNING THE IMPERIAL HOTEL, TOKYO, JAPAN, 1923: DEMOCRACY: A MAN-SEARCH, 1961; EMOTIONAL ARCHITECTURE AS COMPARED WITH CLASSICAL, 1894; ESSAY ON INSPIRA-

TION, 1886; KINDERGARTEN CHATS, 1947 (first published in the INTERSTATE ARCHITECT AND BUILDER, 1901-2, with various editions including one by Bragdon, 1934, and another, 1947); REFLECTIONS ON THE TOKYO DISASTER, 1924; WHAT IS ARCHITECTURE: A STUDY IN THE AMERICAN PEOPLE OF TODAY, 1906.

Avery Library, Columbia University, has drawings, letters, notebook while Sullivan was at Massachusetts Institute of Technology, 1872, and other sketches, 1873-80; studies and working sketches, preliminary studies, three sheets of the Chicago Auditorium Building. The Frank Lloyd Wright Foundation gave 122 drawings in 1965 (see catalog below). Harwell Hamilton Harris gave photographs and pamphlets of the Owatonna, Minnesota, Security Bank and Trust Co. after restoration and remodeling, 1958. Burnham Library, Chicago, has drawings of thirteen projects; Brown Hall Library, Ohio University, one project; and the University of Michigan, two projects.

Obituaries: ARCHITECTURAL RECORD 55 (1924): 503, 586-87; AMERICAN INSTITUTE OF ARCHITECTS' JOURNAL 12 (1924): 241, 275, 294, 401; AMERICAN ARCHITECTURE 125 (May 7, 1924): 426.

Narcisco G. Menocal is working on a doctoral dissertation at the University of Illinois, on "Louis Sullivan: A Re-evaluation of his Architectural Thought." Suzanne Shulof wrote a master's thesis at Columbia University in 1962 on "An Interpretation of Louis Sullivan's Architectural Ornament Based on His Philosophy of Organic Expression."

148:2 Bennett, Carl K. A BANK BUILT FOR FARMERS: LOUIS SULLIVAN DESIGNS A BUILDING WHICH MARKS A NEW EPOCH IN AMERICAN ARCHITECTURE. New York: The United Crafts, 1908. 185 p.

148:3 Bragdon, Claude Fayette. "An American Architect: Being an Appreciation of LHS." HOUSE AND GARDEN 7 (January 1905): 47-55.

As part of Chicago's business world, Adler and Sullivan produced architecture for the utilitarian city. Adler as engineer and businessman and Sullivan the designer and artist made the perfect partnership for this commercial city. Sullivan's philosophy, as seen in his architecture, is clearly defined.

148:4 _____. "Louis Sullivan: Prophet of Democracy." ARCHITECTURE AND DEMOCRACY. New York: A.A. Knopf, 1918. Pp. 141-59.

The subject of this book ranges "from skyscraper to symbols....The appreciation of Louis Sullivan as a writer appears here for the first time...." The discussion centers around KINDERGARTEN CHATS, from which many quotations are included.

148:5 Bush-Brown, Albert. LOUIS SULLIVAN. New York: G. Braziller, 1960. 128 p.

Twenty-five pages outline the early life, education, early buildings set against the taste of the 1870's, philosophy, evolving style, writings, and twentieth-century architecture of Sullivan. Illustrations show the impact of Frank Furness, Ware and Van Brunt, Paxton, Viollet-le-Duc, and Richardson; in all 112 figures, plus a selected chronological list of buildings and projects, selected bibliography, and a selection of Sullivan's articles and publications.

148:6 Chamberlain, Betty. "Louis Sullivan." ARTS AND ARCHITECTURE 73 (December 1956): 12-15.

A misleading article on "Inventor of the Skyscraper," stating that the steel salesmen of Pittsburgh and Bethlehem had little success in New York because their suggestions "first fell on disinterested ears." This article is a review of a retrospective exhibition at the Art Institute of Chicago organized by Edgar Kaufmann, but tends to churn out the usual, popular narrative of the opening of the auditorium in 1889, with President Harrison in attendance for a performance including Adelina Patti, etc.

148:7 Columbia University, Avery Architectural Library. CATALOGUE OF THE FRANK LLOYD WRIGHT COLLECTION OF DRAWINGS BY L.H. SULLIVAN. New York: 1965. 2 p.

Presented by Olgivana Lloyd Wright to President of Columbia, Grayson Kirk, in 1965, these 122 drawings are the largest collection of Sullivan drawings anywhere.

148:8 Connely, Willard. "The Last Years of Louis Sullivan." AMERICAN INSTITUTE OF ARCHITECTS' JOURNAL 23 (January 1955): 32-38.

Sullivan had numerous setbacks in the 1907-10 period, then came the commissions for seven country banks until 1919, and the Krause Music Store of 1921, the last commission. The American Institute of Architects also engineered the publication of his THE AUTOBIOGRAPHY OF OF AN IDEA, before his death.

148:9 _____. "The Later Years of Louis Sullivan." AMERICAN INSTITUTE OF ARCHITECTS' JOURNAL 21 (May 1954): 223-28.

One reason for the Adler and Sullivan split in 1895 was that Adler wanted to bring his two sons into the firm, one of whom was a mechanical engineer. Sullivan's marriage to Margaret Davies Hattabough in 1899 and the death of Adler in 1900 both had an effect on Sullivan. Commissions were also few at the turn of the century, and except for a few minor works, Sullivan languished until commissions for banks in small towns began.

148:10 _____. "Louis Sullivan and his Younger Staff." AMERICAN INSTITUTE OF ARCHITECTS' JOURNAL 22 (December 1954): 266-68.

After Elmslie came Parker Berry as Sullivan's assistant in 1909, and in 1911, Homer Sailor, and they stayed for seven and five years respectively, until they took their licensing exams. Both assistants planned to practice together, but Berry died in 1918.

148:11 _____. LOUIS SULLIVAN AS HE LIVED: THE SHAPING OF AMERICAN ARCHITECTURE, A BIOGRAPHY. New York: Horizon Press, 1960. 322 p.

Connely considered that Sullivan was a major contributor to American architecture, who "has remained in eclipse." Family friends, background, marriage, partnership with Adler and its 1894 severance, loneliness, and poverty are all touched upon.

148:12 _____. "The Mystery of Louis Sullivan and His Brother." AMERICAN INSTITUTE OF ARCHITECTS' JOURNAL 20 (November 1953): 226-29; 20 (December 1953): 292-96.

Louis' brother, Albert, was a railway inventor and engineer. Both brothers sketched well, a quality handed down from their mother, but it was athletics that brought the two brothers together, especially in the field of wrestling. Only when the thirty-eight-year-old Albert married a twenty-three-year-old wife, a woman "possessive, hypercritical, managing and not charitable in her judgments" did a split come between the brothers, a split never to mend.

148:13 _____. "New Chapters in the Life of Louis Sullivan." AMERICAN INSTITUTE OF ARCHITECTS' JOURNAL 20 (September 1953): 107-14.

Facts on Sullivan from a 217-page notebook owned by the family have clarified facts in the life of Sullivan. Sullivan's stay at the Ecole des Beaux Arts, Paris, was short and when he returned to the United States, he worked for an old friend, John Edelmann, who was partner in the prosperous firm of Johnson and Edelmann. Sullivan designed the Sinai Synagogue, Chicago, in 1875 for the firm, his first known design. (Earlier than the Central Music Hall, 1879, for Adler, as previously suggested.)

148:14 _____. "New Sullivan Letters." AMERICAN INSTITUTE OF ARCHI-

TECTS' JOURNAL 20 (July 1953): 9-13.

Two letters came to light while Connely was writing his monograph on Sullivan. Both were from Louis to his older brother Albert, the first of December 7, 1874, when he had passed his examinations to enter the Ecole des Beaux Arts, Paris, and the second, January 20, 1887, when Adler and Sullivan were awarded the contract for the Auditorium Building, Chicago.

148:15 Crook, David H. "Louis Sullivan and the Golden Door." JOURNAL OF THE SOCIETY OF ARCHITECTURAL HISTORIANS 26 (December 1967): 250-58.

This transportation "shed" with its doorway, as an "isolated fragment," was a protest by Sullivan against the "White City of Classical motifs." The article discusses the chronology of events at the 1893 Chicago Fair and the architects involved - Chicagoans and easterners.

148:16 Desmond, H.W. "The Schlesinger and Meyer Building. An Attempt to Give Functional Expression to the Architecture of a Department Store." ARCHITECTURAL RECORD 16 (July 1904): 53-67.

"The entire scheme is one organic whole and is carried out in full harmony and balance" from the protective terra-cotta encasing the structural steel frame, the flexibility of the organic architecture to be enlarged as necessary, and the delicacy of feminine ornamentation. "Mr. Sullivan is really our only Modernist."

148:17 Duncan, Hugh Dalziel. CULTURE AND DEMOCRACY, THE STRUGGLE FOR FORM IN SOCIETY AND ARCHITECTURE IN CHICAGO AND THE MIDDLE WEST DURING THE LIFE AND TIMES OF LOUIS H. SULLIVAN. Totowa, N.J.: Bedminster Press, 1965. 616 p. Illus.

An extension of Sullivan's influence beyond architecture and decoration into his social philosophies. Like-minded philosophies by Dewey, Veblen, and Addams are analyzed and the contributions, both positive and negative of John Wellborn Root, D.H. Burnham, Dankmar Adler, and John Edelmann are considered together with the social life of the period: Pullman strike, Haymarket riots, Hull House program through to the Columbian Exposition of 1893.

148:18 Eaton, Leonard K. "Richardson and Sullivan in Scandinavia." PROGRESSIVE ARCHITECTURE, March 1966, pp. 168-71.

Sullivan had an impact in Sweden and Denmark. See also under Richardson.

148:19 Elmslie, G.G. "Sullivan Ornamentation." AMERICAN INSTITUTE OF ARCHITECTS' JOURNAL 6 (October 1946): 155-58. Reprint. MONTHLY

BULLETIN OF THE ILLINOIS SOCIETY OF ARCHITECTS, June-July 1935.

Gray's BOTANY was the source of Sullivan's drawings, many of which are housed in the Burnham Library of the Art Institute of Chicago and in debased form on lesser-known architects' work in the United States and Canada. Sullivan, however, wanted his ornamentation as organic as nature.

148:20 English, Maurice, ed. THE TESTAMENT OF STONE: THEMES OF IDEALISM AND INDIGNATION FROM THE WRITINGS OF LOUIS SULLIVAN. Evanston, Ill.: Northwestern University Press, 1963. 227 p.

Sullivan is presented as a hero figure around which a younger generation of idealistic designers could rally. Not a great articulator of the English language, nor able to communicate well, Sullivan's writings are important in understanding the architect as a person. The eighteen selected articles and excerpts range from unpublished manuscripts and lesser known works to KINDERGARTEN CHATS and AUTOBIOGRAPHY OF AN IDEA.

148:21 Gebhard, David. "Louis Sullivan and George Grant Elmslie." JOURNAL OF THE SOCIETY OF ARCHITECTURAL HISTORIANS 19 (May 1960): 62-68.

"Contrary to accepted fact Wright was never the chief draftsman of the Adler and Sullivan office." Elmslie shared a drafting office with Wright from 1888, and after Wright's dismissal in 1892, became the mainstay of Sullivan until 1909, especially after the breakup of the Adler and Sullivan partnership in 1895. The Gage Building, Carson, Pirie-Scott Store and Owatonna Bank were a combined effort, in decoration at least, of Sullivan and Elmslie.

148:22 Greenyard, Bernard C. "Sullivan, Presto The Krause Music Store." THE PRAIRIE SCHOOL REVIEW 6 (Third Quarter, 1969).

Sullivan's last commission: The Krause Music Store, 4611 N. Lincoln Avenue, 1922, still stands. The commission was given by William Krause to William C. Presto, the last of Sullivan's assistants who had become licensed and was in 1922 practicing in his own right. Presto approached Sullivan and they worked together on this terra-cotta facaded jewel box.

148:23 Hamlin, T.F. "Sullivan Letters at Columbia." AMERICAN ARCHITECTURE 149 (November 1936): 100-104.

Avery Architectural Library, Columbia University, was given a scrapbook of Lyndon P. Smith, a close friend of Sullivan. The scrapbook contains clippings of KINDERGARTEN CHATS and letters signed "Louis" written to Smith at Palisades, New Jersey. Some of the manuscript was written by Sullivan at Palisades.

148:24 Hitchcock, Henry Russell. "Sullivan and the Skyscraper." BUILDER 185 (August 7, 1953): 197-200. [Also ROYAL INSTITUTE OF BRITISH ARCHITECTS' JOURNAL 60 (July 1953): 253-61.]

Hitchcock chose Sullivan as one of the triumvirate for his lecture at the Royal Institute of British Architects on June 23, 1953, because he was more particularly linked to skyscraper construction. "Sullivan was the first master architect of the skyscraper." A brief history of structures using component parts, necessary in high-rise structures is provided, in addition to the links between early structural developments, the Chicago scene, and Sullivan's place therein. Most of Sullivan's high-rise Chicago structures are mentioned with concluding remarks of their impact upon later buildings.

148:25 Hoffmann, Donald. "The Setback Skyscraper City of 1891: An Unknown Essay by Louis H. Sullivan." ROYAL INSTITUTE OF BRITISH ARCHITECTS' JOURNAL 29 (May 1970): 181-87.

Sullivan's brief essay "The High Building Question" is an appendix to this article. It attempts to justify light and air for the populace of an urban area plus sufficient profitable rentable space for the owner-realtor. Adler and Sullivan's Schiller Building, Chicago, 1891-92, and the Odd Fellows Temple project of 1891 fit into the category of a high-rise building diminishing to a slender tower above a block square podium.

148:26 Hope, Henry R. "Louis Sullivan's Architectural Ornament." ARCHITECTURAL REVIEW 102 (October 1947): 111-14. [Also MAGAZINE OF ART 40 (March 1947): 110-17.]

A survey of Sullivan's career and buildings but with a special emphasis on his decorative style and how it developed to its richest forms in the 1890-95 period. KINDERGARTEN CHATS provides ample quotations to support Sullivan's decorative intentions: "The decoration of a structure is in truth, when done with understanding, the more mobile, delicate and sumptuous expression of the creative impulse...expressed in the structure."

148:27 Huxtable, Ada Louise. "And This Time the Good Banks." THE NEW YORK TIMES, Sunday, April 30, 1972, section 2, p. 22.

Examples of good conversions of historic properties into banks are provided but the article is essentially concerned with the Security Bank and Trust Co., Owatonna,

Minnesota, 1908, by Sullivan, aided by George Grant Elmslie. A brief historic sketch of this particular bank is provided, up to the period of its restoration in 1958 by Harwell Hamilton Harris.

148:28 _____. "Architecture: Sullivan's Powerful Inspired Legacy." THE NEW YORK TIMES, January 27, 1966, p. 66.

Columbia University was exhibiting fifty-four fragile drawings of a total of 122 given by Sullivan to Wright in 1924. Avery Library purchased them from Mrs. Wright.

148:29 _____. "Arts Group Saves Bits of Landmark." THE NEW YORK TIMES, October 6, 1964.

Sullivan's only New York building, The Bayard at 65 Bleeker Street, has had its facade mutilated and changed. Some pieces of decoration are being saved.

148:30 _____. "Handling a Hot Potato." THE NEW YORK TIMES, Sunday, March 1, "The Chicago Style - On Its Way Out?", November 29, 1970, section 2, p. 27.

Adler and Sullivan's Chicago Stock Exchange, 1893, was one of seventeen structures proposed for designation as landmarks by the Chicago Landmarks Commission. But the Chicago City Council will have to compensate the owners if they accept the designation status. The build-is functional and rents well, but yields less in taxes than would a new building on the same site built to maximum zoning height. Mrs. Huxtable suggests that the "air rights" above the building should be saleable as in New York City, thus aleviating the need for demolition.

148:31 _____. A SYSTEM OF ARCHITECTURAL ORNAMENT ACCORDING WITH A PHILOSOPHY OF MAN'S POWERS. New York: Eakins Press, 1967. 75 p. 20 pl.

This publication includes drawings for the Farmers' and Merchants' Union Bank, Columbus, Wisconsin, and the twenty plates are reduced in size from an earlier edition of 1924.

148:32 Ianelli, Alfonso. "Evaluation of Louis H. Sullivan's Ornament." THE PRAIRIE SCHOOL REVIEW 1 (Second Quarter, 1964): 25-26.

Ianelli, a sculptor who worked on Wright's Midway Gardens, Chicago, discusses Sullivan's "play of light, dark and texture."

148:33 Jeanneret-Gris, Charles Edouard. "Letter from le Corbusier to Mayor Daley of Chicago." PROGRESSIVE ARCHITECTURE 42 (June 1961): 208.

"I should not want to give the impression of busying myself with issues that do not concern me, but. . . ." Corbusier is concerned about Sullivan's Garrick Theater and the Republic Building of Holabird and Roche.

148:34 Johnson, Philip. "Is Sullivan the Father of Functionalism?" ART NEWS 55 (December 1956): 44-46, 56-57.

At the centennial of Sullivan's birth, the Chicago Art Institute had an exhibition and John Szarkowski published a book based upon the show (148:60). Johnson here adds his piece as an architect under Sullivan's influence, admitting that John Root was a better Richardsonian than Sullivan. Even McKim "in his Boston Public Library. . . created a design far purer, and much more inspiring to look at than nine-tenths of Sullivan's buildings." Johnson doesn't even think that the "father of functionalism" is particularly functional in his designs.

148:35 Kimball, Sydney Fiske. "Louis Sullivan an Old Master." ARCHITECTURAL RECORD 57 (April 1925): 289-304.

Ruskin is quoted at length with the statement that "the predominance of these ideas was fundamentally hostile to every survival or revival of historical forms, but the new principles were only gradually driven to their extreme consequences. . . . In Louis Sullivan, Chicago found its poet." The article glorifies Sullivan's approach to design, notably in the case of the skyscraper. Included in the illustrations is a little-known project: the Trust and Savings Building, St. Louis.

148:36 Line, Ralph Marlowe. "Art and Architecture - The Past: Louis H. Sullivan." CRAFT HORIZONS 22 (May-June 1962): 18-21.

Excerpts from Line's introduction to Dover Publication's 1956 edition of Sullivan's THE AUTOBIOGRAPHY OF AN IDEA, emphasizing at the end that Sullivan designed only twenty-four buildings in the last thirty-one years of his life.

148:37 McQuade, Walter. "Sullivan Survives." ARCHITECTURAL FORUM 105 (October 1956): 156-61.

A review of John Szarkowski's THE IDEA OF LOUIS SULLIVAN (see).

148:38 Manson, Grant. "Sullivan and Wright, An Uneasy Union of Celts." ARCHITECTURAL REVIEW 118 (November 1955): 297-300.

"The interplay of two creative Celtic minds in transient and unstable union." Wright needed Sullivan, "the towering force" at the beginning of his career, but Wright gave a new and significant direction to the occasional piece of domestic architecture which came, uncourted, into the office. The Charnley House, Chicago, 1891, was symbolically the last of Adler and Sullivan's domestic architecture and the beginning for Wright. Sullivan played no part in the design of the Charnley House and too little in the Schiller Building, which when compared to the house, became an "aberration in Sullivan's career."

148:39 Millett, Louis J. "The National Farmer's Bank of Owatonna, Minnesota." ARCHITECTURAL RECORD 24 (October 1908): 248-58.

Why would the businessmen of a dairy-farming community, 6000 strong, want a bank "with its new forms telling of new Thoughts?" Was it the individual spirit of which the United States is made?

148:40 Morrison, Hugh. LOUIS SULLIVAN, PROPHET OF MODERN ARCHITECTURE. New York: Peter Smith, 1952. (1st ed. 1935). 391 p.

Morrison proposed Louis Sullivan's architecture as a subject for a doctoral dissertation at Harvard. It was turned down as being a subject of too recent vintage, so Morrison went ahead and produced the most satisfying book on Sullivan to date. Others have discovered additional research material, but the basic judgments of Morrison hold true. Sullivan growing up, developing, and turning to various schools and architects for training precede detailed considerations of each major structure by Adler and Sullivan, and Sullivan alone after 1895. Architectural theory and critical evaluations form part of this excellent biography.

148:41 _____. "Louis Sullivan Today." AMERICAN INSTITUTE OF ARCHITECTS' JOURNAL 26 (September 1956): 98-100.

Morrison reassessed the Wainwright Building, St. Louis, as a masterpiece leading on to Carson, Pirie, and Scott, a leap forward into the twentieth century. Morrison's book on Sullivan was the first, and in many respects, the best, but he like many others was satisfied to see others, including Richard S. Nickel and Willard Connely, following in his footsteps to provide greater understanding of an architect of the ability of Sullivan.

148:42 Mumford, Lewis. ROOTS OF CONTEMPORARY AMERICAN ARCHITECTURE. New York: Reinhold Publishing Corporation, 1952. Pp. 432-33.

"One of the hardest figures to place in American Architecture...," Mumford seems to think that he was a graduate of Massachusetts Institute of Technology where, in fact, he studied for only a few months, and then he became a partner of Adler as late as 1883, instead of 1881.

148:43 Paris, W. Franklyn. "Louis Sullivan." AMERICAN SOCIETY LEGION

OF HONOR MAGAZINE 23 (Summer 1952): 153-70.

An emphasis on the appreciation by the French of Sullivan in their awards for his designs and exhibitions at the Musee des Arts Decoratifs. The article also covers his education, association with Adler, brief discussion of some of his architecture, attitudes of people who knew him, and mention of his writings and philosophy.

148:44 _____. "Louis Sullivan." THE HALL OF AMERICAN ARTISTS. Vol. 9. New York: New York University Press, 1952. Pp. 67-84.

Sullivan's AUTOBIOGRAPHY provides valuable information on his early career and his partnership with Dankmar Adler. Together they designed numerous notable structures and employed Frank Lloyd Wright for several years, but Sullivan gained less respect in his own country where he made derogatory statements concerning the classical designs of his contemporaries. The French were first to recognize and honor his ability. His theories are briefly noted.

148:45 Sherman, Paul. LOUIS SULLIVAN: AN ARCHITECT IN AMERICAN THOUGHT. Englewood Cliffs, N.J.: Prentice-Hall, 1962. 176 p.

An assessment of Sullivan, not only as architect but equally as writer and philosopher with strong overtones in sociology and economics. Although no great author, Sullivan is linked to the Transcendentalists and Pragmatists. A bibliography lists thirty-seven articles and publications by Sullivan.

148:46 Purcell, William Gray. "Louis H. Sullivan, Prophet of Democracy." AMERICAN INSTITUTE OF ARCHITECTS' JOURNAL 16 (December 1951): 265-71.

Purcell comes to the defense of Sullivan whom he complains is continually maligned and misquoted by those who do not understand. In Sullivan's day and age they were answered by the master or Montgomery Schuyler, but when Denison B. Hull published "Freedom in Architecture," AMERICAN INSTITUTE OF ARCHITECTS' JOURNAL, June 1951, Purcell saw the need to counter misconceptions.

148:47 _____. "Sullivan at Work." NORTHWEST ARCHITECT 8 (January-February 1944): 11.

Purcell began work for Sullivan "over forty years" earlier, and in 1944 he reminiscences on Sullivan, the Thinker, in drawing and draftsmanship. A brief half-page article.

148:48 Randall, John D. THE WAINWRIGHT BUILDING, A PUBLIC APPEAL FOR PRESERVATION. Edwardsville, Ill.: Privately printed, n.d. 53 p.

An open letter signed by a large number of concerned people was sent to President Lyndon B. Johnson and others on October 12, 1967, in order to preserve the building. Cost estimates, recommendations, evaluations regarding its importance, and a chronological list of references emphasize the building's importance. A log of demolished and desecrated designs of Sullivan ends this attention-getting booklet.

148:49 Rebori, A.N. "An Architecture of Democracy." ARCHITECTURAL RECORE 39 (May 1916): 436-65.

Subtitled "Three Recent Examples from the Work of Louis H. Sullivan," Rebori relates the work of Sullivan to the American scene rather than "reproductions of monuments of the old world." Mr. Sullivan's approach is to visit the client or committee and the site, and familiarize himself with all aspects of the problem. The article illustrates original plans with notations as well as finished drawings and photographs of the Merchants National Bank, Grinnell, Iowa; the Homebuilding Association Co., Newark, Ohio; and the Land and Loan Office, Algona, Iowa.

148:50 Roosevelt University. ANNOUNCES PLANS FOR THE RESTORATION OF ADLER AND SULLIVAN'S AUDITORIUM BUILDING. Chicago, Ill.: N. pub., n.d. 23 p.

Roosevelt University purchased parts of the building in 1946 for conversion into college facilities. Many areas were restored, although for student use and not for luxury and lavish uses originally intended. Comparing photographs from the 1890's with those of the university's occupation show the changes and achievements. A list of advisors wanting the restoration of the actual auditorium is provided.

148:51 Salerno, Joseph. "Louis Sullivan - Return to Principle." LITURGICAL ARTS 16 (February 1948): 49-50.

"Organic law is inherent in all great architecture," and Sullivan (and Wright) are praised for a return to this as well as other basic principles which would seem compatible with Catholic architecture. Sullivan's works and philosophies are listed with the conclusion that "is it not time the Church accepted the validity of this truth once more and demanded its recognition by those charged with the building of churches."

148:52 Schuyler, Montgomery. "The People's Savings Bank of Cedar Rapids, Iowa." ARCHITECTURAL RECORD 31 (January 1912): 44-56.

In 1912, Schuyler could begin his article "There is no

denying that a new work by Louis Sullivan is the most interesting event which can happen in the American architectural world today." Owatonna was a success but not a prototype. Schuyler considers this bank in Cedar Rapids, Iowa, to be just as individualistic in form and detail. It was designed from the interior outward, so that the form is an envelope, stark and simple, with an internal emphasis on decoration, yet an openness to express the workings of the bank.

148:53 _____. "The Skyscraper up to Date." ARCHITECTURAL RECORD 8 (January-March 1899): 231-60.

After stating the problems of the steel-framed tall building, Schuyler discusses numerous examples by well-known architects and at p. 255 comes to the Bayard Building, New York City, by Sullivan, "the nearest approach yet made, in New York, at least to solving the problem of the Skyscraper."

148:54 Scully, Vincent., Jr. "Louis Sullivan's Architectural Ornament." PERSPECTA 5 (1959): 73-80.

Subtitled "A brief note concerning humanist design in the age of force." This essay is a reassessment of Johnson's criticism of Sullivan's lack of function by the application of ornamentation (ART NEWS, December 1956, pp. 44-46, 56-57 above). The Guaranty Building, Buffalo, becomes "a skeleton clad with what appears to be integral force, stepping out toward its corner, standing, stretching and physically potent." Ornamentation was also used elsewhere to "deny any expression of physical weight or solidity to certain surfaces."

148:55 Smith, Lyndon P. "The Home of an Artist-Architect. Louis H. Sullivan's Place at Ocean Springs, Mississippi." ARCHITECTURAL RECORD 17 (June 1905): 471-90.

An outdoor retreat with house was built by Sullivan at Biloxi Bay between New Orleans and Mobile on the Gulf Coast, set in luxurious growth with rose, fig, and many cultivated blooming varieties. Numerous photographs and a site plan from which can be seen the detailed plan of this T-shaped house.

148:56 Sprague, Paul Edward. "The Architectural Ornament of Louis Sullivan and His Chief Draftsmen." Doctoral dissertation, Princeton University, 1969. 490 p.

Devoted to the study of Sullivan's architectural and ornamental theory and the development and influence on Frank Lloyd Wright, George Elmslie, and Parker Berry. Sullivan is discussed in relation to European trends of the period and as deriving from his contemporaries such as Frank Furness and William Ware.

148:57 ____. "The National Farmer's Bank, Owatonna, Minnesota." THE PRAIRIE SCHOOL REVIEW 4 (Second Quarter, 1967): 5-21.

Carl Bennett, vice president of the Owatonna Bank read Sullivan's essay, "What is Architecture: A Study of the American People Today," published in the CRAFTSMAN, May 1906, and decided upon Sullivan as the bank's architect. Sullivan worked closely with his chief assistant, Elmslie, on the $90,000 structure. Sprague questions David Gebhard's assumption that Elmslie was the designer [JOURNAL OF THE SOCIETY OF ARCHITECTURAL HISTORIANS 19 (May 1960): 66], even though he admits Sullivan's strong reliance upon the younger man.

148:58 Starrett, Theodore. "The Architecture of Louis Henri Sullivan." ARCHITECTS' AND BUILDERS' MAGAZINE 44 (December 1912): 469-75.

As much a discussion of the place of great architects in listings of world famous figures as a discussion on the architecture of Sullivan, the skyscraper in Chicago, and more particularly Sullivan's contribution.

148:59 Sturgis, Russell. "New Frank Lloyd Wright and Louis H. Sullivan Papers in the Burnham Library of Architecture." CALENDAR OF THE ART INSTITUTE OF CHICAGO 65 (January 1971): 6-15.

The Sullivan papers, 1910-14, are concerned with the construction of a dry goods store for John D. Van Allen and Sons of Clinton, Iowa. Some interesting construction photographs.

148:60 Szarkowski, John. THE IDEA OF LOUIS SULLIVAN. Minneapolis: University of Minnesota Press, 1956. 161 p.

The author and photographer of THE IDEA OF LOUIS SULLIVAN has sought to juxtapose Sullivan's designs with the works of his contemporaries, to introduce people and objects into close relationships with the architecture. Szarkowski forwards the humanist attitude that Sullivan was building for people, to enhance their environment and make life more rewarding.

148:61 Tallmadge, Thomas Eddy. "The Peoples' Savings and Loan Association Building of Sidney, Ohio." AMERICAN ARCHITECTURE 114 (October 23, 1918): 497-500.

Daylight, artificial lighting, ventilation by natural and fan-blown circulation, exhaust, and air washing are briefly discussed in relation to this bank. Plans and sections of the mechanical equipment are provided.

148:62 Tselos, Dimitri. "The Chicago Fair and the Myth of the 'Lost Cause.'" JOURNAL OF THE SOCIETY OF ARCHITECTURAL HISTORIANS 26 (December 1967): 259-68.

A general discussion of the Romanesque Revival of John W. Root and the classicism after his death of Daniel Burnham as the styles considered for the 1893 Chicago Columbian Exposition. In detail, however, the main theme concerns the retardataire quality of Sullivan's Transportation Building compared to George B. Post's ultra-modern Manufacturer's Building. Inspiration for Sullivan came from Islamic Morocco and medieval Notre Dame, Paris, added to a simplistic clumsiness.

148:63 Turak, Theodore. "A Celt Among Slavs: Louis Sullivan's Holy Trinity Cathedral." THE PRAIRIE SCHOOL REVIEW 9 (Fourth Quarter, 1972): 5-22.

"The sole religious structure designed by Sullivan to survive as he intended," is Holy Trinity Russian Orthodox Cathedral, Chicago, a building of great originality designed for ritual and with economy ($27,104.37), and the decoration based possibly upon Viollet-le-Duc's L'ART RUSSE....

148:64 Vaughn, Edward J. "Sullivan and Elmslie at Michigan." THE PRAIRIE SCHOOL REVIEW 6 (Second Quarter, 1969): 20-23.

Two alumni of the University of Michigan commissioned Sullivan in 1895 to design a medal to be awarded annually for the Northern Oratorical League Contest. "Elmslie was responsible for its execution, refinement and elaboration." Elmslie also designed the Angell Loving Cup, 1909, and the Testimonial Book for retiring president James B. Angell. All items are illustrated.

148:65 _____. "Sullivan and the University of Michigan." THE PRAIRIE SCHOOL REVIEW 6 (First Quarter, 1969): 21-23.

"When in 1905 the University of Michigan proposed to reestablish a Chair of Architecture in their Department of Engineering, surprisingly, one of the applicants was Louis Sullivan." Emil Lorch (1870-1963) was given the position.

148:66 Weisman, Winston. "Philadelphia Functionalism and Sullivan." JOURNAL OF THE SOCIETY OF ARCHITECTURAL HISTORIANS 20 (March 1961): 3-19.

Was the Jayne Building, Philadelphia, 1849, by William L. Johnston, a precursor of Sullivan's Wainwright Building, St. Louis? "This in turn raises the query of whether the form of functionalism practiced in the Midwest was an independent phenomenon attributable to Chicago or was it merely the extension of an earlier tradition rooted in. . . Philadelphia?" Both Sullivan and the Philadelphians used the same principles, building methods, verticality, and materials.

148:67 Wofford, Theodore J. RECOMMENDATIONS FOR RESTORING AND REJUVENATING THE WAINWRIGHT BUILDING, ST. LOUIS, MISSOURI. St. Louis: 1966. Plates and plans.

Not meant as an answer to all the problems of saving the building, the booklet recommends means by which the structure can be repaired, made to comply with codes and satisfy planning and mechanical needs. Plans are provided and an early perspective.

148:68 Wright, Frank Lloyd. GENIUS AND THE MOBOCRACY. New York: Duell, Sloan and Pearce, 1949. 112 p. Reprint. New York: Horizon Press, 1971. 247 p.

The 1971 edition contains drawings by Wright and Sullivan in addition to the thirty-nine by Sullivan in the 1949 edition. The text links the two great architects together in philosophy and design. "I have tried - with honest arrogance - to describe the tragedy, triumph and significance of the great man. . ." wrote Wright.

148:69 _____. "Louis H. Sullivan, his Work." ARCHITECTURAL RECORD 56 (July 1924): 28-32.

Wright compares Sullivan to "the insensate period of General Grant Gothic." Wright preferred the simplicity of the Auditorium with its free-form ornamentation and richness. The Getty Tomb, Wainwright Building, and Transportation Building are also mentioned as showing the "creative activity that was Sullivan's genius." Sullivan predicted more mediocrity in the future and the difficulty of younger generations achieving what he had set out to do.

148:70 _____. "Louis Sullivan's Words and Work: Kindergarten Chats." ARCHITECTURAL REVIEW 77 (March 1935): 116-17.

A review by Wright of KINDERGARTEN CHATS.

148:71 _____. "On Louis Sullivan." ARCHITECTURAL FORUM 91 (August 1949): 94-97.

"Louis Sullivan taught me nothing nor did he ever pretend to do so. . . ." (Wright) The article has numerous quotations and illustrations of Sullivan's drawings (one hundred of which were given to Wright a week before Sullivan died) from Wright's GENIUS AND THE MOBOCRACY.

148:72 ______. "Sullivan Against The World." ARCHITECTURAL REVIEW 105 (June 1949): 295-98.

A reprint of "Truth Against The World," a chapter from Wright's book on Sullivan: GENIUS AND THE MOBOCRACY. At this time Wright had just received the gold medal of the American Institute of Architects.

149:1 TALLMADGE AND WATSON (Partnership 1905- ?)

Thomas Eddy Tallmadge (1876-1940). Educated Massachusetts Institute of Technology and worked for Daniel H. Burnham.

Publications: ARCHITECTURE IN OLD CHICAGO, 1941; THE STORY OF ARCHITECTURE IN AMERICA, 1927; THE STORY OF ENGLAND'S ARCHITECTURE, 1934.

Obituary of Tallmadge: ARCHITECTURAL FORUM 72 (March 1940): 58; ARCHITECTURAL RECORD 87 (February 1940): 116.

149:2 THE WESTERN ARCHITECT. "The Work of Tallmadge and Watson." Vol. 22 (December 1915): 47-50.

Domestic architecture with a feeling for the Gothic was the vogue of this Chicago firm, which utilized local and inexpensive materials. Background, biographical information, and seventeen plates provide adequate material on the firm.

150:1 TROST, HENRY C. (c. 1860-1933)

Trained in Toledo, Ohio; Tucson, Arizona; and Colorado Springs where he practiced as Weston and Trost. He also practiced in Pueblo; Galveston, Texas; and Chicago, c. 1886-96, where he worked for Adler and Sullivan.

150:2 Engelbrecht, Lloyd C. "Henry Trost: The Prairie School in the Southwest." THE PRAIRIE SCHOOL REVIEW 6 (Fourth Quarter, 1969): 5-29.

Trost was an illusive architect who practiced throughout his life over a wide geographic area. Much of his history is difficult to trace or substantiate. His buildings range from the strictest classical through the local pueblo styles, the commercialisms of Sullivan, the Chicago School in all its variations, and the Prairie style of Wright. Most of the work is a trifle clumsy and heavy-handed, irrespective of Trost's historicism, which Engelbrecht attempts to justify.

151:1 TRUMBAUER, HORACE (1869-1938)

Self-trained and practiced from 1892.

Avery Library, Columbia University, has two blueprints of buildings at 720 Fifth Avenue and 56th Street, New York City, 1910-12. The School of Library Service, Columbia University, has a list of books from Trumbauer's Library at a Public Sale, February 2, 1939, in Philadelphia, S.T. Freeman and Co. The Philadelphia Museum of Art has drawings of thirty-five projects. The Rare Book Room of the University of Pennsylvania has one sheet of the Philadelphia Parkway and the Philadelphia Museum of Art, one sheet of the museum, both by Trumbauer, C.C. Zantzinger and Paul Cret.

Obituary: ARCHITECTURAL FORUM 70 (January 1939): 46.

151:2 ARCHITECTURAL RECORD. "A New Influence in the Architecture of Philadelphia." Vol. 15 (February 1904): 93-121.

Philadelphia in 1904 was one of the "unmitigated spots ...of wildly bad design," but with some good showing through. Trumbauer's residences, rural and urban, are palatial whether in a strictly classical style or with the rusticity of a medieval castle, or a half-timbered Elizabethan mansion. One church and a school for crippled children, of less pretension, are also illustrated.

152:1 UPJOHN, RICHARD MITCHELL (1827-1903)

Son of the famous American Gothic Revivalist, Richard Upjohn, for whom he worked. In 1851 he became a partner in Upjohn and Co. Major designer in the firm, 1860-76.

Avery Library, Columbia University, has a drawing of the State Capitol, Hartford, Connecticut; a collection of Upjohn drawings including those of Richard M. Upjohn (see index below) and Manuscript Record, July 1846 to April 1854. Museum of the City of New York has drawings. Richard M. Upjohn became the chief designer in the office of Richard Upjohn and Associates after Richard Upjohn's retirement.

Avery Library, Columbia University, has 189 projects by Richard Upjohn; Richard Upjohn and Associates, some of which are by Richard M. Upjohn.

Obituaries: AMERICAN ARCHITECT AND BUILDING NEWS 79 (1903): 81-82; AMERICAN INSTITUTE OF ARCHITECTS' QUARTERLY BULLETIN 4 (April 1903): 20-21; INLAND ARCHITECT

AND NEWS RECORD 41 (March 1903).

Ticknor of Boston published twenty-two plates of the State Capitol, Hartford, Connecticut, 1886, in their Monographs of American Architecture Series.

152:2 Albany, New York, St. Peter's Church. ST. PETER'S CHURCH IN THE CITY OF ALBANY: HISTORICAL SKETCH AND DESCRIPTION OF THE EDIFICE. New York: Fort Orange Press, 1907. 51 p. 15 pl.

The second church on the site was demolished on St. Peter's Day, June 29, 1859. Thereafter the third church was built with alterations taking place in 1885. Memorial windows, tablets, and the like are described in detail.

152:3 Columbia University. Avery Architectural Library. INDEX OF THE UPJOHN COLLECTION. New York: 1944. 69 p.

Includes material of Richard Upjohn, Richard Upjohn and Co., and Richard Mitchell Upjohn.

152:4 Hersey, G.L. "Replication Replicated." PERSPECTA 9-10 (1965): 211-48.

Upjohn's Connecticut State Capitol at Hartford, Connecticut, 1872-78, "proclaims with crude clarity a certain American concept of architecture...and how it seems to be reappearing in the present wave of brutalism." Other structures of the period and other submissions for the Hartford Capitol are discussed and illustrated, with numerous nineteenth-century photographs of the Upjohn building.

152:5 Upjohn, Everard [Miller]. RICHARD UPJOHN: ARCHITECT AND CHURCHMAN. New York: Columbia University Press, 1939. Reprint. New York: Da Capo Press, 1968. 243 p.

Although this work is on Richard Upjohn, father of Richard M. Upjohn, the book by Richard's grandson included data on the experience gained by the son in his father's office, the partnership of father and son, and a comparison of their work. Richard M. Upjohn became designer in the firm after 1860 and the Appendix lists important, secondary, and minor works by the firm, some by the father, others by Richard M. Upjohn, and yet further collaborative efforts by both.

153:1 URBAN, JOSEPH (1872-1933)

Obituaries: ARCHITECTURAL FORUM 59 (August 1933): 4; AMERI-

CAN ARCHITECTURE 145 (September 1933): 137; ARCHITECTURAL RECORD 74 (August 1933): 148.

153:2 LONDON STUDIO. "Joseph Urban: Architect - Theatre Designer - Industrial Designer." Vol. 7 (January 1934): 34-37.

"America owes much to the late Joseph Urban, architect, theatre designer, and latterly industrial designer." Born in Vienna, 1872, he studied under Baron Hasenaeur and worked for him and later in private practice until 1904. After several visits to the United States he began practice both in stage scenery and exhibition architecture. Includes Art Deco illustrations.

153:3 Roberts, Mary Fanton. "Timeless Modernism." ARTS AND DECORATION 44 (August 1936): 10-13, 47.

Neither modern nor traditional, but rather personal and forwarding a new way of living - "young, gay, simple and extravagant." This is Art Deco at its best in color, form, and interior space arrangements.

153:4 Scott, Irvin L. "'Maralajo,' Estate of Edward F. Hutton, Palm Beach, Florida." AMERICAN ARCHITECTURE 133 (June 20, 1928): 795-811.

Maralajo is an extensive house for seasonal entertainment with a "picturesque and dramatic quality." Italian stone, Hispano-Moresque tiles, and Cuban roof tiles help to make this spread a veritable Hadrian's Villa in Florida, with all the imaginative richness, albeit not the Art Nouveau of Antonio Gaudi.

153:5 Taylor, Deems. "The Scenic Art of Joseph Urban. His Protean Work in the Theater." ARCHITECTURE (New York) 69 (May 1934): 275-90.

Famous for his stage sets, Urban's emergence in this field was more by accident than of choice, through an invitation from the Vienna Royal Theater for scene designs for a production of Faust. The numerous drawings and photographs of this article present an all-round picture of this man's contribution to the theater arts.

153:6 Teegen, Otto. "Joseph Urban." ARCHITECTURE (New York) 69 (May 1934): 251-56.

A biographical sketch of Carl Maria Georg Joseph Urban, from the years and training in Vienna, London, and the United States. Sketches of early work and illustrations.

153:7 ______. "Joseph Urban's Philosophy of Color." ARCHITECTURE (New York) 69 (May 1934): 257-71.

"Color was...one of the principal interests of the early

groups of Viennese artists of which he was a member and leader." Floriated patterns were a preference in the early years, but in the 1930's he used large masses of bright color. Numerous and varied examples of his work are illustrated but all in black and white.

153:8 Walter, Ralph. "Joseph Urban, the Man." ARCHITECTURE 69 (May 1934): 271-72.

An appreciation of some of the operatic sets which Urban designed and a tribute to his design ability.

154:1 VAN BRUNT, HENRY (1832-1903)

Educated at Harvard and worked for George Snell, Boston, and Hunt, in New York City. Partnerships with William R. Ware (see) and Frank M. Howe. See also Ware and Van Brunt.

Publications: ARCHITECTURE AT THE WORLD'S COLUMBIAN EXPOSITION, 1892; GREEK LINES AND OTHER ARCHITECTURAL ESSAYS, 1893; GROWTH AND CHARACTERISTIC ARCHITECTURE STYLE IN THE U.S., 1894; Translated the DISCOURSES ON ARCHITECTURE, 1875-81, of Viollet-le-Duc.

Obituaries: ARCHITECTURAL REVIEW 10 (April 1903); INLAND ARCHITECT AND NEWS RECORD 51 (April 1903); AMERICAN INSTITUTE OF ARCHITECTS' QUARTERLY BULLETIN 3 (April 1903): 21-22.

154:2 ARCHITECTURAL REVIEW (Boston). "Henry Van Brunt, 1832-1903." Vol. 10 (1903): 44.

After the Civil War a generation of men stimulated by Richard M. Hunt began a new era of architecture in the United States. "It is to be remembered that even at present, with much of our architecture influenced by French tradition of space, we are still prone to small scale and petty cubules, and that Memorial Hall (Harvard) is an admirable antidote for such littleness."

154:3 Coles, William A. ARCHITECTURE AND SOCIETY. Cambridge, Mass.: The Belknap Press of Harvard University Press, 1969. 562 p.

Subtitled "Selected Essays of Henry Van Brunt," the book contains a short biography and essay on his writings followed by twenty-two essays ranging from monographs on Eidlitz, Richardson, Root, and Hunt in whose atelier Van Brunt began after graduating from Harvard. Van Brunt set up an office in Kansas City and thus there is an essay on the architecture of the West as well as another on the World's Columbian Exposition, Chicago,

1893, where Van Brunt and Howe designed the Electricity Building. Illustrations complement the essay topics. There is also a survey of the work of Van Brunt and his various partners.

154:4 Howe, Frank Maynard. "The Development of Architecture in Kansas City, Missouri." ARCHITECTURAL RECORD 15 (February 1904): 135-57.

This article written by Howe includes several structures designed by Van Brunt and Howe including several residences, some lavishly extravagant, and Howe's own home. They also extended the Federal Building; designed a commercial building, the Bryant; and a hotel called Coates House.

154:5 Wight, P.B. "Henry Van Brunt - Architect, Writer and Philosopher." INLAND ARCHITECT AND NEWS RECORD 23 (April 1894): 29-30; 23 (May 1894): 41-42; 23 (June 1894): 49-50; 23 (July 1894): 60-61.

A book review of Van Brunt's GROWTH AND CHARACTERISTIC ARCHITECTURAL STYLE IN THE UNITED STATES and GREEK LINES AND OTHER ARCHITECTURAL ESSAYS, but also an evaluation of his contribution to American architecture. Van Brunt attempted to synthesize the stylistic trends of the nineteenth century and to achieve progress through cooperation and intelligent unity.

155:1 VAUGHAN, HENRY (1846-1917)

Born in Boston, but trained in England under George F. Bodley.

Obituaries: AMERICAN ARCHITECT AND BUILDING NEWS 112 (1917): 31, 40; ARCHITECTURAL RECORD 42 (1917): 266; AMERICAN INSTITUTE OF ARCHITECTS' JOURNAL 5 (1917): 352, 518.

William Morgan has recently completed a doctoral dissertation on Vaughan at the University of Delaware.

155:2 Frohman, Philip Hubert. "The Cathedral of St. Peter and St. Paul, Washington, D.C." AMERICAN ARCHITECTURE 127 (April 22, 1925): 355-68.

Frohman, Robb and Little revised the designs of Vaughan and Bodley. Medieval cathedrals and those at Liverpool, England, and in New York, are discussed in relation to the various parts of the cathedral at Washington. The Lady Chapel, for example, is considered more original than beautiful but does "impress us with the modern trend toward self expression of the individual, rather than the medieval spirit of self forgetfulness. . . . " The accurate Gothic of Cram is praised and so too is the choice of English above the French Gothic style by Vaughan. Frohman, Robb and Little intend to proceed in this spirit of detailed accuracy.

155:3 Morgan, William. "The Architecture of Henry Vaughan and the Episcopal Church." HISTORICAL MAGAZINE OF THE PROTESTANT CHURCH 42 (June 1973): 125-35.

Material abstracted from Morgan's doctoral dissertation.

155:4 PROGRESSIVE ARCHITECTURE. "What's Progressive about a Gothic Cathedral," December 1972, pp. 68-75.

Although the Cathedral Church of St. Peter and St. Paul, Washington, D.C., was won in competition by Vaughan and Bodley, several architects were instrumental in the work, including Philip H. Frohman (1887-1972) who designed fifty other churches and cathedrals in the Gothic and Romanesque styles. His contribution to the advancement of the construction of the cathedral is assessed.

155:5 Vaughan, Henry. "The Late George Frederick Bodley, an Appreciation." ARCHITECTURAL REVIEW (Boston) 14 (1907): 213-15.

Bodley was working on designs for the San Francisco Cathedral at his death. His preferred style of Gothic was the fourteenth-century of France, a style used by Vaughan and Bodley in the new Episcopal Cathedral, Washington.

155:6 Washington, D.C. Cathedral of St. Peter and St. Paul. THE CATHEDRAL IN THE NATION'S CAPITOL. Washington, D.C.: Washington Cathedral Executive Committee, 1930. 75 p.

A series of annotated sketches and photographs of the building as planned and won in competition, the various stages of construction, and detailed considerations of each portion of the proposed fabric.

156:1 VAUX, CALVERT (1824-95)

Educated in England and emigrated c.1850, when he worked for and later practiced with Andrew J. Downing and with Frederick Law Olmsted and Frederick C. Withers.

Publications: HINTS FOR COUNTRY HOUSE BUILDERS, 1855; VILLAS AND COTTAGES, 1857; and with Frederick L. Olmsted, DESCRIPTION OF A PLAN FOR THE IMPROVEMENT OF CENTRAL PARK, 1868.

Free Library of Philadelphia has one plan of the Main Building, International Exposition at Philadelphia, 1874-75; and Museum of Fine Arts, Boston, has one sheet of a town house for Brooklyn, New York, by Vaux and Withers, 1866.

Obituary: AMERICAN ARCHITECT AND BUILDING NEWS 50 (1895): 25.

156:2 Andrews, Wayne. "Olana Falling." ARCHITECTURAL REVIEW 140 (September 1965): 215-18.

Built in 1874, Olana was the home of Frederick Edwin Church, painter and pupil of Thomas Cole. Vaux was the possible collaborator in this extravaganza where East complemented West in all aspects of historical styles.

156:3 Huxtable, Ada Louise. "Just A Little Love, A Little Care." THE NEW YORK TIMES, Sunday, December 9, 1973, section 2, p. 28.

The argument is in the title of the article, and it is: if continuous maintenance were provided for Central Park there would be no need to spend $21,000 plus labor for a nine by fifteen foot ladies pavilion designed by Vaux. Likewise a ninety foot bridge repair would not cost $327,000.

156:4 Mumford, Lewis. ROOTS OF CONTEMPORARY AMERICAN ARCHITECTURE. New York: Reinhold Publishing Corp., 1952. 434 p.

Brought to the United States by Andrew J. Downing, Vaux complemented much of what Olmsted achieved and designed the first portion of the Metropolitan Museum of Art.

156:5 Sigle, John David. BIBLIOGRAPHY OF THE LIFE AND WORKS OF CALVERT VAUX. Vol. 5. Charlottesville: The American Association of Architectural Bibliographers, 1968. Pp. 69-94.

An historical essay on Vaux and his contemporaries is followed by primary, contemporary, modern, and background source books and a similar listing of articles. Manuscript collections, unpublished studies, maps and drawings, and list of works completes this bibliography.

156:6 Steese, Edward. "Villas and Cottages by Calvert Vaux, Condensed by Edward Steese." JOURNAL OF THE SOCIETY OF ARCHITECTURAL HISTORIANS 6 (January-June 1947): 1-12.

The parlance of Vaux's time is omitted and his attitudes condensed and commented upon.

157:1 WALTER, THOMAS USTICK (1804-87)

Worked for William Strickland and gained his first commission in

1830. Became architect of the United States Capitol in 1861.

Publications: A GUIDE TO WORKERS IN METALS AND STONE, 1846; TWO HUNDRED DESIGNS FOR COTTAGES AND VILLAS, 1847.

The Royal Institute of British Architects Library, London, has three drawings (Avery has photographic copies); the Office of the Architect of the Capitol, Army and Navy Branch of the National Archives, and the American Institute of Architects, Washington, have numerous drawings of the United States Capitol. Free Library of Philadelphia has three sheets of the James Dundes Mansion, Philadelphia; Pennsylvania Hospital, eleven sheets; Historical Society of Pennsylvania, thirty-six sheets of Girard Collection, Arch Street Prison, and an unidentified building.

Obituaries: BUILDING 7 (November 5, 1889): 149; 9 (October 27, 1888): 148; ARCHITECTURE 38 (1887): 345; 40 (1888): 282-84; AMERICAN INSTITUTE AND BUILDING NEWS 22 (1887): 225; AMERICAN INSTITUTE OF ARCHITECTS PROCEEDINGS, 1888, pp. 101-8.

Robert Ennis is working on a doctoral dissertation at the University of Pennsylvania.

157:2 Bannister, Turpin C. "The Genealogy of the Dome of the United States Capitol." JOURNAL OF THE SOCIETY OF ARCHITECTURAL HISTORIANS 7 (January-June, 1948): 1-9.

"The first room ever made exclusively of iron" was Walter's way of describing his dome, built in association with August Schoenborn and Captain M.C. Meigs, and inspired by the dome of St. Isaac's Cathedral, St. Petersburg, Russia, of 1840-42. The United States Capitol dome was erected 1856-64.

157:3 Burnham, Smith. FIRST HUNDRED YEARS OF THE NATIONAL BANK OF CHESTER CO. WEST CHESTER, PENNSYLVANIA, 1814-1914. Philadelphia: 1914. 48 p.

The bank was completed in 1837 and thus is beyond the scope of the bibliography. This pamphlet emphasizes the history of the bank, subscribers, stockholders, eras of prosperity and panic, as well as detailed information on the building.

157:4 Davis, Frohman Paul. "Early Metal Space Frame Investigated." PROGRESSIVE ARCHITECTURE 41 (December 1960): 164-73.

Inspection of the dome of the United States Capitol began in 1955. A brief history of the dome, its cost and the construction betwen 1856 and 1865 is given, and the conflict between Walter and Montgomery Meigs is discussed. (Walter was supported by the President and Meigs was replaced by W.B. Franklin, Captain of Topographical Engineers.) Movement, deterioration, and replaced portions are listed, including the removal of up to thirty layers of paint on the external surface of the metal dome.

157:5 Hall, Louise. "Mills, Strickland and Walter: Their Adventures in the World of Science." MAGAZINE OF ART 40 (November 1947): 266-71.

A pictorially-descriptive account of the fire in 1877 of the north and west walls of the United States Patent Office Building, in addition to a survey of the talents and skills of Mills, Strickland and T.U. Walter, notably as structural innovators.

157:6 Mason, George C., Jr. "Thomas Ustick Walter, FAIA, 1804-87." AMERICAN INSTITUTE OF ARCHITECTS' JOURNAL 8 (November 1947): 225-30.

Background, education, training, achievements, awards, service to the profession, and major structures designed by Walter are the basic facts of this article.

157:7 Newcomb, Rexford. "American Architects." THE ARCHITECT 10 (August 1928): 585-89.

As much an article of Strickland under whom Walter trained as on Walter. Most of Walter's major commissions including the United States Capitol are mentioned, in addition to his interest in the profession as Secretary, American Institute of Architects.

157:8 Wischnitzer, Rachel. "Thomas U. Walter's Crown Street Synagogue, 1848-49." JOURNAL OF THE SOCIETY OF ARCHITECTURAL HISTORIANS 13 (December 1954): 29-31.

An example of the Egyptian Revival, dated 1849, as in the case of Strickland's Cherry Street Synagogue, 1824.

158:1 WARE, WILLIAM ROBERT (1832-1915)

Educated Harvard, 1852, and Lawrence Scientific and Technical School, Cambridge, Massachusetts. Worked for E.C. Cabot and later associated with Henry Van Brunt (see). Became the first Professor of Architecture at Massachusetts Institute of Technology in 1866 and at Columbia University 1881-1903. See Ware and Van Brunt.

Publications: THE AMERICAN VIGNOLA, 1905; GREEK ORNAMENT, 1878; MODERN PERSPECTIVE, 1895; REPORT (new site for Columbia), 1893; SHADES AND SHADOWS, 1912.

Avery Library, Columbia University, has letters on American Academy, Rome, lectures and papers, course teaching, descriptions, correspondence, and reminiscences by alumni.

Obituaries: AMERICAN ARCHITECT AND BUILDING NEWS 107 (1915); AMERICAN INSTITUTE OF ARCHITECTS' JOURNAL 3 (1915): 305, 382; ARCHITECTURE 9-10 (1904): 7; ROYAL INSTITUTE OF BRITISH ARCHITECTS' JOURNAL 22 (1914-15): 427, 506.

158:2 ARCHITECTURAL RECORD. "The Work of Professor Ware." Vol. 13 (January 1903): 91-94.

An account of a testimonial building in honor of Professor Ware who chaired the first school of architecture at Massachusetts Institute of Technology and later at Columbia University when a school was established there. The architectural contribution of his pupils during twenty-one years attest to his ability as a teacher.

158:3 THE BRICKBUILDER. "Professor William R. Ware." Vol. 12 (June 1903): 112.

A tribute to Ware upon his retirement from the Columbia School of Architecture after twenty-two years during which time he must have trained a considerable percentage of the architectural profession.

158:4 Columbia University. School of Architecture, Alumni Association. WILLIAM ROBERT WARE. New York: Privately printed, 1915. 5 p.

Education, training, partnership, and career as educator precede a resolution recording the reverence for his achievements made by the Alumni Association.

158:5 Hamlin, A.D.F. "William Robert Ware." ARCHITECT AND ENGINEER IN CALIFORNIA 42 (July 1915): 100-101.

An obituary of the organizer of the first American School of Architecture, Massachusetts Institute of Technology, 1866, who died June 9, 1915, at the age of eighty-four. He practiced 1865-80 with Van Brunt but his greatest work was in education. He was a pioneer at Massachusetts Institute of Technology, 1866-80, and at Columbia, 1881 to 1903.

158:6 _____. "William Robert Ware." COLUMBIA UNIVERSITY QUARTERLY 17 (September 1915): 376-80.

Two weeks after his eighty-third birthday and a tribute paid by the Alumni Association of Columbia University, Ware passed away at Milton, Massachusetts. Hamlin sums up his achievements as first professor of architecture at Columbia from 1881, his twenty-two years of service, his publications, lectures, and his friendships.

159:1 **WARE AND VAN BRUNT (Partnership c. 1865-81)**

William Robert Ware (1832-1915) and Henry Van Brunt (1832-1903) were partners after the Civil War and until 1881 when Ware became head of the Columbia University School of Architecture.

Avery Library, Columbia University, has one sheet of a house, 1865, and fourteen plates of Memorial Hall, Harvard University. Ticknor of Boston published fourteen plates of Memorial Hall, Harvard, 1887, in their Monographs of American Architects Series.

159:2 Reiff, Daniel D. "Harvard's Memorial Hall and Its Tower." THE VICTORIAN SOCIETY IN AMERICA, NEWSLETTER 5 (Spring-Summer 1973): 3-6.

An excellent example of the High Victorian Gothic, Memorial Hall, built in memory of Harvard men who died in the Civil War, was used as theater, dining facilities, having a memorial vestibule between. The story of the tower is provided. The March 1972 issue of the HARVARD BULLETIN and part of the Spring 1949 HARVARD LIBRARY BULLETIN were devoted to Memorial Hall.

160:1 **WARREN, WHITNEY (1864-1943)**

Educated at the Ecole des Beaux Arts and formed a partnership in 1896 with Charles Wetmore.

Cooper Union, New York, has one sheet of drawings of the New York Public Library and four sheets of a golf club house, Newport, Rhode Island.

Obituaries: ART NEWS 41 (February 1943): 7; INTERIORS 52 (February 1943): 12.

160:2 New York City Improvement Commission. THE REPORT OF THE NEW YORK CITY IMPROVEMENT COMMISSION. New York: Kalkoff Co., 1907. 36 p.

"New York's architectural needs for beauty and convenience by Whitney Warren and illustrations drawn from the official plans of New York City Improvements Commission." The plans tended to concentrate upon plazas, treeplanting, subway terminals, docksides and drives along the rivers, and changes in street grades to allow for overpasses, all of which are illustrated.

160:3 Parke-Bernet Galleries, Inc., New York. THE ARCHITECTURAL WORKING LIBRARY OF WHITNEY WARREN, NEW YORK. CONTAINING IMPORTANT WORKS ON MARINE AND MILITARY ARCHITECTURE. New York: 1940. 35 p.

A public sale was held on Wednesday, May 1, 1940, at which time 243 books on architecture, owned by Whitney Warren, many in French, were sold. All historic periods of architecture, including naval and military, were included plus books on periferal subjects such as furniture, book-bindings, etc.

161:1 **WARREN AND WETMORE (Partnership 1896-1931)**

Whitney Warren (1864-1943) (see) and Charles D. Wetmore (1867-1941).

Avery Library, Columbia University, has many drawings, sheets, and photographs of residential, hotel, commercial buildings, and other types of projects.

161:2 ARCHITECTURAL RECORD. "A Study in Architectural Ethics." Vol. 32 (October 1912): 579.

A suggestion of plagiarism by a firm in Columbus, Ohio, of a New York City store by Warren and Wetmore is discussed in detail in ARCHITECTURAL RECORD 31 (May 1912): 449-69 (see).

161:3 Arnold, Gustavus. "The Homestead." MICHIGAN SOCIETY OF ARCHITECTS MONTHLY BULLETIN 30 (December 1956): 11-15.

Burned on July 2, 1901, and rebuilt by a Cincinnati firm of architects, the main tower, costing $1 million was built in 1929 by Warren and Wetmore. Amenities, social life, and all other aspects of this recreational and sports hotel complex is described, accompanied by photographs and drawings.

161:4 Croly, Herbert. "The Lay-Out of a Large Estate: Harbor Hill, the Country Seat of Mr. Clarence Mackey at Roslyn, Long Island." ARCHITECTURAL RECORD 16 (December 1904): 531-55.

Harbor Hill was the design by Stanford White but stables and other outbuildings were designed in a variety of different styles by Warren and Wetmore.

161:5 Currie, C.W.Y. "Unusual Structural Features in New York Central Skyscraper." AMERICAN ARCHITECTURE 134 (July 5, 1928): 59-61.

A building built on stilts above railroad tracks and separated from Park Avenue automobile traffic lanes which pass through it. Care was thus taken in designing against noise and vibration. Descriptions are given of the lead and asbestos mats placed under concrete foundations.

161:6 Eberlein, Harold D. "Recent Railway Stations in American Cities." ARCHITECTURAL RECORD 36 (August 1914): 98-121.

Michigan Central Railroad Station at Detroit designed in association with Reed and Stem is illustrated and criticized pp. 118-21. The project combines station and office building in two buildings giving the appearance of two different structures, so incongruous are they. The station is dignified, the office "flimsy and insignificant" in detailing and materials.

161:7 Ferree, Barr. "The Art of High Building." ARCHITECTURAL RECORD 15 (May 1904): 445-66.

"High building of today - the typical and most noteworthy architectural creation of our time." Warren and Wetmore's Kean, Van Cortlandt and Co. Building on Pine Street, New York City, "is another structure whose chief interest is the frank way in which it displays Beaux Artism. . . more vigorous by far than that which any French architect would produce, and heavier than seems called for in a building of such moderate dimensions."

161:8 Frohne, H.W. "The Hotel Belmont." ARCHITECTURAL RECORD 20 (July 1906): 63-69.

A critical article on a tall building which made no attempt to solve the skyscraper problem, where interiors change and differ from once space to another and are small in the bargain even though the lobby is vast.

161:9 INTERIORS. "Over Your Head and under Your Nose." Vol. 104 (February 1945): 54-57, 86-88.

INTERIORS considers Grand Central Station, completed in 1913, the most efficiently-planned building of all of Warren and Wetmore's work. The ceiling painting of the 275 by 125-foot concourse was the idea of Paul Hellen and was executed by J. Monroe Hewlett. This article concerns the restoration of this astronomical ceiling by a system of hanging scaffolding, covering 6400 square feet of area. Diagrams and photographs.

161:10 Price, C. Matlack. "The New Aeolian Hall: Some Notes on French Architecture and the Renaissance." ARCHITECTURAL RECORD 32 (1912):

530-51.

In praise of French Renaissance architecture and its adaptation by American architects, notably Warren and Wetmore, to the high-rise structures of New York City and in particular the new Aeolian Hall.

161:11 _____. "A Renaissance in Commercial Architecture: Some Recent Buildings in Uptown New York." ARCHITECTURAL RECORD 31 (May 1912): 449-69.

The article is devoted to the work of several New York City architects, including the firm of Warren and Wetmore. One building on Fifth Avenue is illustrated and critically evaluated.

161:12 Schneider, Walter S. "The Hotel Biltmore." ARCHITECTURAL RECORD 35 (March 1914): 221-45.

The fourth major hotel by Warren and Wetmore, the Biltmore, has several innovative features with regard to scale, planning in relation to railroad transportation, and the lack of sub-surface services. Style, facilities, materials, richness of detailing, and space relationships are enumerated and illustrated; plans are provided.

161:13 Sexton, R.W. "Steward and Co. Building, New York." AMERICAN ARCHITECTURE 136 (December 1929): 46-51.

An essay in the "practical relation between architecture and store sales...sought through architecture and design." An early sketch of the entrance can be compared to the final design.

161:14 Williams, Frank. "Grand Central City." ARCHITECTURAL FORUM, January-February 1968, pp. 48-55.

"Grand Central Terminal remains today the most advanced urban 'mixing chamber' in existence...the prototype of all modern multilevel, multiuse urban distribution centers."

162:1 WELLS, JOSEPH MORRILL (1853-90)

Trained in the offices of Clarence Luce and Peabody and Stearns but is best known as an architect working for McKim, Mead and White; their Villard Mansion is sometimes attributed to him.

Obituaries: AMERICAN ARCHITECT AND BUILDING NEWS 27 (1890): 95; ARCHITECTURE AND BUILDING 12 (January-June 1890): 23.

162:2 Walker C. Howard. "Joseph Wells, Architect. 1853-1890." ARCHITECTURAL RECORD 66 (July 1929): 14-18.

"Joseph Wells, one of the almost forgotten worthies of American architecture was a talented draftsman of the firm McKim, Mead and White, back in the eighties. He has been variously spoken of as McKim's right hand man and as responsible for the adoption by his firm of Italian Renaissance forms." An appreciation with biographical data.

163:1 WELLS, WILLIAM (1878-1938)

Attended University of Kansas; Armour Institute, Chicago; and the Chicago School of Architecture.

163:2 Ramsey, Ronald Lanier. "William Wells: Towers in Oklahoma." THE PRAIRIE SCHOOL REVIEW 8 (Fourth Quarter, 1971): 5-13.

A Richardsonian, Sullivanesque Prairie School designer, who worked for Wright but practiced in Oklahoma, 1904-14.

164:1 WHEELER, GERVASE (n.d.)

Publications: THE CHOICE OF A DWELLING, 1871; HOMES FOR THE PEOPLE, 1855; RURAL HOMES, 1851. Williams College, Massachusetts, has five sheets on Goodrich Hall, Williams College.

164:2 Scully, Vincent J., Jr. "Romantic Rationalism and the Expression of Structure in Wood: Downing, Wheeler, Gardner and the Stick Style, 1840-1876." ART BULLETIN 35 (June 1953): 121-42.

A survey of copybooks written by architects for the use of the profession, up to and including those of Downing and Wheeler. Wheeler's RURAL HOMES was first published in 1851 but was still having an impact in 1868 and ramifications were being felt up to 1875. "By 1876, the Stick Style had developed into an interwoven basketry of sticks. . . ."

165:1 WHEELWRIGHT, EDMUND MARCH (1854-1912)

Graduated from Harvard, 1876, Massachusetts Institute of Technology, and the Ecole des Beaux Arts. Worked for Peabody and Stearns and McKim, Mead and White. Partnership Wheelwright and Haven with Parkman B. Haven. Became Boston City architect, 1891.

Publication: SCHOOL ARCHITECTURE, 1901.

Obituaries: AMERICAN ARCHITECT AND BUILDING NEWS 102 (August 28, 1912): 3; NEW INTERNATIONAL YEARBOOK (1912): 802.

165:2 Chandler, Francis Ward. MUNICIPAL ARCHITECTURE IN BOSTON FROM DESIGNS BY EDMUND MARCH WHEELWRIGHT. Boston: Bates and Guild Co., 1898.

Contains an introductory historical sketch of the city's architects' department and details concerning the designs of schools, their heating and ventilation, furnishings, sanitation, from 1891 to 1895. Hospital design and other institutional buildings are also considered.

166:1 WHITE, STANFORD (1853-1906)

See also McKim, Mead and White.

Obituaries: AMERICAN ARCHITECT AND BUILDING NEWS 89 (1906): 215; 90 (1906): 54; AMERICAN INSTITUTE OF ARCHITECTS QUARTERLY BULLETIN 7 (1906): 100-108; ARCHITECTURAL REVIEW 13 (1908): 101; THE BRICKBUILDER 15 (1906): 243-59.

166:2 AMERICAN ARCHITECT AND BUILDING NEWS. "The Artist in our World." Vol. 90 (July 7, 1906): 6.

A reprint of an article in the NEW YORK EVENING POST criticizing Stanford White for selling his taste "to a wealthy but half trained society, his taste condescended to their ignorance and vanity. The time that he should have given to creative design, he spent in despoiling French and Italian country houses of their furnishings. . . ." See Lawrence Grant White, SKETCHES AND DESIGNS OF STANFORD WHITE, for a rebuttal of this type of criticism.

166:3 Baldwin, Charles. STANFORD WHITE. New York: Dodd, Mead and Co., 1931. 399 p. (Facsimile edition: New York: Da Capo Press, 1971.)

This is the only life of White published to date and sympathetically portrays White as an all-round designer with several illustrations of jewelry, book plates, picture frames and the like as a back-up to his architectural achievement. Major buildings and, collectively, building types are discussed, as are the relationships between White, his two partners, clients, and artistic collaborators, such as Augustus Saint-Gaudens. Additionally the book is illustrated with drawings of the architecture of White by Birch Burdette Long.

166:4 Blake, Channing. "Stanford White's New York City Interiors." ANTIQUES, December 1972, pp. 1060-67.

White "had an eye for beautifully designed and embellished objects and an ability to combine heterogeneous elements to form a lavish whole." White used walls as surfaces upon which to hang beautiful objects, whereas furniture gave form to the interior spaces. Thoroughly illustrated.

166:5 Bouton, Margaret I. "Early Works of Augustus Saint-Gaudens." Doctoral dissertation, Radcliffe College, 1946. 485 p.

Stanford White designed three bases for New York sculptures of Saint-Gaudens and they collaborated on other projects. This is an excellent detailed study, and in part, clears up some of the questions regarding the contributing ideas of the Admiral Farragut statue.

166:6 Brown, Elmer Ellsworth, et al. MEMORIAL MEETING IN HONOR OF THE LATE STANFORD WHITE. New York: Privately printed, 1921. 15 p. Pamphlet.

Includes tributes by Chancellor Elmer Ellsworth Brown; Thomas Hastings, Chairman of the Memorial Committee; and Royal Cortissoz, art critic of the New York Times. The memorial consisted of a pair of bronze doors for the Gould Library, New York University, Bronx Campus, dedicated December 10, 1921, sculpted by James W. O'Connor, Herbert Adams, Philip Martiny, A.A. Weinman, and Ulysses Ricci, and cast by Attilio Piccirilli and Ardolino Di Lorenzo.

166:7 Davis, Richard Harding. "Stanford White." COLLIER'S WEEKLY, August 18, 1906, and quoted in AMERICAN ARCHITECTURE 90 (August 18, 1906): 54.

Davis, a newspaper man for fifteen years and a friend of White, was one of the few who defended White after his murder on June 25, 1906. Most newspapers judged White according to the accusations made by Evelyn Nesbit Thaw, wife of White's murderer, a "silly child" who went to any lengths to defend Thaw, the "sadistic paranoiac," as Gerald Langford (see) termed him. Davis saw in White all the qualities of a genius in architecture and interior design, a person who thought everything in life was "bully, wonderful, gorgeous."

166:8 Hewlett, J. Monroe, et al. "Stanford White as Those Trained in His Office Knew Him." THE BRICKBUILDER 15 (December 1906): 245.

Personal recollections.

166:9 Ketchum, R.M. "Faces from the Past: E. Nesbit at Thaw-White Murder Trial." AMERICAN HERITAGE 20 (June 1969): 64-65.

"To Charles Dana Gibson, a lovely model. To Harry Thaw, an inconstant wife. To Stanford White, a mortal danger!"

166:10 Koch, Robert. "The Stained Glass Decades. A Study of Louis Comfort Tiffany (1848-1933) and the Art Nouveau in America." Doctoral dissertation, Yale University, 1964. 635 p.

Tiffany's association with Stanford White, John La Farge and others of the Decorative Arts Society in New York is discussed. Richardson and Sullivan are also introduced but the major portion of the dissertation is on Tiffany's training, influence, and association with the movement of Art Nouveau.

166:11 Langford, Gerald. THE MURDER OF STANFORD WHITE. Indianapolis: The Bobbs-Merrill Co. Inc., 1962. 270 p.

Harry Kendall Thaw, son of a wealthy railroad and coke magnate of Pittsburgh, shot to death Stanford White on the roof of Madison Square Garden, June 25, 1906, while a performance of "Mamzelle Champagne" was in progress. Thaw, a "crazed profligate" as McKim's biographer Moore termed him, was goaded into murder by his wife, Evelyn Nesbit Thaw, who before marriage had apparently had relations with White. This book covers the background of the period, the trial and aftermath, and comes to some logical conclusions.

166:12 Logan, Andy. "That Was New York, The Palace of Delight." NEW YORKER 41 (February 27, 1965): 41, 93.

An account of Madison Square Garden from its inception as a public open space to the building of Stanford White's "Garden," opened in 1890 and closed 1925. All activities of the Garden, its financial backers, the boxing, circus, political conventions, and other forms of public entertainment are enumerated. So too, is the firm of McKim, Mead and White and the sculptor-collaborator of White, Augustus Saint-Gaudens.

166:13 McQuade, W. "White and the Wherewithal." THE ARCHITECTURAL FORUM 123 (November 1965): 70.

A one-page series of quotations from Baldwin's biography. Confused, and with some facts muddled. If White left the employ of Richardson in 1878, as he did, how could he have had independent commissions at the age of twenty-eight (1881) "before leaving H.H. Richardson's employ."

166:14 Myer, John Walden. "The New York Work of Stanford White." MUSEUM OF THE CITY OF NEW YORK BULLETIN 5 (March 1942): 42-52.

Illustrations and discussion of banks, hotels, churches, commercial and residential buildings, private clubs, and religious architecture in New York City. Stylistic differentiation is a dominant theme whether the Francis I. William Vanderbilt Mansion on Fifth Avenue, the Venetian Renaissance Vendramini Palace for Tiffany and Co. at 37th Street and Fifth Avenue, or the utilitarian sturdy chimneys and subtle classical emphasis of the Interborough Power House, Eleventh Avenue, 59th Street.

166:15 Nelson, Lee H. "White, Furness, McNally and the Capital National Bank of Salem, Oregon." JOURNAL OF THE SOCIETY OF ARCHITECTURAL HISTORIANS 19 (May 1960): 57-61.

White had nothing to do with the design of this bank and that is about all this article has to say concerning Stanford White!

166:16 Saarinen, Aileen. "Splendid World of Stanford White, with Photographs by T. Frissell." LIFE 61 (September 16, 1966): 87-108.

"Half a century after an era embellished by American Society's most flamboyant architect, his master works endure as stately monuments to this day - and his great-grandchildren pay them nostalgic visits. He saw Architecture as the Permanent Stage Set of an Age. His buildings helped satisfy his clients' yearning for beauty and reassurance. He often masked structure to make a statement of dignity and importance. Right through to his last day of life, he thrived on acclaim and clamor." Well illustrated in color, with White's descendants.

166:17 Saint-Gaudens, Homer, ed. "Intimate Letters of Stanford White, Correspondence with His Friend and Co-Worker, Augustus Saint-Gaudens." ARCHITECTURAL RECORD 30 (1911): 107-16, 283-98, 399-406.

These series of letters were incorporated into THE REMINISCENCES OF AUGUSTUS SAINT-GAUDENS, edited and amplified by his son, Homer Saint-Gaudens (see).

166:18 _____. THE REMINISCENCES OF AUGUSTUS SAINT-GAUDENS. 2 vols. New York: The Century Co., 1913. 381 and 393 p., respectively.

White gains considerable mention, from the initial meeting with the sculptor, their travels, professional associates, but most notably on their combined efforts. White provided bases for many of Saint-Gaudens' sculptures. Both men believed in complementing architecture with sculptural groups.

166:19 Schroeder, Francis de N. "Stanford White and the Second Blossoming of the Renaissance." INTERIORS 110 (February 1951): 106-9.

An over-generalized article which again drags in the Thaw murder trial.

166:20 Schuyler, Montgomery. "The Romanesque Revival in America." ARCHITECTURAL RECORD 1 (October-December 1891): 151-98.

Considerable attention is logically devoted to Richardson in this article and to his immediate followers including his most famed assistant, Stanford White. The Church of St. Peter, Baltimore, is the only Richardsonian structure by McKim, Mead and White. Illustrated and discussed in a lengthy, well-illustrated article.

166:21 Tharp, Louise Hall. SAINT-GAUDENS AND THE GILDED ERA. Boston: Little, Brown and Co., 1969. 419 p.

Saint-Gaudens and White were not only the greatest of friends, but collaborated on numerous works. White designed sculpture bases and Saint-Gaudens helped decorate interiors mainly of residential architecture. These facets of their lives and work complement their travels and learning experiences in this biography of the sculptor.

166:22 Van Rensselaer, Mrs. Mariana Griswold. "Mr. St. Gaudens' Statue of Admiral Farragut in New York." AMERICAN ARCHITECT AND BUILDING NEWS 10 (September 10, 1881): 119-20.

Mrs. Van Rensselaer as architectural critic objected to the shape of the base of the statue by White as looking too much like a couch and noted that the substructure would have better fitted into the angle of a building. She realized that the Saint-Gaudens reliefs of "Loyalty" and "Courage" on the base were unconventional. They are proto-Art Nouveau.

166:23 White, Lawrence Grant. SKETCHES AND DESIGNS BY STANFORD WHITE. New York: The Architectural Book Publishing Co., 1920. 33 p. plus 56 pls.

The son of Stanford White defends his father against attacks, including the argument that he pilfered from Europe for the wealthy of the United States. Lawrence Grant White portrays his father as a lover and designer of beautiful things many of which are illustrated, including picture frames, jewelry, book covers and plates, monuments, architectural drawings, and numerous sketches made while traveling in Europe.

166:24 White, Stanford. Bound volume of photographs of Stanford White Residence at St. James, Long Island, owned by the New York Historical Society and deposited in their Map and Print Room.

Stanford and his young wife Bessie spent the summers at St. James where they purchased a cubic-shaped building having gables on all four sides of the house. White enlarged this cubic mass to three or four times its size adding verandahs, porches, and a wealth of internal furniture, decoration, and ornamentation.

166:25 _____. "The Buildings of the University of Virginia." CORKS AND CURLS 2 (1898): 127-30.

A justification by White in his reconstruction of Thomas Jefferson's rotunda library at University of Virginia which burned in 1895. White also added Rouss, Cocke, and Cabell Halls at the far end of the lawn from the library. Asked why he placed them so far apart from the original Jefferson plan, White remarked that he did not have the temerity and audacity to locate them closer.

166:26 Zion, Robert L. "How Our Half Lives, a Stanford White is Restored and Redesigned." LANDSCAPE ARCHITECTURE 44 (April 1954): 127-31.

Robert and Beatrice Zion took possession of Stanford White's gatehouse to "Harbor Hill," the Mackay's estate at Roslyn, Long Island, in June 1951. They had a two-year lease and redesigned this building which was in poor repair as best they could.

167:1 WHITNEY, WILLIAM CHANNING (1851-1945)

Studied at Harvard and Massachusetts State College, 1872. Practiced Minneapolis, Minnesota, 1880 until 1925.

Minnesota Historical Society has eighteen sheets of the Minnesota building for the World's Columbian Exposition, Chicago, 1893.

167:2 Nutter, F.H. "Highcroft, Lake Minnetonka, Minnesota." THE WESTERN ARCHITECT 2 (February 1903): 16-17.

"...among the finest country places in the Northwest." Brief descriptions with small photographs. Olmsted was the landscape architect.

168:1 WIGHT, PETER B. (1838-1925)

Graduated from New York City College, 1855, and worked for Thomas R. Jackson. In 1862 he opened his own office but moved to Chicago, 1871, where he worked with Asher Carter and later

William Drake in the partnership Drake and Wight. See his articles on Daniel H. Burnham, Henry Van Brunt, Rafael Guastavino, and Russell Sturgis. Yale Art Gallery has five sheets of Street Hall, Yale.

Obituaries: AMERICAN ARCHITECTURE 128 (October-December 1925): 389-90; AMERICAN INSTITUTE OF ARCHITECTS' JOURNAL 13 (1925): 386; ARCHITECTURAL RECORD 58 (1925): 513.

168:2 THE BUILDER. "The New York National Academy of Design." Vol. 25 (January 12, 1867): 21-22, 28-29.

Foundation stone laid October 21, 1863, on land costing $50,000 on the northwest corner of Fourth Avenue and 23rd Street. The building cost $150,000. Decorations are discussed and illustrated together with plans and a full-page perspective.

169:1 WILSON, JAMES KEYS (1828-94)

Trained under Charles A. Mountain of Philadelphia, Martin E. Thompson and James Renwick of New York, and in Europe, prior to returning to his native Cincinnati. Sometime a partner of Henry Walter.

Obituaries: AMERICAN ARCHITECT AND BUILDING NEWS 46 (1894): 41-42; INLAND ARCHITECT AND NEWS RECORD 24 (December 1894): 49.

169:2 Patton, Glenn. "James Keys Wilson (1828-1894). Architect of the Gothic Revival in Cincinnati." JOURNAL OF THE SOCIETY OF ARCHITECTURAL HISTORIANS 26 (December 1967): 285-93.

A general survey of Cincinnati architecture and architects at mid-century with detailed considerations of some of Wilson's religious, residential, collegiate, and funerary architecture. The fine pseudo Gothic-Moorish Isaac M. Wise Temple Synagogue with its two tall (minaret) towers still stands as a notable landmark in a Cincinnati that has little left of the mid-nineteenth century.

170:1 WINDRIM, JAMES H. (d. 1919)

Supervising Architect of the Treasury Department, 1889-91. Masonic Temple Library, Philadelphia, has one sheet of the Temple; Pennsylvania Hospital, seven sheets; Historical Society of Pennsylvania, two sheets of the International Exposition Agriculture Building; National Archives, Washington, twenty-one sets of drawings of post offices, court rooms, and custom houses.

George Thomas is working on a dissertation on Windrim at the University of Pennsylvania.

Obituary: AMERICAN INSTITUTE OF ARCHITECTS' JOURNAL 7 (1919): 281.

170:2 Poppeliers, John C. "The 1867 Philadelphia Masonic Competition." JOURNAL OF THE SOCIETY OF ARCHITECTURAL HISTORIANS 26 (December 1967): 279-84.

When Sloan and Stewart's Chestnut Street Masonic Temple, 1853-55, became too small, the Building Committee purchased a large site on the north side of Pennsylvania Square, Philadelphia, and held a competition for the construction of a new temple. Schemes by Sloan and Stewart, John McArthur, Jr., George Summers, and several unidentified entries, in addition to James H. Windrim's were received. Windrim's structure still stands as the oldest building on Pennsylvania Square.

171:1 WITHERS, FREDERICK C. (1828-1901)

English by birth and training and brought to the States by A.J. Downing, the collaborator of Calvert Vaux.

Published CHURCH ARCHITECTURE, New York, 1873. Avery Library, Columbia University, has eleven original ink and wash drawings and miscellaneous material. The Fine Arts Library, University of Pennsylvania, has twelve sheets of ink drawings of churches and a library by Withers and three sheets emanating from the partnership of Withers in association with Walter Dickson.

Obituary: AMERICAN ARCHITECT AND BUILDING NEWS 71 (1901): 17.

Francis R. Kowsky has recently completed a doctoral dissertation at Johns Hopkins University on Withers. It is, as yet, unavailable.

171:2 Kidney, Walter C. "The Return of Old Jeff." PROGRESSIVE ARCHITECTURE, October 1967, pp. 174-79.

The Jefferson Market Courthouse was built by Withers in 1875. Concerned Greenwich Villagers fought to save the building which was refurbished as a library by Giorgio Cavaglieri. Plans, and before and after photographs.

171:3 Kowsky, Francis R. "Frederick C. Withers: In Recognition." THE VICTORIAN SOCIETY IN AMERICA NEWSLETTER. Christmas 1970, unpaged, but in fact pages 2-3 of this four-sided pamphlet.

Provides background, career, a list of his most notable works and the styles in which they were designed. Structures by Withers which are being preserved are carefully noted.

172:1 WRIGHT, FRANK LLOYD (1867*-1959)

Part time education for two semesters at the University of Wisconsin. Worked for James Lyman Silsbee (see) for one year before joining Adler and Sullivan (see). Began accepting commissions while working for them and slowly branched out on his own. *Thomas S. Hines. "Frank Lloyd Wright, The Madison Years." JOURNAL OF THE SOCIETY OF ARCHITECTURAL HISTORIANS 24 (December 1967): 227-33, established Wright's birth as June 8, 1867.

Olin Library, Cornell University, has six sheets of drawings of the Avery Coonley residence, Forest Park, Illinois; Burnham Library, Chicago, six sheets of the Moore residence, Oak Park, Illinois, and ten sheets of the Robie house; American Institute of Architects, Washington, four projects; Harvey P. Sutton, eleven sheets of his own house, McCook, Nebraska; Avery Library, Columbia, two sheets of Crater Resort, Meteor, Arizona.

Publications: AN AUTOBIOGRAPHY, 1952; THE DISAPPEARING CITY, 1932; THE FUTURE OF ARCHITECTURE, 1953; THE JAPANESE PRINT, 1912; THE LIVING CITY, 1958; MODERN ARCHITECTURE (The Kahn Lectures for 1930 given at the Department of Art and Archaeology, Princeton University), 1931; THE NATURAL HOUSE, 1954; AN ORGANIC ARCHITECTURE: THE ARCHITECTURE OF DEMOCRACY, 1939; THE STORY OF THE TOWER: THE TREE THAT ESCAPED THE CROWDED FOREST, 1956; A TESTAMENT, 1957; WHEN DEMOCRACY BUILDS, 1945. See under Sullivan for his GENIUS AND THE MOBOCRACY, 1949.

Obituaries: ARCHITECTURAL REVIEW 125 (June 1959): 373; JOURNAL OF HOUSING 16 (May 1959): 147; ROYAL INSTITUTE OF BRITISH ARCHITECTS' JOURNAL 66 (September 1959): 369; ARCHITECTS' JOURNAL 129 (April 16, 1959): 571-75 by Fello Atkinson; PROGRESSIVE ARCHITECTURE 40 (May 1959): 135; THE BUILDER 196 (April 17, 1959): 735; ART NEWS 58 (May 1959): 25 by H.R. Hitchcock; ARCHITECT AND BUILDING NEWS 215 (April 22, 1959): 464-67 by R. Furneaux Jordan; ARTS AND ARCHITECTURE 76 (May 1959): 12-13, 32; HOUSE AND HOME 15 (May 1959): 95, 98; MICHIGAN SOCIETY OF ARCHITECTS MONTHLY BULLETIN 33 (May 1959): 11.

Kathryn A. Smith is working toward a doctoral dissertation on

Wright and Ezra Pound at the University of California, Santa Barbara.

172:2 Akashi, Shindo. "The Imperial Comes Tumbling Down." AMERICAN INSTITUTE OF ARCHITECTS JOURNAL 50 (December 1968): 42-47.

It was inevitable that the Imperial would be demolished. One positive aspect of such vandalism is that it has been possible to analyze the construction techniques and innovations in reverse order, notably the pilings and foundation construction.

172:3 Anderson Galleries. "The Frank Lloyd Wright Collection of Japanese Antique Prints." CATALOG. New York: Anderson Galleries, 1927. 163 p.

The 346 items mainly by Hiroshige, Shunsho, Shunyei, Utamaro--a total of twenty-six artists--went for reasonable prices. Hiroshige's "The Ocean Wave" from the thirty-six views of Fujiyama went for $300 although two Komuso by Toyonobu sold for $2500. A total price of $36,975 was realized. Wright wrote the five-page introduction. The reason for the auction was Wright's indebtedness to the Madison-based Bank of Wisconsin, which forced the sale. For details see THE NEW YORK TIMES, January 7, 1927, p. 19.

172:4 Andrews, Leonard E.B., ed. DALLAS THEATER CENTER. Dallas, Tex.: N. pub., 1959. 36 p. Illus.

Andrews edited a series of essays on various aspects of the theater, including the need for the theater; the director's view; financial support; technician, audience, and author viewpoints; and an essay by Harwell Hamilton Harris on the architecture (a very brief appreciation).

172:5 ARCHITECTURAL FORUM. Issue devoted to work of Wright from 1938 to 1947. Vol. 88 (January 1948).

A message from Wright, plus numerous illustrations, sketches, photographs, plans, sections, and elevations of projects and finished work, with descriptions and annotations.

172:6 ARCHITECTURAL FORUM. "A Special Portfolio." Vol. 110 (June 1959): 115-45.

Again a series of historically important structures illustrated with photographs and compared to the work of Wright's contemporaries. One house of 1894, by George W. Rapp, condemned in the article, is not really so different from Wright's Blossom House, Chicago, 1893, which illustrates the superficiality of such articles, attempting to glorify Wright at the expense of accuracy.

Current and, at that time in 1959, future projects are also covered.

172:7 ARCHITECTURAL RECORD. "Wright, Frank Lloyd. A Selection of Current Work." Vol. 123 (May 1958): 167-90.

Devoted to projects and structures, some proposed but never built and others in process of construction. Many sketches and plans and progress photographs.

172:8 Ashbee, C.R. FRANK LLOYD WRIGHT: THE EARLY WORK. New introduction by Edgar Kaufmann. New York: Horizon Press, 1968. 144 p.

Originally published in Berlin, 1911, to complement the Wasmuth portfolio of drawings. It has an interesting series of photographs with text by Ashbee, the English arts and crafts designer, but with additional text in German, not by Ashbee, as editor Kaufmann discovered.

172:9 Banham, Reyner. "The Wilderness Years of Frank Lloyd Wright." ROYAL INSTITUTE OF BRITISH ARCHITECTS' JOURNAL 76 (December 1969): 512-19.

On the centennial of Wright's birth (actually the 102nd anniversary), Banham lectured on the middle years of Wright's career about which little is known, "a triple wilderness of professional solitude, psychological disruption, and retreat to the Arizona desert, where Wright finally achieved freedom in planning and dreamed - a dream that eventually led to Broadacre City." The arguments begin with Wright's displacement with Mrs. Cheney to Germany, Italy, and Japan, continue with concrete construction of the Los Angeles houses of the mid-1920's, and end with the Jeffersonian ideals of Broadacres and Usonia.

172:10 Barnett, Jonathan. "Rethinking Wright." ARCHITECTURAL FORUM, June 1972, p. 42.

"Frank Lloyd Wright is being rediscovered as his views about our society and cities take on new meaning in the midst of urban chaos." This is the antithesis of Peter Blake's attitude that, as a child of the nineteenth century, Wright could not conceive of buildings as groups. The article cites several examples of Wright's schemes of a comprehensive redevelopment scale to support the theory.

172:11 Barney, Maginel Wright, and Burke, Tom. THE VALLEY OF THE GOD-ALMIGHTY JONESES. New York: Appleton-Century, 1965. 156 p. Illus.

Subtitled "Reminiscences of Frank Lloyd Wright's Sister,"

this chatty, but informative book, similar to Wright's own AUTOBIOGRAPHY provides background, not only of Wright but all his kin folks!

172:12 Barr, Alfred H., Jr., and Hitchcock, H.R. MODERN ARCHITECTS, New York: Museum of Modern Art, 1932. Pp. 29-55.

This early exhibition catalog on modern architecture lists Wright's achievement and his place in the modern movement, his early years, Sullivan's office, early houses and the Prairie architecture. Individual projects are described and illustrated. There is also a bibliography, chronology of Wright's life and a list of works, 1887-1932.

172:13 Besinger, Curtis. "Comment on 'The Early Drawings of Frank Lloyd Wright Reconsidered.'" JOURNAL OF THE SOCIETY OF ARCHITECTURAL HISTORIANS 31 (October 1972): 216-20.

Besinger was a member of the Taliesin Fellowship from 1939 to 1955, and in this article rebuts and questions information by Eileen Michel's article on "The Early Drawings of Frank Lloyd Wright Reconsidered." (JOURNAL OF THE SOCIETY OF ARCHITECTURAL HISTORIANS 30 (December 1971): 294-330 below) Ms. Michels, for example, did not question the use of the drawings, which are relevant in discussing their content. Was Wright a "gifted draftsman" and did he have the "ability to draw"? As a practicing architect Mr. Besinger counters well some of Ms. Michels misunderstandings. Ms. Michels felt Mr. Besinger hostile towards her as an art historian and her letter to the editor contained little else. (JOURNAL OF THE SOCIETY OF ARCHITECTURAL HISTORIANS 31 (December 1972): 340.

172:14 Blake, Peter. FRANK LLOYD WRIGHT: ARCHITECTURE AND SPACE. Harmondsworth, Middlesex, England: Penguin Books, 1963? 138 p.

Originally published in the United States as one of three lengthy essays on THE MASTER BUILDERS, 1960, this offering presents Wright as out of harmony with what American architects were trying to achieve at the time of his death in 1959. Wright's early developments leading into the Prairie style of the first ten years of the twentieth century constitute the first half of the book. Thereafter his major contributions are commented upon, including the structural, aesthetic, and philosophic considerations.

172:15 Brooks, H. Allen. "Architectural Drawings by Frank Lloyd Wright." BURLINGTON MAGAZINE 104 (May 1962): 210-12.

A review of an exhibition of 250 drawings of Wright and his assistants shown at the New York Museum of Modern Art. The Frank Lloyd Wright Foundation has 8000 drawings and from these, a series of project sketches were assembled for display, in addition to sketches of a few completed works. Plans per se were omitted. See Arthur Drexler's book THE DRAWINGS OF FRANK LLOYD WRIGHT, which was, in fact, the exhibition catalog.

172:16 _____. "Frank Lloyd Wright and The Wasmuth Drawings." ART BULLETIN 58 (June 1966): 193-201.

Of the seventy-one plates in the Wasmuth publication, twenty are by Marion Mahony (Griffin), Wright's most prolific and successful draftsperson. Other draftspeople who contributed were Birch Burdette Long, and William Drummond; and Wright contributed at least ten. Many drawings cannot be attributed to any particular individual since Wright reworked several probably to give a sense of unity.

172:17 _____. THE PRAIRIE SCHOOL, FRANK LLOYD WRIGHT AND HIS MID-WEST CONTEMPORARIES. Toronto: University of Toronto Press, 1972. 352 p.

This book is not only concerned with Wright and Louis Sullivan but also seventeen architects of the following generation, some of whom were employed as assistants, one is a Canadian architect. When Wright left for Europe in 1910, many of his clients turned to his assistants, who then became successful in their own rights. All were part of the arts and crafts movement which tended to die after the First World War. Many reasons could be given for its demise, but the resurgence of historic and traditional modes of design was a major cause.

172:18 _____. "Steinway Hall, Architects and Dreams." JOURNAL OF THE SOCIETY OF ARCHITECTURAL HISTORIANS 22 (October 1963): 171-75.

"Steinway Hall soon became a rallying point and symbol of the avant-garde and a variety of occupants were attracted to the eleventh floor." Among them was Wright and many of his contemporaries. These architects, through the admiration of Sullivan, founded the Architectural League of America. This article is concerned with the influence of this young group of architects.

172:19 Byrne, Barry. "On Frank Lloyd Wright and His Atelier." AMERICAN INSTITUTE OF ARCHITECTS' JOURNAL 39 (June 1963): 109-12.

A discussion of the apprenticeship system of architectural education as reviewed by Byrne and his early twentieth-century contemporaries in the studio of Wright, as opposed to the academic type of education. Byrne was an apprentice, 1902-9, and provides personal reminiscences.

172:20 _____. "Wright and Iannelli." ARCHITECTURAL RECORD 129 (January 1961): 242, 246.

Byrne's letter, not attempting to detract from the greatness of Wright, points out that Wright was architect of Midway Gardens, Chicago, in collaboration with Alfonso Iannelli, sculptor. Iannelli did not execute designs by Wright but was the originator of the sculptures which he carved.

172:21 Cary, James. THE IMPERIAL HOTEL. Rutland, Vt.: C.E. Tuttle and Co., 1969. 46 p.

The text, which includes quotations from the writings of Wright, complements a series of good photographs by James, an architect of California. The hotel, built from 1917-22, was on the point of demolition when the book was published.

172:22 Cavanaugh, Tom R., and Thomas, Payne E.L. A FRANK LLOYD WRIGHT HOUSE: BANNERSTONE HOUSE, SPRINGFIELD, ILLINOIS. Springfield, Ill.: Charles C. Thomas, 1970. 41 p.

The Susan Lawrence Dana House, Springfield, was begun in 1902. This booklet compares the house to other earlier houses of Wright and its own significance is presented. The client-architect relationship and the present use of the house by a publisher is discussed. A bibliography of articles and books in which the house is mentioned is included.

172:23 Churchill, Henry S. "Notes on Frank Lloyd Wright." MAGAZINE OF ART 41 (February 1948): 62-66.

Churchill, a New York architect, laments the lack of written evaluations of Wright's work, excepting two by Hitchcock and Gutheim respectively. He then proceeds to chat about Wright's life, philosophy, concepts in architecture and city planning, his failings and prophecy.

172:24 Cohen, Rabbi Mortimer J. BETH SHOLOM SYNAGOGUE, A DESCRIPTION AND INTERPRETATION. Elkins Park, Pa.: Congregation Beth Sholom, 1959. 34 p. Illus.

Brief essay with emphasis on religious symbolism.

172:25 Cooke, Alistair. "Memories of Frank Lloyd Wright." AMERICAN INSTITUTE OF ARCHITECTS' JOURNAL 32 (October 1959): 42-44.

"It is difficult to avoid these theological images [in relation to Wright] in introducing him because his reputation, his public pronouncements...all conspire to suggest a sort of Buddha, a high priest....It may be that I knew him too late." He called Cooke, "young man," and asked what was on his mind (a television program on Wright). Cooke describes the television debut and a debate which took place sometime later. The essay is reprinted from THE MANCHESTER GUARDIAN WEEKLY, April 16, 1959.

172:26 Cuscaden, R.R. "Frank Lloyd Wright's Drawings Preserved." THE PRAIRIE SCHOOL REVIEW 1 (First Quarter, 1964): 18.

Lists 144 drawings of seventeen projects by Frank Lloyd Wright, now deposited at the American Institute of Architects, The Octagon, Washington, D.C. (see 172:72).

172:27 Cutler, Anthony. "The Tyranny of Hagia Sophia: Notes on Greek Orthodox Church Design in the United States." JOURNAL OF THE SOCIETY OF ARCHITECTURAL HISTORIANS 31 (March 1972): 38-50.

A brief statement concerning the historic revivals and spirit of Byzantine, Greek, and Orthodox styles prior to a discussion of three churches, one of which is Wright's Annunciation Church at Milwaukee, 1956-59. (The other two are Church of the Ascension, East Oakland, California, 1960, by Reid, Rockwell, Banwell and Tarics; Church of the Ascension, Atlanta, 1967, by D.A. Polychrone.) Edgar Kaufmann and Dimitri Tselos are quoted as having recalled Hagia Sophia as Wright's last church. Cutler expands the idea.

172:28 Decker, Paul. "Prophet Not without Honor." CALIFORNIA ARTS AND ARCHITECTURE 57 (February 1940): 15.

Dedicatory address by Wright at the University of Southern California at the opening of the May Omerod Harris Hall of Architecture and Fine Arts.

172:29 Drexler, Arthur. THE DRAWINGS OF FRANK LLOYD WRIGHT. New York: Horizon Press for Museum of Modern Art, 1962. 320 p.

Drexler worked for Wright from 1902 to 1908, when many of the drawings in this publication were produced. He differentiates between Wright's drawings, made with a total understanding of the third dimension and those by William Drummond and Marion Mahony, whose style contributed most to Wright's renderings and according to some, were superior to Wright as a draftsman.

172:30 Dull, Elizabeth Helsing. "The Domestic Architecture of Oak Park, Illinois: 1900-1930." Doctoral dissertation, Northwestern University, 1973, 266 p.

An indepth analysis of this Chicago suburb in which Wright and so many of his followers lived, practiced, and built. Many other architects practiced there after Wright had moved.

172:31 Eaton, Leonard K. TWO CHICAGO ARCHITECTS AND THEIR CLIENTS: FRANK LLOYD WRIGHT AND HOWARD VAN DOREN SHAW. Cambridge, Mass.: The M.I.T. Press, 1969. 259 p.

Shaw, an almost totally unknown architect had many things in common with Wright - age, background, craftsman traditions - but Shaw had the more affluent clients. Eaton provides detailed information on fourteen of Wright's clients and thirteen of Shaw's in a total listing of forty and fifty clients respectively.

172:32 _____. "W.H. Winslow and the Winslow House." THE PRAIRIE SCHOOL REVIEW 1 (Third Quarter, 1964): 12-14.

A study of client-architect relationships. Photographs of Winslow and family.

172:33 Farr, Finis. FRANK LLOYD WRIGHT, A BIOGRAPHY. New York: Scribners, 1961. 293 p.

Published as a series of articles in the SATURDAY EVENING POST, this biography, attempting to cover ninety years of the famous architect's full life, presents anecdotes and details. However, he does little to relate them to Wright, the architect or the man. It is a biography for the general public and does not attempt to add to the scholarship and research on Wright.

172:34 Fern, Alan M. "The Midway Gardens of Frank Lloyd Wright." ARCHITECTURAL REVIEW 134 (August 1963): 113-16.

A sketchy descriptive article, with plans, sections and photographs of what was a significant nonresidential structure by Wright. Only five large nonresidential projects apparently remained standing when this article was written.

172:35 _____. THE MIDWAY GARDENS, 1914-1929, AN EXHIBITION... APRIL 24 TO MAY 20, 1961. Chicago: College of Humanities, University of Chicago Press, 1961. 10 p.

Exhibition material consisted of photographs, photocopies of drawings, plaster scale models, and original preparatory sketches of sculptures by Iannelli. The three-page Fern introduction is followed by essays on Wright and Iannelli and a letter from the sculptor to the architect.

172:36 Fitch, James Marston. "Frank Lloyd Wright, 1869-1959." ARCHITECTURAL FORUM 110 (May 1959): 108-12.

An obituary covering Wright's origins, his personality, his stylistic development, and his writings. But "it is to his buildings, rather than his writings, that we must turn for the clearest exposition of his principles."

172:37 Forsee, Aylesa. FRANK LLOYD WRIGHT, A REBEL IN CONCRETE. Philadelphia: Macrae Smith, 1959. 181 p.

Written as a stimulus to the imagination of high school students, the author provides anecdotes of Wright's early life and background, shows his rise to fame and the philosophy of design which guided his architectural contributions. Twenty photographs of his work are included.

172:38 Gannett, William Channing. THE HOUSE BEAUTIFUL...IN A SETTING DESIGNED BY FRANK LLOYD WRIGHT. River Forest, Ill.: Auvergne Press, 1897. 55 p. Reprint. Park Forest, Ill.: W.R. Hasbrouck, 1963.

This book was printed in the basement of William Herman Winslow's house, Forest River, Illinois, designed in 1894 by Wright. Winslow and Wright printed the book by hand in the tradition of the arts and crafts movement and bound it in half calf with gilt top.

172:39 Gebhard, David. "A Note on the Chicago Fair of 1893 and Frank Lloyd Wright." JOURNAL OF THE SOCIETY OF ARCHITECTURAL HISTORIANS 18 (May 1959): 63-65.

Dimitri Tselos (below) has emphasized the impact of the 1893 Japanese Pavilion. In Gebhard's article the Turkish Pavilion is discussed as being an additional possible source of influence upon Wright. Projecting hipped roof, geometric decorations, and continuous line of horizontal windows are similar characteristics to the houses of the Prairie years, notably the Winslow house, 1893-94.

172:40 Gloag, John. "Frank Lloyd Wright and the Significance of the Taliesin Fellowship." ARCHITECTURAL REVIEW 77 (January 1935): 1-2.

"My real destination [was] Spring Green [where] there lived one of the great men who gave form and feeling to the Modern Movement...." The Fellowship was not an "art colony," not an "escapist school," but an attempt to produce well-rounded designers who read Butler's THE WAY OF ALL FLESH. Gloag's 1935 statement that the Fellowship's influence "may be far greater than anybody at Taliesin yet suspects" is interesting in the light of today's attitudes toward Wright's successors.

172:41 Griggs, Joseph. "Alfonso Iannelli, The Prairie Spirit in Sculpture." THE PRAIRIE SCHOOL REVIEW 2 (Fourth Quarter, 1965): 5-23.

Iannelli, 1888-1965, was a sculptor in collaboration with architects, including Irving Gill, Purcell and Elmslie, and Barry Byrne, but most notably with Frank Lloyd Wright at Midway Gardens, Chicago, 1914.

172:42 Gutheim, Frederick. FRANK LLOYD WRIGHT ON ARCHITECTURE: SE-

LECTED WRITINGS 1894-1940. New York: Duell, Sloan and Pearce, 1941. 275 p. (republished 1959).

Includes a complete listing of published writings by Wright up to publication date. The emphasis of his writings is upon organic architecture - as in the Gothic but not in the Renaissance Baroque or Rococo - "they are not developed from within. There is little or nothing organic in their nature[!!!!]" "Architecture is a living art and will not live again until we break away entirely from adherence to the false ideals of the Renaissance." Wright rejected America's reliance upon her European past and thus completely misunderstood the spirit of the Renaissance, interpreting it as a negative force in his own time.

172:43 H., G.J. "Wright, Frank Lloyd. A Reassessment." THE BUILDER 174 (March 5, 1948): 274-76.

A brief introduction to Wright's philosophy of an organic architecture with a discussion of his current work, notably of his Florida Southern College, which is illustrated.

172:44 Hamlin, Talbot F. "Frank Lloyd Wright. An Analysis." PENCIL POINTS 19 (March 1938): 137-44.

Hamlin considers Wright's designs as the products of a genius, eternally young, who subordinates all aspects of a design to a basic idea. In the Kaufmann house it was site and structure; Johnson Wax, industrial concrete forms; the Hanna house, hexagonal shapes, but with poetry and a "varied and magnificent passion for rhythm." Admitting that this approach to design has defects, and Wright too conceded as much, Hamlin feels that Wright is totally justified.

172:45 _____. "Frank Lloyd Wright." THE NATION 151 (November 30, 1940): 541-42.

Review of a half-century of work by Wright at the New York Museum of Modern Art. "Creative use of materials ...truth in expression...creative structural conceptions...sensitivity to site...astonishing plastic sense ...which stand out in Wright's work and make it unique in contemporary architecture."

172:46 Hasbrouck, Wilbert R. "The Earliest Work of Frank Lloyd Wright." THE PRAIRIE SCHOOL REVIEW 7 (Fourth Quarter, 1970): 14-16.

"The Earliest Known published Drawing by Frank Lloyd Wright. Drawing from FOURTH ANNUAL, ALL SOULS CHURCH, January 6, 1887." Unity Chapel as it was known at Helena, Wisconsin, and the drawing was probably made in 1886, when Wright was eighteen. Other facts concerning Wright's early years, including two commissions given to Silsbee by Wright's uncle, Jenkins Lloyd Jones, are mentioned.

172:47 Hasbrouck, W.R., ed. A GUIDE TO THE ARCHITECTURE OF FRANK LLOYD WRIGHT IN OAK PARK AND RIVER FOREST, ILLINOIS. Oak Park, Ill.: Oak Park Public Library, 1966. 32 p.

Thirty-one structures are listed with original owner's name, address, date of construction, photograph, descriptive information, and location map.

172:48 Hines, Thomas S. Jr. "Frank Lloyd Wright - The Madison Years, Records Versus Recollections." JOURNAL OF THE SOCIETY OF ARCHITECTURAL HISTORIANS 26 (December 1967): 227-33.

Wright always claimed that he was born in 1869 and that on an impulse he abandoned engineering in his senior year at the University of Wisconsin to become an architect. Hines questions these romantic myths, and his detective work in court records and university archives has shown that Wright was born in 1867, and only spent two semesters as a part-time student at the university. Edgar Kaufmann in the December 1966 JOURNAL OF THE SOCIETY OF ARCHITECTURAL HISTORIANS gave other evidence for Wright's birth in 1867.

172:49 Historic American Buildings Survey. THE ROBIE HOUSE. Palos Park, Ill.: The Prairie School Press, 1968. 14 sheets of drawings.

The Historic American Buildings Survey began in 1933, and during summer months, students and faculty of architecture schools measure and record architectural structures of historic and stylistic significance. This set of fourteen drawings, eleven by fifteen inches, consists of a site plan, three floor plans, three elevations, and details of glazing, furniture, and services.

172:50 Hitchcock, Henry Russell. "The Evolution of Wright, Mies and Le Corbusier." PERSPECTA 1 (Summer 1952): 8-15.

Their education, apprenticeship, practice, point of maturity, and first masterpieces are compared. Wright is considered to be mature in the Prairie houses period, all buildings prior to that being a series of educational exercises in development. "The study of Wright's early work still continues to reveal new sources of influence."

172:51_____. "Frank Lloyd Wright and the Academic Tradition of the Early 1890's." WARBURG AND COURTAULD INSTITUTE'S JOURNAL 7 (January-June, 1944): 46-63.

Some interesting aspects of Wright's early career including his entry in the Milwaukee Museum and Library competition based upon the seventeenth-century classical east facade of the Louvre, Paris, and the Blossom House, Chicago, of 1893, inspired by the H.A.C. Taylor House, Newport, Rhode Island, of McKim, Mead and White, a Colonial Revival house with Adamesque and Palladian overtones.

172:52 _____. "Frank Lloyd Wright at the Museum of Modern Art." ART BULLETIN 23 (March 1941): 73-76.

"The most important architectural exhibition...since the international exhibition of Modern Architecture of 1932," in which Hitchcock also lauded Wright, even though "the year 1932 was a difficult one in which to show sympathetically the work of Wright." Hitchcock explains the difficulty and complexity on the part of the public in understanding Wright's work, spread, as it is, over a wide geographic area. For this reason Wright requested Hitchcock to publish a biography which Hitchcock advises that he is doing.

172:53 _____. "Frank Lloyd Wright, 1867-1967." THE PRAIRIE SCHOOL REVIEW 4 (Fourth Quarter, 1967): 5-9.

Hitchcock quotes the source (Thomas S. Hines, Jr. - above) which proves Wright was born in 1867, and assesses the hundred-year span to 1967. Unlike Olbrich whose centennial occurred also in 1967, or Richardson's in 1938, Wright is well known, has had and will continue to have much written about him, although numerous scholars are turning to his contemporaries, many of whom were his assistants.

172:54 _____. IN THE NATURE OF MATERIALS: 1887-1941. New York: Duell Sloan and Pearce, 1942. 130 p.

The first major biography of Wright still stands as the basic text, even though different interpretations have since been forwarded and new material and research have modified some of the data. The book emphasizes the importance of Wright to the development of Sullivan. Early houses, all aspects of the Prairie style, Broadacres and Usonian houses are all discussed.

172:55 _____. "Notes of a Traveler: Wright and Kahn." ZODIAC 6 (1960): 14-21.

An essay on the Guggenheim Museum, New York City, finished and opened after Wright's death, with crowds of people coming, not to view paintings but to experience the architecture as a work of art. Hitchcock analyzes space, structure, and materials, relating the building to other current movements and architects.

172:56 Hoffmann, Donald. "Frank Lloyd Wright and Viollet-le-Duc." JOURNAL OF THE SOCIETY OF ARCHITECTURAL HISTORIANS 28 (October 1969): 173-83.

Wright readily admitted his indebtedness to John Ruskin and Eugene Viollet-le-Duc, especially the influence of the latter. Parallels in philosophical attitudes between Wright and the Frenchman, as Hoffmann points out in a series of sub-headings, included ornamentation, truth, reason, axiality, nationalism, and organic analogies. Theories are related to the practice of architecture, especially in le-Duc's medievalism and Wright's romanticism in the Prairie years, notably in the Larkin Building, Buffalo.

172:57 HOUSE BEAUTIFUL. "Wright, Frank Lloyd. Special Issue devoted to Frank Lloyd Wright." Vol. 98 (November 1955): 233-379.

Devoted to the residential architecture of Wright with numerous photographs, many in color, the accompanying essays include such topics as: the man who liberated architecture, poetry of structure, character of the site, materials, the house as a home, individuality, and furnishings. The writings, movies, and what men have written about Wright attempt to give as rounded a picture of Wright as possible.

172:58 Hunter, Paul. "Mr. Wright Goes to Los Angeles." PENCIL POINTS 21 (March 1940 supplement): 34, 36.

Mr. Wright was at the dedication of the new College of Architecture, University Southern California, and spoke (after a three-minute ovation) to 2500 people on a variety of topics but demanded that "architecture must be the center line of any indigenous American culture."

172:59 Huxtable, Ada Louise. "Anatomy of a Failure." THE NEW YORK TIMES, March 17, 1968, section 2, p. 35.

Art has values but architecture does not. The only value is in the land on which the architecture stands. This is true of Wright's Imperial Hotel, Tokyo; not a single spatial element was saved for posterity.

172:60 _____. "Art: Wright Mythology. Twentieth Century on CBS TV Aims at Perpetrating Legend of Architect." THE NEW YORK TIMES, February 19, 1962, p. 14.

The myth but not the facts of Wright's greatness were presented in the CBS television program, here reviewed.

172:61 _____. "Drawings and Dreams of Frank Lloyd Wright." NEW YORK

TIMES, March 11, 1962, Magazine section, pp. 24-25.

A brief comment with illustrations of Wright's drawings, 1895-1969, from an exhibition at the New York Museum of Modern Art.

172:62 _____. "The Facts of Wright's Greatness." THE NEW YORK TIMES, March 18, 1962, p. 21.

250 of the 8,000 drawings in the Wright Foundation archives were on display at the New York Museum of Modern Art. Wright's greatness is in his foresight and development of ideas.

172:63 _____. "Metropolitan to Set up Wright Interior." THE NEW YORK TIMES, May 15, 1972, p. 42.

The Francis W. Little house, Wayzata, Minnesota, 1912-15, has been demolished and one room will be installed in the American Wing of the New York Museum of Modern Art. It is the first museum display of architecture by a modern master.

172:64 _____. "Natural Houses of Frank Lloyd Wright." NEW YORK TIMES, Sunday, November 17, 1963, Magazine section, p. 78.

Between 1893 and 1959, Wright designed 262 houses. One was destroyed by fire, another demolished, but in 1963 the remainder still stood. Edgar Kaufmann donated "Falling Water" to Western Pennsylvania Conservancy, and photographs of this house were exhibited at the New York Museum of Modern Art in November 1963.

172:65 _____. "That Museum: Wright or Wrong." THE NEW YORK TIMES, October 25, 1959, Magazine section, cover and pp. 16-17, 91.

Wright claimed that the Guggenheim Muesum would be "an unusual container for an unusual collection.... Here for the first time, you will see twentieth-century arts and architecture in their true relation.... This is the liberation of painting by architecture."

172:66 _____. "Triple Legacy of Mr. Wright." NEW YORK TIMES, Sunday, November 15, 1959, Magazine section, pp. 18-19.

"The extraordinary public response to the new Guggenheim Museum again puts the limelight on the lifetime of accomplishment of its creator." This two-page spread illustrates several of Wright's projects in addition to containing a brief statement.

172:67 _____. "Wright House at Bear Run, Pa., Will Be Given Away to Save It." THE NEW YORK TIMES, September 7, 1963, p. 21.

Edgar J. Kaufmann, Jr., studied with Wright in the

1930's and induced his father to commission Wright to design "Falling Water," the summer retreat which is now being turned over to the Western Pennsylvania Conservancy. An endowment fund, grants, and 500 acres accompany the gift of the house.

172:68 _____. "Wright Show Tells of the Wrangles in Creation of a Landmark House." THE NEW YORK TIMES, May 5, 1973, p. 41.

"An architect and his client," is the title of an exhibition on Wright at the New York Metropolitan Museum of Art which relates to a future American Wing installation of two rooms from the Francis W. Little house, Wayzata, Minnesota, 1912-15. One of the two rooms is the living room measuring thirty-five by thirty-five by fourteen and a half feet high.

172:69 Jacobs, Herbert, FRANK LLOYD WRIGHT, AMERICA'S GREATEST ARCHITECT. New York: Harcourt, Brace and World, 1965. 224 p. Illus.

Herbert Jacobs employed Wright on two different residences, and the one at Madison, Wisconsin, was constructed for only $5500, including the architect's fee. Jacobs obviously admired Wright, enough to have employed him to design a third house, (not built), and this adulation comes through.

172:70 Johnson, Philip. "The Frontiersman." ARCHITECTURAL REVIEW 106 (August 1949): 105-10.

After stating that "Wright is the greatest living architect for many reasons," Johnson then analyzes Wright in relation to his major, mainly European, contemporaries, as leaders in the modern movement: Corbusier the "Mediterranean culture," Wright the exuberant individualism of an ever-expanding frontier. Illustrations of Taliesin West.

172:71 Johonnot, Rodney F. THE NEW EDIFICE OF UNITY CHURCH, OAK PARK, ILLINOIS. Oak Park, Ill.: New Unity Church Club, 1961. 16 p.

Johonnot was the pastor at the time of publication, and wrote these historical and descriptive notes.

172:72 Kamrath, Karl. "Frank Lloyd Wright Drawings in the American Institute of Architects Archives." AMERICAN INSTITUTE OF ARCHITECTS' JOURNAL 42 (July 1964): 50-51.

Kamrath was responsible for making negatives of 144 drawings of thirteen projects by Wright from the Wright Fellowship archives. The thirteen projects are listed. "Mrs. Wright, however, requested that the two Taliesins not be printed. The tracings of two other projects, the Johnson Wax Administration Building and the famous Robie House, have not yet been found." Three drawings are illustrated. See Cuscaden (above).

172:73 _____. "The Stubborn Hotel is Shaking." AMERICAN INSTITUTE OF ARCHITECTS' JOURNAL 48 (November 1967): 70-72.

The value of land in downtown Tokyo and the low income realized by the hotel will result in its demolition after standing for forty-four years. Its run-down condition is described.

172:74 Karpel, Bernard. "What Men have Written about Frank Lloyd Wright." HOUSE BEAUTIFUL, November 1955.

Mr. Karpel, then librarian of the Museum of Modern Art, New York City, has compiled a list of 330 articles and publications of "every worthwhile biography of Wright listed at ten year intervals from 1900 to 1949 and 1950 to 1955 in English and foreign languages." This listing, like so many bibliographies, "is a comprehensive rather than exhaustive statement."

172:75 _____. "Selected Works by Wright." HOUSE BEAUTIFUL, October 1959.

This is an extended listing, comprehensive but not exhaustive, of 120 periodical articles and publications by and on Wright from 1955 to 1959. Mr. Karpel's November 1955 listing covered the years 1900 to 1955.

172:76 Kaufmann, Edgar. Jr. "Crisis and Creativity: Frank Lloyd Wright, 1904-1914." JOURNAL OF THE SOCIETY OF ARCHITECTURAL HISTORIANS 25 (December 1966): 292-96.

"...tumultuous emotions...slowed but did not stop or deflect the surge of Wright's art." His first marital separation and travel in Europe broke the continuity of his Chicago practice. Kaufmann touches upon Wright's family, his six teenage children, and his mother's influence, when he was forty-two years of age in 1909. (Kaufmann establishes that Wright was born in 1867, a fact of importance discussed later by Thomas S. Hines in the December 1967 JOURNAL OF THE SOCIETY OF ARCHITECTURAL HISTORIANS.) Frank's son Lloyd was also in Europe helping with the Wasmuth publication.

172:77 _____. "The Form of Space for Art: Wright's Guggenheim Museum." ART IN AMERICA 46 (Winter 1958-59): 74-77.

The building was still in construction when it was photographed and discussed in this article.

172:78 _____. "Frank Lloyd Wright and the Fine Arts." PERSPECTA 8 (1963): 37-42.

"Wright's heritage in the arts centered on ideals common to liberal British intellectuals of the mid-nineteenth century...." (He could abhor modern art and yet design a museum to house it!) Beauty had to be associated with the useful and the romantic. This romantic naturalism in architecture began for Wright with Sullivan. Wright's career is briefly surveyed to analyze his relationships to the fine arts.

172:79 _____. "Frank Lloyd Wright at the Strozzi." MAGAZINE OF ART 44 (May 1951): 190-92.

Oskar Stonorov assembled the Wright exhibit at the Strozzi Palace, Florence, financed by A.C. Kaufmann, executive head of Gimbel Brothers, Philadelphia. It is Europe which has continued to honor Wright: Germany at the beginning followed by Holland, England, and in 1951, Italy. All this while America was demolishing its architectural heritage.

172:80 _____. "Frank Lloyd Wright: The Eleventh Decade." ARCHITECTURAL FORUM, June 1969, pp. 38-41.

Wright's "territoriality" or a response to the environment led to his "clustering" or grouping of buildings around a nucleus. His final phase of development included "indeterminacy" whereby the simple geometry of a design predominated.

172:81 _____. "Frank Lloyd Wright: Three New Churches." ART IN AMERICA 45 (Fall 1957): 22-25.

Three different expressions for three different religions: Jewish, Greek Orthodox, and Christian Scientist, but "each one is richly inventive, intensely pure, and eloquent of the praise, the search, the art which unites all worships."

172:82 _____. FRANK LLOYD WRIGHT'S FALLING WATER, 25 YEARS AFTER. Milan, Italy: ET/AS Kompass, 1963. 64 p. 127 illus.

Good color photographs of Wright's famed house on the Mesa, seen at all seasons of the year.

172:83 _____. TALIESIN DRAWINGS: RECENT ARCHITECTURE OF FRANK LLOYD WRIGHT, SELECTED FROM HIS DRAWINGS. New York: Wittenborn, Schultz, 1952. 62 p.

Nineteen projects and buildings are illustrated with descriptive notes and as Kaufmann says in his all too brief introduction, this is the first publication of drawings from the office of Wright in forty years.

172:84 _____. "Three New Buildings on the Pacific Coast." ARCHITECTS' YEAR BOOK 4 (1951): 55-63.

Pages 61-63 are concerned with Wright's V.C. Morris Gift Shop, San Francisco, an inward-looking space as are the Larkin Building and Johnson Wax. The shop is praised for its space relationships in relation to displays of gifts which the shop purveys.

172:85 _____. "Undampened Wright." ARCHITECTURAL FORUM 87 (July 1947): 22.

A letter concerning "Falling Water" built by Wright for the Kaufmanns. Kaufmann admits that the building leaks but awards the blame to the contractors and not the architect.

172:86 Kaufmann, Edgar, and Raeburn, Ben. WRITINGS AND BUILDINGS. New York: Horizon Press, 1960. 346 p. 150 pls. (Paperback by Meridan Books.)

The importance of this book is that it has the address of every notable work of Frank Lloyd Wright. There are one or two errors and omissions, but this is an invaluable source for anyone seeking out buildings by Wright.

172:87 Kienitz, John Fabian. "The Romanticism of Frank Lloyd Wright." ART IN AMERICA 32 (April 1940): 91-101.

Spaces in two of Wright's houses in California termed "fastidious clarification...for people of more than moderate means." Picturesque effect achieved by silhouette, tranquil effects seen in painting and European influences from several architectural movements are given as sources for many of Wright's achievements.

172:88 Kimball, Sidney Fiske. "Builder and Poet - Frank Lloyd Wright." ARCHITECTURAL RECORD 71 (June 1932): 379-80.

"The individual creations of the inspired artist," is the theme of this review of Wright's AUTOBIOGRAPHY. Wright's attitudes, his reliance upon Sullivan, his buildings, materials, and expressions are all briefly touched upon.

172:89 Kostka, Robert. "Frank Lloyd Wright in Japan." THE PRAIRIE SCHOOL REVIEW 3 (Third Quarter, 1966): 5-23.

Japanese art and architecture had an influence on Wright from the period of 1893 when he saw the Japanese Pavillion at the Chicago World's Fair. His own print collection acted as a stimulus to his architecture and made him the logical non-Japanese choice as architect of the Imperial Hotel, Tokyo. Wright designed eight other projects in Japan, including residences, a theater, and a hotel. Well-illustrated article.

172:90 Laporte, Paul M. "Architecture and Democracy." ARCHITECT'S YEAR BOOK 3 (1949): 12-19.

Quoting Wright's dictum that "A new space concept is needed. And it is evident that it has come...the Architecture of Democracy," the author discussed Konrad Wachsmann's mobilar structure of a hangar and Wright's Kaufmann house, "Falling Water," a house of complete freedom, not only because of the architect's role but also because the wealthy clients had freedom to move from settled areas and thus build for rational, emotional, social, and recreational reasons.

172:91 McAuliffe, George. "The Guggenheim: Great Architecture, Difficult Installation." INDUSTRIAL DESIGN 6 (November 1959): 66-69.

The curved walls of the spiral ramp necessitated each painting be projected from the wall on steel rods to the center back of the painting. Wright actually wanted them tilted as on an easel, but either way McAuliffe argues that the paintings appear askew.

172:92 MacCormac, Richard C. "The Anatomy of Wright's Aesthetic." ARCHITECTURAL REVIEW 143 (February 1968): 143-46.

The Froebel educational system was not necessarily meant to have an aesthetic appeal, but in fact it had a profound influence upon the early work of Wright. Solid and void, circulation and non-circulation spaces are as clearly defined as the building blocks which Wright played with as a child. Numerous plans, diagrams, and isometrics complement the argument.

172:93 Manson, Grant Carpenter. FRANK LLOYD WRIGHT TO 1910. New York: Reinhold, 1958. 222 p.

Wright's early years are covered in some detail, especially in his Froebelian Kindergarten and the architectural practice of the Prairie years when he made an "avowed attempt to give expression to the nature of materials and forms they naturally suggest." This book developed from a Ph.D. dissertation at Harvard, 1941, entitled "The Work of Frank Lloyd Wright Before 1910."

172:94 _____. "Wright in the Nursery. The Influence of Froebel Education on the Work of Frank Lloyd Wright." ARCHITECTURAL REVIEW 113 (June 1953): 348-51.

Froebelian toys were searched out by Mrs. Wright at the 1876 Philadelphia Exposition, and in turn they supposedly influenced the volumetric quality in Wright's work. Madame Kraus-Boelte's Boston Kindergarten of 1872, when Wright was five, would have been a more likely influence on the architect, since he would have been nine in 1876!

172:95 Masselnk, Eugene, ed. BUILDINGS BY FRANK LLOYD WRIGHT IN SEVEN MIDDLE WESTERN STATES: ILLINOIS, INDIANA, IOWA, MICHIGAN, MINNESOTA, OHIO, WISCONSIN. Chicago: Chicago Art Institute, 1963. 28 p.

An extension of a similar 1949 listing with material taken from H.R. Hitchcock's IN THE NATURE OF MATERIALS, and an extended listing published in 1954.

172:96 Michels, Eileen. "The Early Drawings of Frank Lloyd Wright Reconsidered." JOURNAL OF THE SOCIETY OF ARCHITECTURAL HISTORIANS 30 (December 1971): 294-303.

Some articles question the accuracy of Wright's AN AUTOBIOGRAPHY. Ms. Michels goes further and questions the accuracy of Wright's contention that he was a competent draftsman while an assistant of Adler and Sullivan. The firm invariably used the services of Paul Loutrup, a professional delineator, and from 1887 they employed Oliver Smith, another delineator of note. Wright's style is examined in relation to that of his contemporaries.

172:97 Miller, Richard A., et al. FOUR GREAT MAKERS OF MODERN ARCHITECTURE. New York: Trustees of Columbia University, 1963. 296 p.

Includes Gropius, Corbusier, and Mies, in addition to Wright, who were subjects of a symposium at the Columbia School of Architecture, March to May 1961. Thirty-five papers were presented including a translation of a statement by Le Corbusier and another by Gropius. Theory, philosophy, influence, concepts, ideas, and aesthetics of the four men were the basis of topics offered.

172:98 Mock, Elizabeth B. "Taliesin West." HOUSE AND GARDEN 94 (August 1948): 52-55.

"Frank Lloyd Wright looked at the Southern Arizona desert and saw that it was good." The reasons for its goodness and the means of living in such an environment are forwarded with plan and photographs.

172:99 Moholy-Nagy, Sibyl. "Frank Lloyd Wright and the Aging of Modern Architecture. PROGRESSIVE ARCHITECTURE 40 (May 1959): 136-42.

His work after 1892 always had "a transcendental message

linking it to Christianity, Ethnography, Democracy, Humanism," with the profession of architecture inseparably linked to religion, sometimes to the extent that Wright became more prophet than architect, although always the technologist.

172:100 Montgomery, Roger. "Frank Lloyd Wright's Hall of Justice." ARCHITECTURAL FORUM, December 1970, pp. 54-59.

A quarter-mile long, the Marin County Court House is a low but dominant structure, a stucco extravaganza backdrop for the lurid tragedies of modern life.

172:101 Morgan, Don L. "A Wright House on the Prairie." THE PRAIRIE SCHOOL REVIEW 2 (Third Quarter, 1965): 5-19, 23.

A detailed discussion of the only Wright house in Nebraska, at McCook for Harold P. Sutton, 1905. The article relates the Sutton house to Wright's early work and his work en toto. Photographs, plans, letters owned by the Sutton family including a facsimile on page 23.

172:102 Morton, Terry Brust. "Wright's Pope-Leighey House." THE PRAIRIE SCHOOL REVIEW 4 (Fourth Quarter, 1967): 20-26.

The Loren Popes commissioned the house in 1940, and sold it when they left Washington in 1946 to Robert Leighey for $17,000. The State Department of Highways condemned the house in 1963, and although the highway was never built, the house was moved to Woodlawn Plantation. The Department of the Interior paid Mrs. Leighey $31,500 for the house. This amount and other contributions were used to move the house.

172:103 Muggenburg, James R. "Frank Lloyd Wright in Print, 1959-1970." THE AMERICAN ASSOCIATION OF ARCHITECTURAL BIBLIOGRAPHERS. Papers 9. William B. O'Neal, ed. Charlottesville: University of Virginia, 1972. Pp. 85-132.

Lists 134 books, catalogs, and general works, including book reviews and doctoral dissertations, eleven motion pictures, one recording, ten manuscript collections, 414 periodical articles, and fifteen obituaries and portraits. It's a pity that the three-page introduction is so subjective and patronizing. "The uniform, if bland architecture of the fifties..." is the sort of statement that will be questioned in a few years.

172:104 Mumford, Lewis. "The Skyline: At Home, Indoors and Out." THE NEW YORKER, February 12, 1938, p. 31.

A review of the Kaufmann House, "Falling Water" at Bear Run, Pennsylvania, the subject of an exhibit at the New York Museum of Modern Art until March 1, 1938.

172:105 Nelson, George. "Wright's Houses: Two Residences Built by a Great Architect for Himself." FORTUNE 34 (August 1946): 116-25.

The article is concerned with the two Taliesins, the one north of Phoenix, Arizona, known as Taliesin West and the other at Spring Green, Wisconsin, known as Taliesin East. All plates, interior and exterior, are in color.

172:106 New York, Museum of Modern Art. A NEW HOUSE BY FRANK LLOYD WRIGHT ON BEAR RUN, PENNSYLVANIA. New York: Museum of Modern Art, 1938. 20 p.

"Falling Water" was the subject of an exhibit at Museum of Modern Art in 1938, and this catalog resulted. It consists of a one-page description by Wright and photographs.

172:107 O'Gorman, J.F. "Henry Hobson Richardson and Frank Lloyd Wright." ART QUARTERLY 32 (Autumn 1969): 292-315.

See under Richardson.

172:108 Osman, Mary E. "The Imperial Comes Tumbling Down." AMERICAN INSTITUTE OF ARCHITECTS' JOURNAL 50 (December 1968): 42-49.

Illustrations of the demolition, with accompanying text, but also construction drawings and photographs of the piling layed bare after the demolition. Stanford University has a one and a half ton urn from the hotel.

172:109 Parke-Bernet Galleries, Inc. ORIENTAL ART. New York: Parke-Bernet Galleries, 1967. 90 p.

Another auction of oriental works of art owned by Frank Lloyd Wright. A total of ninety-seven pieces were sold by "an Arizona Educational Institution."

172:110 Pawley, Martin. FRANK LLOYD WRIGHT I: PUBLIC BUILDINGS. New York: Simon and Schuster, 1970. 130 p.

It is incredible that after so much research on the early life of Wright, the introduction should begin, "In 1869, the year of Frank Lloyd Wright's birth. . . " when it has now been established that he was born in 1867! "All of Wright's public buildings reveal the extent of the architect's pioneering techniques and ideas." This volume in a series on a Library of Contemporary Architects has seventy-four plates, thirteen in color with notes and twenty-three plans and sections.

172:111 Pevsner, Nikolaus. "Frank Lloyd Wright's Peaceful Penetration of Europe. ARCHITECTS' JOURNAL 89 (May 4, 1939): 731-34, 756.

A report on the Sir George Watson Lectures of the Sulgrave Manor Board for 1939 given by Wright. Pevsner discusses the impact of Wright on modern architecture, crediting C.R. Ashbee with having introduced the Wrightian philosophies to Europe after his trip to Chicago in 1900. Professor Kuno Franke introduced Wright into Germany. Wright's greatest impact, however, was in Holland as illustrated in the article. An outstanding article.

172:112 Pfeiffer, Bruce Brooks. "Out of the Desert's Mystery." AMERICAN INSTITUTE OF ARCHITECTS' JOURNAL 59 (May 1973): 54-55.

Half of the article consists of a lengthy quotation from Wright's AUTOBIOGRAPHY on choosing the Arizona site for Taliesin West. "The same feeling prevails. . . today."

172:113 Pundt, Hermann G. FRANK LLOYD WRIGHT: VISION AND LEGACY. Chicago: Prairie School Press, 1966. 32 p.

A catalog of an exhibition organized by the University of Illinois Committee of Architectural Heritage.

172:114 Reed, Henry H., Jr. "Frank Lloyd Wright Conquers Paris: and Vice Versa." ARCHITECTURAL RECORD 112 (July 1952): 22, 268, 272.

Everyone in Paris, including the Communist literary weekly, admired Wright's work exhibited at the Ecole des Beaux Arts. Some of the French traditionalists upheld Wright because they felt that he had divorced himself from certain attitudes of modern design which they abhorred.

172:115 Rebori, A.N. "Frank Lloyd Wright's Textile-Block Slab Construction." ARCHITECTURAL RECORD 62 (December 1927): 448-56.

"Wright's work is based on a unit system of measure sufficiently flexible to meet exacting plan requirements or the particular needs and then proceeds to his own individual and inimitable manner. . . ." Residences of the mid-1920's are analyzed.

172:116 Rudd, J. William. "Frank Lloyd Wright's First Independent Commission." THE PRAIRIE SCHOOL REVIEW 1 (Third Quarter, 1964): 5-11.

Report of the Historic American Building Survey of the Chicago area, 1963-64. Photographs and Historic American Building Survey drawings of W.H. Winslow House, River Forest, Illinois, 1893.

172:117 Samona, Joseph. "Man, Matter and Space, on the Architecture of Frank Lloyd Wright." THE ARCHITECTS' YEARBOOK 5 (1953): 110-22.

Edgar Kaufmann, Jr. translated this address given by the rector of the University of Venice when Wright was given an honorary doctorate. The paper's emphasis is on space, the "natural flow of matter differentiated according to various qualities," as seen in a selection of examples of Wright's work spanning from the Prairie years through to the 1950's.

172:118 Schuyler, Montgomery. "An Architectural Pioneer; Review of the Portfolios Containing the Works of Frank Lloyd Wright." ARCHITECTURAL RECORD 31 (April 1912): 427-36.

A review of the portfolio of Wright's drawings published in Berlin by Ernst Wasmuth, stating that "Germany is more hospitable to new ideas" than France or England, and thereby referring the reason for Wright's work being printed in Germany. Wright is justified in his design philosophy as a rationalist against the illogicality of copying the historic styles. Wright is "Rhapsodie Prariale . . . in contrast with the rehandling and rehashing of admired historical forms."

172:119 Scully, Vincent Joseph. FRANK LLOYD WRIGHT. New York: G. Braziller, 1960. 125 p.

The 21-page introduction complements the 127 pages of illustrations, discussing Wright's major works, his role in American architecture, his reliance upon Europe and other movements. The plates are followed by a bibliographical note and a chronological list of buildings and projects, 1889-1959.

172:120 _____. "The Heritage of Wright." ZODIAC 8 (1961): 8-13.

Scully comments on Wright's attitudes against the city, his reliance upon traditional architecture and architects, and his geometry which pilots his whole course of development toward oneness. Wright's influence in Europe is looked upon as a positive contribution, compared to his influence in the 1940's and 1950's when he set up a smokescreen behind which he hid. Most students went elsewhere for inspiration, but those who stayed were part of incubator inbreeding. Thus his heritage in 1961 seemed weak and the future will view his contributions in perspective by new values.

172:121 _____. "Wright vs. The International Style." ART NEWS 53 (March 1954): 32-35, 64-66.

Until 1910, Wright was influencing European architects and ultimately the International style, but in 1929, European architects were having an impact upon him. Van der Rohe's brick house, 1923, is one example cited as influencing Wright's house on the Mesa, 1932. Mondrian's De Stijl paintings and Corbusier's concrete can be traced through to Wright. Wright, Corbusier, and

Mies "must all know in their hearts that the differences between them does not really matter; their meanings vary widely but are still the same."

172:122 Shank, Wesley I. "The Residence in Des Moines." JOURNAL OF THE SOCIETY OF ARCHITECTURAL HISTORICANS 29 (March 1970): 56-59.

Discussed as a house attributed to Frank Lloyd Wright and stylistically similar to his work of the early 1890's, Mr. Shank waits until the close of the article before admitting the house as being in the Prairie style, but by Heun.

172:123 Smith, Dean. GRADY GAMMAGE MEMORIAL AUDITORIUM, DESIGNED BY FRANK LLOYD WRIGHT. Tempe, Ariz.: Bureau of Publications, Arizona State University, 1964. 32 p.

This brash, crude, garish building is by the Frank Lloyd Wright Fellowship and not by Wright, who must still be spinning in his grave.

172:124 Smith, Norris Kelly. FRANK LLOYD WRIGHT: A STUDY IN ARCHITECTURAL CONTENT. Englewood Cliffs, N.J.: Prentice-Hall, 1966. 178 p.

Wright saw architecture as an embodying idea whether designing a house or a "city" of the dimensions of Broadacres. All were created as a contribution to the good life of democratic America. But the realization that this dream was not to be, for Wright or any other utopian idealist, led Wright into a phase of design associative to historical precedents, eclectic as nineteenth-century architecture and just as romantic. This is the theme of this well-illustrated offering.

172:125 _____. "Frank Lloyd Wright and the Problem of Historical Perspective." JOURNAL OF THE SOCIETY OF ARCHITECTURAL HISTORIANS 26 (December 1967): 234.

In 1952 the idea for a new State Capitol for Arizona had its nemesis. In 1956 four architectural firms formed into the Associated State Capitol Architects group and produced a Miesian design. ARCHITECTURAL FORUM for April 1957 published Wright's alternative proposal for a state Capitol. This article makes two major points: 1) if this controversy were written at the time of the events, would it be architectural history, since history needs an ingredient of backward looking perspective; 2) Wright's aims and designs for the capitol were to identify "his Cause with the public life of the nation," even though he was periferal to society and its conventions.

172:126 _____. "A Study of the Architectural Imagery of Frank Lloyd Wright." Doctoral dissertation, Columbia University, 1961. 251 p.

The relationship of Wright's writings to his architectural expression, 1892 to 1940, as governed by a conservative attitude toward the sober and restrained, and in relation to the family, Unitarianism, the Transcendental philosophers, and general concepts of romanticism (European and American). Wright's abandonment of family, practice, and accepted social values in 1909 is reflected at Taliesin East begun in 1911. Thereafter the influence of Rousseau led to Wright's anti-urban attitudes at "Falling Water," and the Johnson Way Building. Rousseau's SOCIAL CONTRACT paved the way for Broadacre (non)-city.

172:127 Solomon R. Guggenheim Foundation. THE SOLOMON R. GUGGENHEIM MUSEUM. ARCHITECT: FRANK LLOYD WRIGHT. New York: 1960. 72 p.

Harry F. Guggenheim provides a short history of the museum and Wright, a statement on his concept. Photographs illustrate construction, internal and external spaces and views, and a few of the treasures of the collection.

172:128 Solomon R. Guggenheim Museum. SIXTY YEARS OF LIVING ARCHITECTURE. New York: Solomon R. Guggenheim Museum, 1953. (40) p.

This is a catalog of an exhibition of Wright's work displayed at the Strozzi Palace, Florence, in 1951, then Switzerland, Holland, Germany, France, Mexico, and Philadelphia before New York City. There were 151 panels in the exhibition, some of which form the illustrations of this catalog.

172:129 Spencer, Robert C. "The Work of Frank Lloyd Wright." ARCHITECTURAL REVIEW (Boston) 7 (May 1900): 61-72. Reprint. The Prairie School Press, n.d. (See Spencer below).

As opposed to architects "busily engaged in the transplanting of exotics," Wright is presented as having "given us more poetic translations of material into structure." His original and varied work is surveyed with numerous thumbnail-size photographs, drawings, perspectives, and plans.

172:130 _____. THE WORK OF FRANK LLOYD WRIGHT FROM 1893 TO 1900. Park Forest, Ill.: The Prairie School Press, n.d., 12 p.

This is a facsimile from THE ARCHITECTURAL REVIEW (Boston), 1900, and illustrates many early projects by Wright, many of which are not to be found elsewhere. Spencer, an architect and friend of Wright, produced double-page renderings of the Winslow, Husser, and Heller houses.

172:131 Starosciak, Kenneth and Jane. FRANK LLOYD WRIGHT: A BIBLIOGRAPHY. New Brighton, Minn.: Kenneth Starosciak, 1973. Unpaged.

Subtitled "Issued on the occasion of the destruction of the Francis W. Little House, Deep Haven, Minnesota, 1913-1972," this limited edition of 750 lists forty-two publications from 1896 to 1962. It is a checklist of first editions. The occasion of this publication was the rape and destruction of the Little house, with a note on further information to be found in the MINNEAPOLIS TRIBUNE, August 20, 1972, picture magazine section, pages 6-21.

172:132 Stillman, Seymour. "Comparing Wright and Le Corbusier." AMERICAN INSTITUTE OF ARCHITECTS' JOURNAL 9 (April 1948): 171-78; 9 (May 1948): 226-33.

The comparison is of their attitudes to city (or non-city) planning and the backup philosophy associated with the urban environment, the individual, and his home. Social, economic, and cultural attitudes of the two men are touched upon.

172:133 Storrer, William Allin. THE ARCHITECTURE OF FRANK LLOYD WRIGHT. A COMPLETE CATALOG. Cambridge, Mass,: MIT Press, 1974. Unpaged.

A complete listing of all of Wright's structures which were actually built, plus commentary. Over a hundred of the buildings have never before appeared in a publication. Storrer tracked down and photographed every building where possible. Addresses are provided numerically by zip code.

172:134 Sturgis, Russell. "The Larkin Building in Buffalo." ARCHITECTURAL RECORD 23 (1908): 310-21.

This "Shock of Surprise" from the "traditional styles" as Sturgis termed the Larkin building at the time of its construction, was to him "a monster of awkwardness" in lines and masses. Nevertheless as a major architectural critic he took a "sympathetic position" in regard to the building, explaining it, and justifying Wright's attitude in designing such a building at a period when eclecticism was rife.

172:35 ______. "New Frank Lloyd Wright and Louis H. Sullivan Papers in the Burnham Library of Architecture." CALENDAR OF THE ART INSTITUTE OF CHICAGO 65 (January 1971): 6-15.

The letters of Wright's office were written by Walter Burley Griffin who site supervised the First National

Bank, Dwight, Illinois, 1905.

172:136 Sullivan, Louis. "Concerning the Imperial Hotel, Tokyo, Japan." ARCHITECTURAL RECORD 53 (April 1923): 332-52.

Freedom from the slavery of tradition is the poetic theme of this flowery article on Wright's "Masterpiece." This individualistic non-Japanese hotel is described in detail in relation to construction, the utilization of local materials, the function of the parts to the whole, interior design, and furnishings. "Superbly beautiful it stands - a noble prophecy."

172:137 Sweeney, James Johnson. "Chambered Nautilus on Fifth Avenue." MUSEUM NEWS 38 (January 1960): 14-15.

A quarter-mile long ramp, wide at the top and narrower at the bottom, spirals around a great central space capable of holding up to 1500 spectators. From the ramp, paintings can be viewed close at hand or across the space at great visual distances. The Sweeney article is followed by critical opinions by Lewis Mumford (pages 16-17), Alfred Frankenstein (pages 18-19), Peter Blake (pages 20-21), and a letter to the museum director by Philip Johnson (pages 22-25).

172:138 Townsend, Robert. "Frank Lloyd Wright on his Eightieth Birthday." ARCHITECTURAL ASSOCIATION JOURNAL 65 (October 1949): 64-69.

Wright's contribution toward an architecture for public housing as distinct from his designs for millionaires, and his pioneering new structures are discussed and illustrated.

172:139 Tselos, Dimitri. "Exotic Influences in the Architecture of Frank Lloyd Wright" MAGAZINE OF ART 47 (April 1953): 160-69, 184.

International Expositions helped influence stylistic trends in this country and Wright was influenced as much as anyone. Some of the Prairie houses have characteristics of Japanese architecture, however, in the teens and 1920's Wright was equally inspired by the architecture of the civilizations of Central America. Comparative photographs illustrate such influences.

172:140 _____. "Frank Lloyd Wright and World Architecture." JOURNAL OF THE SOCIETY OF ARCHITECTURAL HISTORIANS 28 (March 1969): 58-72.

Stylistic influences in the works of Wright came from wide and divergent sources, both historically and geographically. Mayan detailing from Uxmal, friezes and plans (for Unity Temple, Oak Park) from Mitla, and decoration for Midway Gardens, Chicago, from Kandinsky, Kupka, de la Fresnaye, from European painting movements possibly via the Armory Show of 1913. An appendix quotes a statement on the subject made by Wright following an article in the April 1953 MAGAZINE OF ART.

172:141 Udall, Mary C. "Wright: Great U.S. Architect. First Comprehensive Exhibition at Boston's Modern Institute." ART NEWS 38 (February 24, 1940): 6-7, 16.

Review of an exhibition at the Institute of Modern Art, Boston, when Wright was seventy years old. A brief resume of Wright's life is given with a commentary on the impact of the architecture of the 1930's including Johnson Wax and Kaufmann house. Houses dating from 1901-39 were illustrated in addition to an early model of the Robie house and models of other houses.

172:142 Walker, Ralph A. "Frank Lloyd Wright: His Contribution to Our American Culture." LAND ECONOMICS 32 (November 1956): 357-60.

Wright "denies the mediocre, acclaims the individual search for beauty, strives for meaning in our democratic way of life; for...democracy, with all its faults is still the best." Quotations from Wright, including his attitudes, experiments, achievements, and specifications of projects from 1911 through 1956 are listed as milestones and memoranda on pages 361-68.

172:143 Wasmuth, Ernst, ed. BUILDINGS, PLANS AND DESIGNS BY FRANK LLOYD WRIGHT. New York: Horizon Press, 1963. 100 pl. 16" x 26".

Facsimile of the Berlin edition of 1910 (72 pl.) and the second edition of 1924 (28 pl.) with a new foreword by William Wesley Peters of the Frank Lloyd Wright Fellowship. This 1963 edition was limited to 2500 copies.

172:144 Watts, Harvey M. "Don Quixote Atilt at His World." THE T-SQUARE CLUB JOURNAL OF PHILADELPHIA 1 (November 1931): 14, 34-35.

A review of Wright's lecture at Princeton "with sententious sentiments and tendentious phrases, some cryptic, some crystalline and some as clear or as obvious as mud."

172:145 Wegg, Talbot. "Frank Lloyd Wright Versus the U.S.A." AMERICAN INSTITUTE OF ARCHITECTS' JOURNAL 53 (February 1970): 48-52.

In 1941, Wright was invited to work for the Division of Defense Housing in producing one hundred houses for workers at a rifle plant. The politics of the situation are described, but also of significance is a conversation with Wright who was asked, "Whom do you regard as the best architect in the country today?" to which he replied, and without hesitation, "Albert Kahn."

172:146 Weisberg, Gabriel. "Frank Lloyd Wright and Pre-Columbia Art - The Background for his Architecture." ART QUARTERLY 30 (1967): 41-51.

A brief survey of the interest in Pre-Columbian art in the United States through publications and exhibitions. Wright expressed a childhood desire to visit Mexico in his A TESTAMENT (page 111). The 1876 and 1893 Expositions had displays; Sullivan incorporated Aztec motifs into his buildings and Wright incorporated Mayan elements into his designs of the 1890's. The Kehl Dance Academy project for Madison, Wisconsin, 1912, was the first design based upon an actual temple (Tulum, Yucatan, Mexico). Others followed at Richland Center, Wisconsin, 1915; at several sites in California during the 1920's and the 1925 Sugar Loaf Mountain Planetarium project, which was based upon a circular watchtower from Oaxaca, Mexico.

172:147 Wheeler, Robert C. "Frank Lloyd Wright Filling Station, 1958." JOURNAL OF THE SOCIETY OF ARCHITECTURAL HISTORIANS 19 (December 1960): 174-75.

Wright's ideal filling station of the 1920's on spacious landscaped highways and overhead pump hoses was not to be, even when the Ray W. Lindholm filling station at Cloquet, Minnesota, was built in 1958.

172:148 Wijdeveld, H. Thied. THE WORK OF FRANK LLOYD WRIGHT. New York: The Great Wendingen Edition, Horizon Press, 1965. 164 p.

A monograph on Wright originally published in Holland, 1925. This is not a facsimile but a new edition with comments by Ben Raeburn and new and added illustrations. Articles of the period and earlier were written by Wright, Sullivan, H.P. Berlage, J.J.P. Oud, Lewis Mumford, Robert Mallet-Stevens, and Erich Mendelsohn.

172:149 Wilson, Stuart. "The Gifts of Friedrich Forebel." JOURNAL OF THE SOCIETY OF ARCHITECTURAL HISTORIANS 26 (December 1967): 238-41.

An explanation of the system established by Forebel (1780-1852) of utilizing the toy as an educational tool, a commonplace occurrence in the twentieth but not in the nineteenth century. Wright in his AUTOBIOGRAPHY states: "Mother would go to Boston, take lessons of a teacher of the Froebel method and come home to teach the children."

172:150 Winston, Elizabeth. "Advocates of Modern Design Rally Strongly to the Defence of Frank Lloyd Wright." MICHIGAN SOCIETY OF ARCHITECTS WEEKLY BULLETIN 21 (July 22, 1947): 1.

This is a reprint of a NEW YORK HERALD TRIBUNE

article praising Wright, with quotations from eminent editors and authors of national magazines against an attack by Robert Moses on modern architecture in general and Wright in particular.

172:151 Wright, Frank Lloyd. AN AUTOBIOGRAPHY. London and New York: Longmans, Green and Co., 1932. 371 p. New York: Duell, Sloan and Pearce, 1943. 581 p. (Books 1-6).

Wright was not only a romantic, a child of the nineteenth century, but he also romanticized on the facts of his life: birth in 1869, instead of 1867, four years of engineering at University of Wisconsin, instead of two semesters part time, a woman who refused overtures to repair a marriage once it had been broken.... He discusses his buildings, his Jeffersonian philosophy, city planning and Broadacres and the new America, Usonia with Usonian houses and architecture. He ends on a positive note concerning Russia of 1937 - "A genuine culture at last!"

172:152 _____. ARCHITECTURAL FORUM 68 (January 1938): 1-107.

The whole issue is devoted to the new and unpublished work of Wright. Photographs, drawings, and plans of Prairie houses of an earlier period complement the work at Taliesin Fellowship, and the work of the 1930's including "Falling Water" and Johnson Wax. Additionally, the philosophies of the Usonian house and Broadacres are illustrated and presented.

172:153 _____. BUILDINGS, PLANS AND DESIGNS. New York: Horizon Press, 1963. 32 p. Portfolio of plates.

Based on the 1910 Ernst Wasmuth Publication, Berlin, this new $75 edition of 100 plates has an introduction by William Wesley Peters discussing the significance of the original work.

172:154 _____. THE STORY OF THE TOWER. New York: Horizon Press, 1956. 134 p.

Harold C. Price, the client of the Price Tower, Bartlesville, Oklahoma, introduces this book dealing with a concept that began as a project development for St. Marks in the Bowery, New York City, 1929. It was later adapted for Oklahoma. Numerous photographs, some in color, and drawings show the development and construction of this building.

172:155 Wright, Henry. "Frank Lloyd Wright: Unity Temple." ARCHITECTURAL FORUM (June 1969): 29-37.

A series of coincidental events led Wright to be chosen as architect for this religious structure. Quotations from

Wright's AUTOBIOGRAPHY provide the reasons for producing this "noble room." Wright had to persuade the congregation to accept his designs, the innovations of which are listed. "It is the seating geometry of the Temple, however, that is its most unusual and successful feature." At the time of the article the building needed repair and renovation.

172:156 Wright, Iovanna Lloyd. ARCHITECTURE: MAN IN POSSESSION OF HIS EARTH. Garden City, N.Y.: Doubleday, 1962. 127 p.

Wright's organic architecture had the "timeless element of beauty." It is this beauty as seen in stone, brick, wood, glass, steel, and concrete that Wright expressed his philosophy. This biography by Wright's daughter is not merely a life of Wright, illustrated with numerous colored sketches and photographs, it also includes the whole realm of architecture - ancient, medieval, vernacular, and modern - as a basis on which to hang the qualities of Wright.

172:157 Wright, John Lloyd. MY FATHER WHO IS ON EARTH. New York: G.P. Putnam's Sons, 1946. 195 p.

This collection of anecdotes, recollections, and reminiscences is not biographical. It doesn's really attempt to add to our understanding of Wright as an architect or an individual. Rather, it is a biased over-exaggerated account; there is also a certain amount of sour grapes.

172:158 Wright, Olgivanna Lloyd. FRANK LLOYD WRIGHT; HIS LIFE, HIS WORK, HIS WORDS. New York: Horizon Press, 1966. 224 p.

This is the fourth book by Mrs. Wright glorifying the memory of her famous architect husband, but this time it is biography strung together with lengthy quotations from the writings of Wright.

172:159 _____. OUR HOUSE. New York: Horizon Press, 1959. 308 p.

Wright had opinions on many subjects both related and unrelated to architecture. All of them came through in his writings and here "Mother" (Wright's wife, Olgivanna) adds her penny's worth!

172:160 _____. THE ROOTS OF LIFE. New York: Horizon Press, 1963. 256 p.

A glorification of the master through his "Art and Architecture in Life," "Meaning of Experience," addresses, "On Science," including attitudes on the hydrogen bomb, "On the Power of Thought," and "Our Inner Growth." These are the chapter headings.

172:161 Zevi, Bruno. "Frank Lloyd Wright and the Conquest of Space." MAGAZINE OF ART 43 (May 1950): 186-91.

Wright was a residential architect in 1910, an expressionist by 1925, and a pioneer in the modern movement by 1930, but who could have foreseen that Wright would have been capable of designing the Guggenheim Museum? Zevi then analyzes the concept of modern architecture and relates Wright's work to it.

173:1 YORK, EDWARD PALMER (1865-1928)

See also York and Sawyer.

Educated Cornell, 1889, and worked for McKim, Mead and White. Joined Philip Sawyer in practice from 1898.

Obituaries: AMERICAN ARCHITECTURE 135 (January 20, 1929): 114; ARCHITECTURAL FORUM 50 (February 1929): 35.

173:2 Sawyer, Philip. "Early Days of Edward Palmer York." AMERICAN INSTITUTE OF ARCHITECTS' JOURNAL 16 (November 1951): 195-200.

Excerpts from Sawyer's book. EDWARD PALMER YORK: PERSONAL REMINISCENCES BY HIS FRIEND AND PARTNER, PHILIP SAWYER (see).

173:3 _____. EDWARD PALMER YORK, PERSONAL REMINISCENCES BY HIS FRIEND AND PARTNER, PHILIP SAWYER AND A BIOGRAPHICAL SKETCH BY ROYAL CORTISSOZ. Stonington: Privately printed, 1951. 68 p.

After the death of York, his partner, Philip Sawyer, imparted numerous incidents and reminiscences to his wife. At her request, they were transcribed and published, with an introduction by Royal Cortissoz. The reminiscences are apocryphal and one would imagine that Sawyer was in his anecdotage when he wrote them.

174:1 YORK AND SAWYER (Partnership 1904-28)

Edward Palmer York (see) and Philip Sawyer (1868-1949). Sawyer trained Columbia and Ecole des Beaux Arts and both worked for McKim, Mead and White. Their practice began in 1904 and continued until York's death in 1928, when Sawyer continued under the firm's name.

Publications: QUEENS BOROUGH PUBLIC LIBRARY, 1955; SPECIFICATIONS FOR A HOSPITAL ERECTED AT WEST CHESTER, PA.,

1927; PROGRESS REPORT ON KILL VAN KULL BRIDGE, 1930; SPECIFICATIONS FOR THE DEPARTMENT OF COMMERCE BUILDING, WASHINGTON, D.C., 1929.

174:2 ARCHITECTURAL REVIEW (Boston). "The Recent Work of York and Sawyer." Vol. 16 (1909): 97-116.

Many office sketches to "express the architectural idea" and numerous photographs illustrate the "brutality" of the Provident Savings Bank of Baltimore, Md., or the simple spaciousness "fresh and individual use of materials" of their other buildings.

174:3 Beach, Wilfred W. SPECIFICATIONS FOR A HOSPITAL AT WEST CHESTER, PA. New York: The Pencil Points Press, 1927. 488 p.

"The publication of this volume is, frankly, an experiment...in order to give the specification writer as well as the designer and draftsman, a chance to discuss his problems." It is thus a teaching-learning tool published by The Pencil Points Library of specifications.

174:4 Butler, Charles, and Franklin, L.M. "Chronic Disease Patients, Housing Them, Large Scale." MODERN HOSPITAL 54 (January 1940): 67-73, 80.

Welfare Island, New York, was the chosen site of this hospital for easy accessibility. Housing 1500 patients in a single-story building even on a large site needed care in planning. However, this site was too small for a single-story building. Details of the plan are described in relation to patients, visitors, admission and transportation of the sick, various services, special features, and administrative procedures.

174:5 Hayes, John H. "Auditorium at Lenox Hill." MODERN HOSPITAL 51 (July 1938): 38-40.

A detailed description of the auditorium wing donated by a doctor "in appreciation of the opportunity to serve Lenox Hill Hospital and Dispensary for more than 50 years...intent on providing the greatest amount of good for the greatest number."

174:6 Laurence, F.S. "The Pershing Square Building, Its Technique of Materials." AMERICAN ARCHITECTURE 124 (October 10, 1923): 319-24.

Mr. Laurence was Executive Secretary of the National Terra-Cotta Society, and thus, it is not surprising that he praises the Pershing Square Skyscraper, a terra-cotta faced building, as having a "vital, logical and beautiful treatment...a satisfying expression of enduring character." He condemns other skyscrapers "not tailored logically and significantly" compared to the anatomical expression and organic nature of the Pershing!

174:7 York and Sawyer. A BRIEF HISTORY, OFFICE OF YORK AND SAWYER. New York: 1948. 25 p.

Founded in 1898, the firm has traversed a considerable amount of ground, even though a fifty-year period in this history of architecture is comparatively small. All commissions, with date and cost, are listed beginning with hospitals (a speciality of the firm), colleges, commercial, and general works. Partners, associates, and staff are also listed.

174:8 _____. QUEENS BOROUGH PUBLIC LIBRARY. New York: 1955. 71 p.

This is a typical example of the firm's brochures. Subtitle tells all: "...a comprehensive survey, study and report of the proposed north west wing addition, services building and alterations to the existing building, for the central building of the Queens Borough Public Library, prepared by the office of York and Sawyer, architects, and Kiff, Colean, Voss and Sounder. Consultants: Smith and Silverman and Jaros Baum and Bolles, in collaboration with the Department of Public Works and the Chief Librarian and his staff."

174:9 Zulauf, G. Walter. "Fifty Years A-Growing - The Allegheny General Hospital." THE MODERN HOSPITAL 48 (March 1937): 47-54.

Begun in 1882, the plans for this twentieth-century new hospital, which cost $8 million, were commenced in 1926. Construction began in 1929, but stopped 1931-35 and only continued with a WPA loan. The new structure was a high rise with 600 beds and all departments closely related. Modern conveniences and services for that day and age were installed.

175:1 YOST, JOSEPH WARREN (1847-1923)

Partnership with Frank L. Packard from 1891, and after 1901, with Albert D'Oench.

Publication: One of four papers at the 30th Annual Convention, American Institute of Architects, Nashville, Tennessee, 1896, on "The Effect of Steel and Glass upon Architectural Design."

175:2 Mumford, Lewis. ROOTS OF CONTEMPORARY AMERICAN ARCHITECTURE. New York: Reinhold Publishing Corp., 1952. 437 p.

Yost attended Harlem College and Mt. Union College 1866-68, later studied civil engineering and architecture.

He settled in Columbus, Ohio, where he enlarged the Capitol. He entered into two partnerships: Yost and Packard from 1891, and D'Oench and Yost in New York City after 1900. The great mystery is how a man of such limited background should at such an early date have made this excellent analysis of the fundamental problems of modern design.

Section 3

SIGNIFICANT ARCHITECTS ABOUT WHOM LITTLE HAS BEEN WRITTEN

Section 3

SIGNIFICANT ARCHITECTS

ABOUT WHOM LITTLE HAS BEEN WRITTEN

176 ALDRICH, CHESTER HOLMES (1870-1940)

Educated at Massachusetts Institute of Technology and Ecole des Beaux Arts, Paris (diploma 1900). 1903 entered into partnership with William A. Delano (see).

Obituaries: PENCIL POINTS 22 (February 1941): 76; ARCHITECTURAL FORUM 74 (February 1941): 43, 46; THE OCTAGON 13 (April 1941): 14-15.

177 ALSCHULER, ALFRED S. (1876-1940)

Educated Armour Institute, Chicago, 1899, and the Art Institute. Worked for Adler and began his own practice 1907.

Obituary: ARCHITECTURE AND ENGINEERING 143 (December 1940): 65.

178 ATWOOD, CHARLES B. (1848-95)

Educated at Harvard and worked for Ware and Van Brunt until setting up practice in Boston, 1872, and later in New York City. Moving to Chicago in 1891, he became a partner in D.H. Burnham and Co.

Obituaries: AMERICAN ARCHITECTURE 50 (1895): 141; ARCHITECTURAL REVIEW 4 (1896): 8.

179 BABCOCK, CHARLES (1829-1913)

Educated at Union College and trained under Richard Upjohn. Became Professor of Architecture at Cornell, 1871, where he designed several buildings.

Obituaries: THE BUILDER 29 (October 28, 1871): 844; ROYAL INSTITUTE OF BRITISH ARCHITECTS' JOURNAL 21 (1913-14): 107; AMERICAN INSTITUTE OF ARCHITECTS' JOURNAL 2 (1914): 51, 249-51.

180 BADGER, DANIEL D. (1806-84)

Manufacturer of cast-iron structures.

Published: ILLUSTRATIONS OF IRON ARCHITECTURE MADE BY THE ARCHITECTURAL IRON WORKS OF THE CITY OF NEW YORK, 1865.

Obituary: AMERICAN ARCHITECT AND BUILDING NEWS 16 (1884): 254.

181 BELL, MIFFLIN EMLEN (1846-1904)

Supervising Architect of the Treasury Department 1884-87. Listed by Daniel Burnham as recommended to participate in the Chicago Exposition, 1893, JOURNAL OF THE SOCIETY OF ARCHITECTURAL HISTORIANS 26 (December 1967): 254. National Archives, Washington, has fifteen sets of drawings of post offices, court houses, and custom houses.

Obituary: AMERICAN ARCHITECT AND BUILDING NEWS 84 (1904): 93.

182 BERG(H), LOUIS DE COPPET (1856-1913)

Studied at Royal Polytechnic at Stuttgart and began working for J. C. Cady, 1873. See Cady, Berg and See.

Publication: SAFE BUILDINGS, 1890-92.

183 BROWN, ARTHUR PAGE (1859-95)

Princeton University, Department of Buildings and Grounds, has drawings of the Museum of Historic Art and Whig Hall, Princeton.

Obituary: AMERICAN ARCHITECT AND BUILDING NEWS 51

(1896): 57-58.

184 **BULLARD, ROGER HARRINGTON (1884-1935)**

Educated at Columbia University and was employed by the American government to build federal buildings in Cuba. Worked for Grosvenor Atterbury and 1916-20 went in partnership as Goodwin, Bullard and Woolsey.

Publication: AMERICA'S LITTLE HOUSE, 1934.

Obituary: AMERICAN ARCHITECTURE 146 (March 1935): 101.

185 **BURGES, WILLIAM (1827-81)**

British architect who designed Trinity College, Hartford, Connecticut.

Obituary: AMERICAN ART REVIEW 2 (1881): 95.

186 **CHANDLER, FRANCIS WARD (1844-1925)**

In partnership with Edward Clark Cabot (1818-1901). They were architects of the Johns Hopkins Hospital, Baltimore, Maryland.

Publications: CONSTRUCTION DETAILS, PREPARED FOR THE USE OF STUDENTS AT MASSACHUSETTS INSTITUTE OF TECHNOLOGY, 1892; MUNICIPAL ARCHITECTURE IN BOSTON FROM DESIGNS BY EDMUND M. WHEELWRIGHT, CITY ARCHITECT, 1891-95, 1898.

Obituaries: AMERICAN ARCHITECTURE 130 (September 20, 1926): 16; AMERICAN INSTITUTE OF ARCHITECTS' JOURNAL 14 (1926): 504; NEW INTERNATIONAL YEARBOOK, 1926. p. 519.

187 **CHASE, FRANK D. (1877-1937)**

Founded Frank D. Chase and Co., 1913.

Obituary: AMERICAN ARCHITECTURE 151 (September 1937): 140.

188 COPE AND LIPPINCOTT (n.d.)

Paul Markely Cope., Jr., and Horace Mather Lippincott, Jr.

189 CUMMINGS AND SEARS (Partnership early 1860s-95)

Charles Amos Cummings (1833-1906) and Willard T. Sears (1837-1920).

Cummings trained at the Rensselaer Polytechnic Institute, Troy, New York, and both worked for Gridley Bryant in Boston. They began practice together in the early 1860's and continued until 1895.

Publication: A HISTORY OF ARCHITECTURE in Italy, 1927.

Obituaries of Cummings: AMERICAN ARCHITECT AND BUILDING NEWS 88 (1905): 57; 88 (1905): 151; AMERICAN INSTITUTE OF ARCHITECTS QUARTERLY BULLETIN 6 (October 1905): 169-73; AMERICAN INSTITUTE OF ARCHITECTS PROCEEDINGS 39 (1906): 256-57; THE BRICKBUILDER 14 (September 1905): 189.

190 CORNELL, JOHN B. (1821-87)

191 COXHEAD, ERNEST A. (1863-1933)

Trained in England and practiced in Los Angeles.

192 DRAPER, FREDERICK (1810-1905)

Trained in London under Sir Robert Smirke. Practiced in New York.

Obituary: AMERICAN ARCHITECT AND BUILDING NEWS 90 (September 22, 1906): 94-95.

193 EDBROOKE, WILLOUGHBY J. (1843-96)

Supervising Architect of the Treasury Department, 1891-93. National Archives, Washington, has sets of drawings for twenty-four post offices, custom houses, and court houses.

194 FAXTON, JOHN LYMAN (1851- ?)

Princeton University, Department of Buildings and Grounds, has twelve sheets of Dod Hall.

195 FERGUSON, FRANK W. (1861-1926)

An engineer who succeeded Charles Wentworth in the firm of Cram, Goodhue and Ferguson (see).

Obituaries: AMERICAN ARCHITECTURE 130 (October-December 1926): 324; AMERICAN INSTITUTE OF ARCHITECTS' JOURNAL 14 (1926): 504.

196 FREDERICK, GEORGE A. (1842-1924)

Worked for Lund and Murdock until 1862 when he began independent practice. The Maryland Historical Society has numerous sheets of eighty-one projects.

Obituaries: AMERICAN ARCHITECTURE 126 (July-September 1924): 294; AMERICAN INSTITUTE OF ARCHITECTS' JOURNAL 12 (1924): 494; AMERICAN ARCHITECTURE 126 (September 24, 1924): 294.

197 FRERET, WILLIAM A. (1833- ?)

Supervising Architect to the Treasury Department, 1887-89. National Archives, Washington, has seven sets of drawings of post offices and court houses and the Royal Institute of British Architects Library, two drawings.

198 GAMBRILL AND RICHARDSON (Partnership 1867-74)

Charles D. Gambrill (d. 1880) and Henry H. Richardson (1838-86) (see). Gambrill worked for Richard M. Hunt and G.B. Post. Houghton Library, Harvard University, has drawings of four projects by Gambrill and Richardson.

Obituary of Gambrill, AMERICAN ART REVIEW 1 (1880): 551; AMERICAN ARCHITECTURE 8 (September 18, 1880); 133.

> Ticknor of Boston published twenty-three plates of Trinity Church, Boston, 1888, in their series Monographs of American Architecture Series.

199 GILBERT, BRADFORD LEE (1853-1911)

Architect of the New York, Lake Erie and Western Railroad.

Obituary: AMERICAN ARCHITECT AND BUILDING NEWS 100 (September 20, 1911): 3.

200 HEINS AND LA FARGE (Partnership 1886-1907)

George Louis Heins (1860-1907) and Christopher Grant La Farge (1862-1938) (see).

Princeton University has drawings of sixteen projects including the Cathedral of St. John the Divine.

Obituary of Heins, AMERICAN ARCHITECT AND BUILDING NEWS 92 (1907): 105.

201 HILL, JAMES G. (1814-1913)

Supervising Architect of the Treasury Department, 1876-84. National Archives, Washington, has drawings of ten projects.

Obituaries: AMERICAN ARCHITECT AND BUILDING NEWS 105 (January 7, 1914): 5; AMERICAN INSTITUTE OF ARCHITECTS' JOURNAL 2 (1914): 51.

202 HOLABIRD, WILLIAM (1854-1923)

Entered United States Military Academy 1873 but worked in Chicago for Major Jenny. Began practice with Ossian C. Simons, c. 1880, and with Martin Roche, 1883.

Obituaries: AMERICAN ARCHITECTURE 124 (August 1, 1923): 135; AMERICAN INSTITUTE OF ARCHITECTS' JOURNAL 11 (1923): 334; ARCHITECTURE AND BUILDING 55 (September 1923): 91.

203 HOWE, FRANK M. (1849-1909)

Educated in the first class at Massachusetts Institute of Technology and worked in Boston for Ware and Van Brunt until 1885 when he opened an office in Kansas City under the title of Van Brunt and Howe. See also Henry Van Brunt.

204 JOHNSTON, WILLIAM L. (n.d.)

205 LAMB AND RICH (n.d.)

Hugo Lamb (1848-1903) and Charles Alonzo Rich (1855-1943).

Avery Library, Columbia University, has three sheets on Barnard College, New York City, 1896, and designs for the T.R. Williams House, Cedarhurst, Long Island, 1886.

206 LELAND, JOSEPH DANIELS (1885- ?)

Educated at Harvard and in Paris before working for Peabody and Stearns. Practiced as Loring and Leland.

207 LINK, THEODORE C. (1850-1923)

Educated Heidelberg and Ecole des Beaux Arts. Partnership 1883-86, Link, Rosenheim and Ittner; with Wilbur T. Trueblood until 1889.

Obituary: AMERICAN INSTITUTE OF ARCHITECTS' JOURNAL 12 (1924): 44.

208 MCLANAHAN, M. HAWLEY (1865-1929)

Practiced with William L. Price, 1900-10, and with Ralph C. Bencker.

209 MURCHISON, KENNETH MACKENZIE (1872-1938)

Educated Columbia, 1894, and Ecole des Beaux Arts, and practiced from 1902, sometimes as Murchison, Hood, Godley and Fouilhoux.

Edited THE ARCO-TEST (for the American Radiator Co.), 1938. Yale University has four sheets of the St. Elmo Club and the Pennsylvania Railroad Company has seven sheets of Johnstown Station.

Obituaries: ARCHITECTURAL FORUM 70 (January 1939): 42, 46; MICHIGAN SOCIETY OF ARCHITECTS' WEEKLY BULLETIN 13 (January 17, 1939): 7; PENCIL POINTS 20 (January 1939): 35.

210 NEWSOM AND NEWSOM (1870-1901)

Samuel (1852-1908) and Joe Cather Newsom. Designed approximately 670 buildings in California from 1870-1901, but some were obviously designed by two other brothers, John Jay and Thomas, plus others by cousins and sons. They published PICTURESQUE CALIFORNIA HOMES, 1884 and 1886; PICTURESQUE AND ARTISTIC HOMES, 1890; and MODERN HOUSES IN CALIFORNIA, 1893. THE CALIFORNIA ARCHITECT illustrated more than 250 of their buildings. David Gebhard has been collecting material since 1969 on the brothers for an exhibition which will be accompanied by a catalog, hopefully of the high calibre of his other works on California architects and architecture.

211 PRICE, WILLIAM L. (1861-1916)

Practiced with brothers Frank and Walter Price, and with M. Hawley McLanahan after 1900.

Publication: MODEL HOUSES FOR LITTLE MONEY, 1898.

212 RUTAN, CHARLES HERCULES (1851-1914)

Worked in Boston for Gambrill and Richardson until 1886 when Shepley, Rutan and Coolidge, Richardson's senior draftsmen, inherited the practice.

Obituaries: AMERICAN ARCHITECT AND BUILDING NEWS 107 (January 6, 1915): 13; AMERICAN INSTITUTE OF ARCHITECTS' JOURNAL 3 (1915): 88.

213 SANDS, JOSEPH (d. 1880)

Of Renwick, Sands and Auchmuty.

Obituary: AMERICAN ARCHITECTURE 7 (April 10, 1880): 154.

214 STEARNS, JOHN GODDARD (1843-1917)

Educated in engineering at the Lawrence Scientific School, Harvard, 1863, and worked for Ware and Van Brunt until entering into partnership in 1870 with Robert Swain Peabody.

Obituaries: AMERICAN ARCHITECTURE 112 (1917): 272; AMERI-

CAN INSTITUTE OF ARCHITECTS' JOURNAL 5 (1917): 517.

215 TAYLOR, ISAAC STOCKTON (1851-1917)

Studied architecture at St. Louis University and worked for George Ingram Barnett, becoming his partner 1874-89. Thereafter opened his own office.

Obituary: AMERICAN INSTITUTE OF ARCHITECTS' JOURNAL 5 (1917): 570.

216 UPJOHN, HOBART BROWN (1876-1949)

Educated Polytechnic Institute of Brooklyn and Stevens Institute of Technology. Avery Library, Columbia University, has drawings of five projects, nine volumes of miscellaneous photographs from his office, perspectives of Grace Methodist Church at Greensboro, North Carolina; Woman's Club, Scarsdale, New York; and Trinity Church, New York.

Publication: CHURCHES IN EIGHT AMERICAN COLONIES DIFFERING IN ELEMENTS OF DESIGN, 1929.

Obituary: ARCHITECTURAL RECORD 106 (October 1949): 158.

217 WALTER, HENRY (n.d.)

Ohio State Architect and Engineer has thirty-two sheets of the Ohio State Capitol Building.

218 WATERMAN, THOMAS TILESTON (1900-51)

Publications: DOMESTIC COLONIAL ARCHITECTURE OF TIDEWATER, VIRGINIA, 1932; THE DWELLINGS OF COLONIAL AMERICA, 1950; ENGLISH ANTECEDENTS OF VIRGINIA ARCHITECTURE, 1939; GOTHIC ARCHITECTURE OF SANTO DOMINGO, 1943; THE MANSIONS OF VIRGINIA, 1945; THE EARLY ARCHITECTURE OF NORTH CAROLINA, 1941.

Obituaries: AMERICAN INSTITUTE OF ARCHITECTS' JOURNAL, 15 (May 1951): 240-41; JOURNAL OF THE SOCIETY OF ARCHITECTURAL HISTORIANS 10 (May 1951): 25.

219 WETMORE, CHARLES DELEVAN (1867-1941)

See Warren and Wetmore.

Obituaries: THE BUILDER 160 (May 16, 1941): 472; MICHIGAN SOCIETY OF ARCHITECTS WEEKLY BULLETIN 15 (June 24, 1941): 3.

220 WILBY, ERNEST (d. 1958)

Partner of Albert Kahn (see).

Obituary: ARCHITECTURAL FORUM 108 (February 1958): 63.

221 WOOD, WILLIAM HALSEY (1855-97)

The New York Historical Society has considerable material on Wood. Ralph Craig Miller wrote a master's thesis on his domestic architecture at the University of Delaware, 1972.

Wood, Mrs. William Halsey. MEMOIRES OF WILLIAM HALSEY WOOD. Philadelphia: Mrs. Halsey Wood, 1938 (?). 56 p.

> Forty years after her husband's death, Mrs. Wood wrote this memoir praising William H. Wood as a devotee of his profession and a faithful and religious man. The introduction is by Ralph Adams Cram who praises Wood's entry for the St. John the Divine competition, which Wood apparently won in 1891, but which was subsequently rejected.

ADDENDUM

The cutoff date for the inclusion of most of the material in this volume was January 1974. At that time, announcements of some forthcoming doctoral dissertations were noted under the biographical notations of individual architects. Since then, the following dissertations have been completed.

Burnham, Daniel Hudson (1846-1912)

19:24 Hines, Thomas S. BURNHAM OF CHICAGO, ARCHITECT AND PLANNER. New York: Oxford University Press, 1974. 445 p.

> This, the first and only biography of Burnham, thoroughly covers his life, work and achievements in his dual profession as architect and planner.

Goodhue, Bertram Grosvenor (1869-1924)

56:18 McCready, Eric Scott. "The Nebraska State Capitol: Its Design, Background and Influence." Doctoral dissertation, University of Delaware, 1973. 266 p.

> The dominant motif of the design is not a dome but a tower. Goodhue and all his architectural-artistic collaborators and their works are discussed.

Maybeck, Bernard Ralph (1862-1957)

90:11 Craig, Robert Michael. "Maybeck at Principia: A Study of an Architect Client Relationship." Doctoral dissertation, Cornell University, 1973, 787 p.

> Frederick E. Morgan was the client of Maybeck's largest commission, Principia College, Elsah, Illinois.

McKim, Mead and White (Partnership 1878-)

94:34 Roth, Leland Martin. "The Urban Architecture of McKim, Mead and White: 1870-1910." Doctoral dissertation, Yale University, 1973. 1146 p.

> Of the 785 designs by the partnership, 360 are discussed with relation to the "spirit of the land and place."

Snook, Jonathan B. (1815-1901)

140:4 Smith, Mary Ann Clegg. "The Commercial Architecture of John Butler Snook." Doctoral dissertation, Pennsylvania State University, 1974. 387 p.

Practicing architecture in New York City, from 1837 to 1910, Snook designed 500 buildings in a wide variety of styles and building types. This dissertation concentrates on the commercial structures, from cast-iron through to the high-rise skyscrapers.

Sturgis and Brigham (Partnership early 1870's-86)

147:3 Floyd, Margaret Henderson. "A Terra Cotta Cornerstone for Copley Square: An Assessment of the Museum of Fine Arts, Boston, by Sturgis and Brigham (1870-1876) in the Context of its English Technological and Stylistic Origins." Doctoral dissertation, Boston University Graduate School, 1974. 226 p.

The terra-cotta for the building came from Stamford, Lincolnshire, England. The "study attempts to establish the nineteenth-century chronology of the terra-cotta revival in England prior to 1870."

Vaux, Calvert (1824-95)

156:7 Goss, Peter L. "An Investigation of Olana, The Home of Frederick Edwin Church, Painter." Doctoral dissertation, Ohio University, 1973. 273 p.

Vaux, Withers and Company created the spatial allocations for Church, who, when he returned from travels in Europe and the Middle East, assumed the design process.

Wright, Frank Lloyd (1867-1959)

172:162 Twombly, Robert C. FRANK LLOYD WRIGHT: AN INTERPRETATIVE BIOGRAPHY. New York; Harper and Row, 1973. 373 p.

Since Wright's heirs are prohibiting the use of his archives, Twombly has resorted to a search through articles in newspapers over a hundred year span. The result is rewarding notably with new interpretations and datings. The bibliography is extensive.

INDEXES

General Index

Building Location Index

GENERAL INDEX

This index is alphabetized letter-by-letter and numbers refer to entry numbers. In the case of individual architects, underlined numbers refer to main entries. Indexed are names and partnerships of major American architects, authors, and titles of books, dissertations, and theses. Subject areas of particular interest and importance to the study of architecture are also indexed. Titles of works written by individual architects are listed under their main heading within the text. Names of firms are not inverted but are indexed as they appear in the annotations. Buildings discussed within the text are separately indexed under the Building Location Index.

A

B

D

G

L

O

Q

R

S

TESTAMENT OF STONE: THEMES OF IDEALISM AND INDIGNATION FROM THE WRITINGS OF LOUIS SULLIVAN, THE 148:20

U

V

W

Y

Z

BUILDING LOCATION INDEX

All buildings are listed first under the state, then city in which they are located. In cases where the building is known to have been demolished, the symbol (D) is used to indicate this fact. (Author's note: a particular building may have two locations listed. The Francis W. Little house by Frank Lloyd Wright, for example, is situated at Wayzata, Minn., according to Ada Louise Huxtable [172:63, 68] and at Deep Haven, Minn., according to the Starosciaks [172:133]. Neither town in question is to be found in the Rand McNally Atlas, therefore both locations are listed.)

ILLINOIS